FROM BAGHDAD
TO BROOKLYN

From Baghdad to Brooklyn

Growing Up in a
Jewish-Arabic Family
in Midcentury America

A MEMOIR BY
JACK MARSHALL

Coffee House Press
Minneapolis
2005

Coffee House Press books are available to the trade through our primary distributor, Consortium Book Sales & Distribution, 1045 Westgate Drive, Saint Paul, MN 55114. For personal orders, catalogs, or other information, write to: Coffee House Press, 27 North Fourth Street, Suite 400, Minneapolis, MN 55401.

Coffee House Press is a nonprofit literary publishing house. Support from private foundations, corporate giving programs, government programs, and generous individuals help make the publication of our books possible. We gratefully acknowledge their support in detail in the back of this book.

Good books are brewing at coffeehousepress.org

LIBRARY OF CONGRESS CATALOGING-IN-PUBLICATION DATA

Marshall, Jack, 1936–
From Baghdad to Brooklyn : growing up in a Jewish-Arabic family in midcentury America / Jack Marshall.— 1st ed.
p. cm.
ISBN-13: 978-1-56689-174-5 (alk. paper)
ISBN-10: 1-56689-174-4 (alk. paper)
1. Marshall, Jack, 1936—Homes and haunts—New York (State)—New York. 2. Brooklyn (New York, N.Y.)—Social life and customs. 3. Children of immigrants—United States—Biography. 4. Marshall, Jack, 1936—Childhood and youth. 5. Poets, American—20th century—Biography. 6. Marshall, Jack, 1936—Family. 7. Jewish families—United States. 8. Sephardim—United States. 9. Arab American families. I. Title.

PS3563.A722Z465 2005
811'.54—dc22
2005012572
FIRST EDITION | FIRST PRINTING
1 3 5 7 9 8 6 4 2
Printed in Canada

"Families are to flee from."

"We shall not cease from exploration
And the end of all our exploring
Will be to arrive where we started
And know the place for the first time."
—T. S. Eliot, *The Four Quartets*

For Nat,
and in memory of
Renee Marshall Zwirn and
Grace and Albert Marshall

ACKNOWLEDGMENTS

I would like to acknowledge *Magic Carpet: Aleppo-in-Flatbush*, by Joseph Sutton, which helped refresh my memory of details about the customs and history of the community I grew up in, and the assistance of my niece Stephane Zavidow in digging out family photos.

I also want to thank my brother Nat, whose phone conversations and e-mails during my work on this book prompted certain sections of dialogue into being and which, in effect, I consider he practically co-authored.

Finally, I want to thank my wife Naomi Schwartz, a poet and teacher in her own right, for being my live-in editor, whose close scrutiny of the several drafts helped clean and clarify the text, and whose patience and support saw the final version through to completion.

Several sections originally appeared, in different form, in *ZYZZYVA*.

PROLOGUE

Some years ago I saw a television news report about Arab gunmen who had burst into a Jewish synagogue in Ankara, Turkey, killing scores of worshipers. A woman passerby was interviewed and remarked in a tone of weary resignation, "My mother is Jewish, my father is Muslim; we have our own Mideast crisis at home."

This irony—one of the many that history never seems able to iron out—struck me as an all-too-accurate description of my own family, given the additional fact that each of my parents were both Arabic *and* Jewish! In the contemporary chaos of political configurations, that combination would seem to rate rather high on the scale of a calamity of errors.

I was born and raised in Brooklyn by parents who had separately emigrated to America during the worldwide Depression in the late twenties. My father, born and raised in Baghdad, Iraq, was sent by his parents, in his late teens, to join his older brothers running a textile business in Manchester, England. From there, in his forties, bankrupt and in debt, he went to New York, taking any menial jobs he could find. All this was explained in letters he wrote to me shortly before his death, in his late eighties. But he never sent them, and I never saw them until recently.

My mother, born and raised in Aleppo, Syria, came as a young woman to New York, and would later enter into an arranged marriage with my father, as was customary among insular immigrant communities at that time. In the old country, these arranged marriages were binding, time-tested, and, in effect, lifelong. In my mother's case, this would later be a disastrous negation of her basically independent nature, for which our family would pay the psychic price. When my siblings and I were growing up, we were not aware of our parents' arranged marriage, which would have explained the flare-ups and resentments between them. At the time, these arguments seemed the natural discord and animosity between a husband and wife.

As an American writing in English while having a mixed Arabic-Jewish heritage, when I try to come to terms with this *meshuggunah* (while we're at it, why not throw in some Yiddish?) mix of battling backgrounds, and to make some kind of survival sense out of it all, where, in what pedigree, or racial lineage, does this put me? What culture, whose rights, what side in the ongoing bloodletting between Arab and Jew am I on, or can I choose? Must I? And when, in my early teens, I told my father that I wanted to be a poet, he answered (and would repeat in one of the letters I would discover later) that if I persisted I would end up in "the madhouse." Though I have written and published ten volumes of poetry, my father's prediction strikes me as no less persistent today as when he made it. This, even though modern science assures us that the body of an elderly man contains not a single cell that is the same as when he was a boy. Can the man and the boy be said to be the same person? Though the older man somewhere retains and often relives certain persistent memories of what the boy once saw, heard, felt, tasted, smelled, he can hardly believe that boy was his earlier self.

Recently, upon listening to the news, when I feel the urge to plead with a God I don't believe in, I hear myself mumble under my breath the plea that Dizzy Gillespie said Charlie Parker made to him one night in a Harlem club: broke, in despair, having hocked his horn to buy drugs, Bird implored his friend, "Save me; why don't you save me?" And Diz, never lacking for a comeback, admitted, for once, he was at a loss for words.

There's a photo of a boy, three or four years old, dressed in a green silk caftan, and an Arab *kaffiyeh* (headdress). Sitting cross-legged on the floor, glancing toward whomever is prompting him, he's caught in a sheepish smile. The photo, cracked and torn in places, had been badly taped together years before. I recognize that expression as an attempt to make the best of an imposed situation. I've seen that look at various times on the faces of pop icons, movie stars, government villains, and corporate thieves, all for an instant camera-friendly. I was told by my mother that that boy was me.

The further back I try to remember, the less sure I am of the time sequence. I don't recall posing for the photo, but I do recall half a century ago my mother telling me that what I had been wearing was the native costume of my Syrian grandfather from Aleppo, who I never knew.

What was I so bashfully grinning about? What am I now to make of that seemingly happy boy to whom I feel no connection—in fact, alien? Since I don't remember posing for the photo, I have to take my mother's word. But as far as I can recall, no other photos exist of me smiling as a boy. So much of what we are given to believe about our childhood selves is hearsay and must be taken on trust. Yet, for all I know, that obligingly grinning kid could've been Yassir Arafat! And from the same family album! The way the races, over the centuries in the Middle East, have come to be Biblically, bloodily, mixed, that's not altogether impossible. Had I a beakier nose (mine, more flattened, is probably of African ancestry), and sleepless, bulging, beady eyes caught in incredulous outrage, the look of a cornered ferret (mine, thank God, at least look like they've gotten some sleep), and a scraggly growth of barbed-wire stubble, topped by a striped *kaffiyeh* on my head, I could have traded places with Chairman Arafat.

And who wouldn't have envied his aides—with PLO funds taxed from the impoverished Palestinian people themselves, plus payoffs by neighboring Arab rulers to keep out of their own hair, and larded with American taxpayers' "aid"—aides who, outfitted in Armani suits, would drive their Mercedes-Benzes to try for further luck at the gaming tables of Monte Carlo?

Whenever I'd see Arafat hunkered in his bunker, hearing him as the embattled underdog try to explain in Arabic the predicament of the Palestinians, I'd feel drawn by a deep genetic pull to the sound and inflection of words familiar to me from my childhood. I'd hear and respond instinctively to the gnarled guttural sounds—Arabic hawked from deep at the back of the throat, a sound made out of a mouthful of olive pits and a gulp of fiery *arak*, gargled, gagging, as if ready to spit—with a corrosive ancestral rage. The difference between spoken English (which emanates more sedately Puritanical—except for curses—from the front of the mouth onto the tip of the tongue) and Arabic (with its hefty, cleaving, throat-clearing vocables) is the difference between being served appetizers on a styrofoam plate and shish kebab on a sizzling spit. By the same token, when I hear Israelis articulating their cause in Hebrew, I feel a similar visceral clench at the sound of rounded vowels and hard, flinty consonants—contracted, elided, enjambed "*dvzzis*" and "*tssitzz*"—ground as from an ancient mill lodged in the Adam's apple in viscid glottals. The two ancient languages, sharing many common words, feel interchangeable, originating out of a common throat, inextricably bound, a double-sided mirror with hardly any coating in between. For me, it's not a matter of taking sides, but rather, in the midst of the ongoing escalating fratricide, of *being* both sides, flooded by each side's hopeless rage.

In Arafat, I had never seen, in public, the likes of such a head of a headless state appear so openly vulnerable, at risk at any moment of blowing it all in an all-out fit of tongue-tied outrage. From that expression of startled impotence, he qualified as, in our old Arabic-speaking neighborhood, what used to be called a "*hazzeet* (pitiful) case." Arab, Jew, Hindu, Bantu: who hasn't seen himself shuffling toward the bank of reporters' microphones in the weary old chairman's *sha-haa-taas* (slippers)? Given his gaunt, pocked-faced glare and gawky ungainliness, I often wondered, could the Palestinians have chosen a less attractive, more fawning representative of their cause and aspirations than this hunted, haunted visage of a wolf? Couldn't they have at least picked someone a bit more conversant in English, at least fairly intelligible, instead of the fractured Ingleezy and slobbering Arabic crudities stammered in Arafat's characteristic hash of mixed signals and duplicitous doublespeak? Former PLO spokesperson Hanan Ashrawi, in trying to perform her negotiations with the U.S. and Israel, finally grew so frustrated with Arafat's ploy of advancing by retreating, giving contradictory mixed messages, and double-dealing, that these tactics (if, by "tactics" we also include the unintentional) soon tarnished the whole Palestinian people in the eyes of the world. Ill-advised, self-defeating strategies added up to a veritable "*hazzeet* case" and prompted Abba Eban's Talmudic quip that the leader of the PLO "never missed an opportunity to miss an opportunity."

Before his recent death, despite numerous attempts on his life (both by Israelis and competing Palestinian militant factions), Arafat had somehow managed to outfox Shamir, Begin, Rabin, Netanyahu, and Barak: the ancient art of outlasting one's enemies without oneself appearing to fire a shot!

And Sharon? Don't get me started. If that heaving hulk were to grow any bulkier, Israel would have to enlarge its borders even further. No wonder that, a few years ago as foreign minister, he urged Israeli militants: "Everybody has to move, run and grab as many hilltops as they can to enlarge the settlements because everything we take now will stay ours . . . Everything we don't grab will go to them" (Agence France Presse report, November 15, 1998). And let's not bring up his deliberately inflammatory visit to one of the holiest sites in Islam, Al-Haram al Sharif, the Temple Mount, in September 2000, which sparked the Second Intifada, triggering waves of suicide bombers followed by deadly reprisals.

Trying to justify a proclaimed course toward a humane social and political end through the means claimed to be necessary, one is drawn to an inevitable conclusion: however noble the ends of such "humane" causes, no matter how much we mean well, most often we unleash disaster.

Yet any Orthodox rabbi worth his kosher Crystal salt will invariably point out: "Does not the Book of *Beresheet* (Genesis) tell us of the enmity of the brothers Jacob and Esau, rivals for their father Isaac's blessing of a Promised Land, eh, *bachur?*" Judaism's patriarch, Abraham, begat Isaac and Ishmael; Isaac begat Jacob and Esau; from Jacob would descend the tribes of Israel, while, according to Jewish tradition, from Esau would descend the ancient Edomites, and Ishmael, the son whom Abraham sent into the desert, would become father to the Arabs.

Each day we witness in the images from Gaza to the West Bank and Jerusalem the shameful treatment of an occupied people who are exiles in their own homeland! And any one of whom could be the uncle my father once mentioned had been interred in a refugee camp; or one of the old women herded by Israeli special forces out of their houses, at gunpoint, could be a distant aunt. In all the confusing generational bloodlines crisscrossing over, who knows anymore?

At this point I should clarify the important differences between the attitudes of the Eastern European (Ashkenazic) Jews and the Arabic-speaking (Sephardic) Jewish immigrants to their countries of origin and to Palestine. Over the centuries, European Jews had formed separate enclaves, or ghettos, within the native cultures they lived among, and developed Yiddish out of a melting pot of languages spoken in those cultures around them. Arabic Jews (also called mizrachim, Eastern Jews), since their ancestors' expulsion from Spain in 1492, were allowed to a large degree to share fully and integrate into the culture and language of the medieval Islamic Arab countries in which they lived. Also, beginning in the early nineteenth century, Jews in Europe who rejected conversion to Christianity were subject to severe religious, economic, and educational restrictions, as well as violent physical assaults culminating in widespread pogroms wiping out entire communities. When those who could emigrated to America, they did so with harsh, embittered memories of the countries they fled. For many, the hope of a Jewish homeland in Palestine was embodied in Zionism.

By contrast, most Arabic Jews came to America during the Depression primarily out of economic necessity, harboring a bittersweet nostalgia for the relatively benign, unchanging life in their former homelands. Along with Zionism, Western revolutionary ideologies such as Socialism and Communism (formulated and aggressively advocated by such European Jews as Karl Marx and Leon Trotsky) had not been widely circulated in the bazaars and *souks* of the Orient, where life remained relatively unchanged since the Middle Ages. For the most part, modern technologies such as electric light, railroads, and indoor toilets were unknown until early in the twentieth century.

In fact, because of their insularity, their ignorance of both Yiddish and English, their unfamiliar Sephardic pronunciation of Hebrew, and their inability to integrate into traditional Ashkenazic Jewish life, these immigrant Arabic Jews seemed to their European counterparts as strange, even alien. And given their ages-old Middle Eastern family lineage and closeness to the Holy Land, these Sephardeem, a minority within a minority, considered themselves more authentic, superior even, having lived for centuries closer to their ancient source. The Ashkenazic disdain toward their unfamiliar observance of Jewish life in a strange land created a cultural wall intensified by Arabic Jews living apart from their fellow Jews as well as from the Gentile values of the American mainstream. Assimilation into the host culture would take several generations. This form of "pecking order" is reflected in the low social status of dark-skinned Yemenite-and-Arabic Jews in the modern state of Israel.

This narrative will not attempt to extricate and unravel my ancestral roots, to pry loose and preen them, or to choose sides between cultural and religious differences, but by a process of re- and dis-membering, to run them together, mix and match the mongrel strains, mingle and merge apparent partitions and genealogical division. This, in order to feed the twin streams into one twined flowing river; not in order to *have* it both ways, but because of the fact of *being* both ways.

Neither an anti-Semitic Arab nor an anti-Arab Jew, I inherited an Old World culture in a traditional Arabic-speaking family while growing up as a studious, observant Jewish boy. In fact, I was a pious *yeshiva* student who (God help me!) was awarded a scholarship to Talmudic Academy for further rabbinical study. Only later, in small angst-ridden stages, would I pause, ponder, and, in progressively confused self-siege, finally feel no sane course was open but to abandon the ancient traditions I had up till then so painstakingly, even fanatically, upheld; fanatic perhaps because, like all zealots, I had an ever-so-fragile hold on what one deems unquestionably sacred.

For me, the hairline fractures in absolute certainty were triggered by my early interest in science, literature, music, and philosophy, which offered a broader view of the world than what I had inherited. The account that follows, while acknowledging that rich Old World heritage, will also trace how the various arts and sciences opened those fractures in me to wider psychic as well as geographic spaces I felt drawn to explore, where the heart is freer to pursue an alternate image of the real, its true desire.

And here, as follows, is how it began.

CHAPTER ONE

MEMORY'S HOOD

It's on the tip of my tongue: "childhood," magical word, conjuring up an endless sky's pale blue hood pulled back to the horizon. Drawn there not for nostalgia's sake, but for what I am now able to see of what our life was then. Now, in my late sixties, I'm trying to remember what I had once left behind to forget.

My memory begins in the dim apartment corridor I walked each day, and especially at night: the narrow hallway leading from the front door to the kitchen, a kind of decompression chamber between public street and private quarters. When, at night, the bare overhead bulb was turned off, on my way to bed in the back room, I walked through that lengthy corridor—about thirty feet long—I grew increasingly unable to distinguish between the darkness inside and the night outside.

Time can be so contracted by dread, that within a dark walk of no more than a few yards, it doesn't take long for a kid's imagination to skip to another level, a further realm, drawn out into astral space. From there, my memory of that early part of my life is vague and erratic.

Start where, then?

Anywhere.

With no beginning or end? It's all middle.

All middle, then; so be it: The center is everywhere.

WHITE CHRISTMAS

An early, perhaps my earliest, memory: night outside our apartment window. Inside it was snug, and a lightbulb overhead, a dim sulfur-yellow, gave off an aura, however insubstantial, of warmth. It was white winter outside. I must have been one or two years old, standing on the carpeted floor, the dimpled corner of a stuffed couch close to my eye level. My father, having returned from work, stood in front of me and held something out: a small figure from a box. After winding it up behind his back, he placed it before me on the floor: a drummer boy in British redcoat, crisscrossed white bands on his chest. With gears whirring and clanking, its miniature arm swung the metal drumstick soldered to each rigid hand and banged the parchment skin, drumming thin, hollow sounds of muted thunder. As it would later turn out, my father had just given me one of the toys that would make a racket he (usually of a quiet, contemplative nature) would later rant against while we noisy kids were growing up. "Don't howl," he'd yell, and add another volume of noise to our own.

An evening or two later, playing with the toy, I was startled by the sudden appearance on the fire escape at the living-room window of a burly figure with a full white beard. Bundled in a bright red, padded jacket, wide black belt, and dangling cap, the figure waved to me with one hand and set a white sack down with the other. Muffled sounds came from the apparition. Seeing my startled expression, my mother turned to the window as the rotund shape was fully backlit by the moon, and uttered curses in Arabic such as I would later hear her repeat in moments of exasperated provocation. My mother, it would turn out, was a connoisseur of what were politely referred to as "swear words." Curses in Arabic originate from deep in the throat, with hawking, gargling, choking vocables, meant to burn their fiery way through the offender's genetic makeup via his inherited rectum all the way back to his ancestors, leaving for their descendants a lineage of scorched waste. A favorite of hers with Gentiles was, "*Yih'rait-dee-nak* (May God burn your religion)!"

As the bulky figure outside reached down to open the window, my mother angrily waved him away. Misinterpreting her motion as a sign of welcome, he straightened, stood still in the snowy background about to wave to her, but stopped as my mother's gestures grew more emphatic. "Getdat-outahere-from-here," she shouted in her mangled but vehement English and again waved him away. This time he understood her unmistakable motions and, picking up his sack, turned back down the fire escape ladder.

She next took me by the hand and led me downstairs to our landlord's flat on the ground floor. I could feel her shaking with rage. She knocked loudly on the door and when it was opened by the Italian landlord's wife, my mother, in her pidgin-Arab-English, unleashed a barrage of accusations at the couple's motives that, even though her language was garbled, made her meaning clear. Her husband had frightened me and they were trying to bribe me with gifts. The woman looked dumbfounded and protested her innocence: they were only offering gifts and good cheer for the season. My mother would have none of it, not goyish gifts nor good cheer nor holiday greetings. She responded the way she did throughout her life, with a characteristic reflex in moments of frustration—blowing out through her lips explosive puffs of indignant air. I could feel her still trembling as she carried me back upstairs. A few weeks later, we moved from that apartment.

That was my introduction to Christmas, which we did not recognize, much less celebrate. However, the following night, when my father brought home a chocolate Santa, my mother, noticing my eager curiosity, didn't put up any resistance. When I broke the hollow brown belly between my fingers, it gave up a richly deep, cavernously sweet aroma, then a dense, delicious flavor that turned my mouth into a jet of watery velvet.

BING, DREAMING

It was indeed white outside the window when I first heard Bing Crosby on the radio crooning "White Christmas." Burbling and bouncingly confident, his tone of easeful entitlement sounded assured of owning all the time and leisure in the world. Gliding like a snowflake over the notes, snug in cozy comfort, his bubbly rendition pictured a vivid landscape where treetops glistened and children listened. Ah, to be so assured was to be royally privileged.

Outside the windows, the surrounding whiteness, no matter how deep, needed no digging out of; was, in fact, the very immaculate cushion on which all this sense of privilege rested. Crooning with all the confidence of an entitled cavalier, Bing's teasing way with the melody—stretching, skipping, tossing—was the way of a playful juggler skating on ice: reaffirmed, the year's finale in a gliding glimpse of sparkle, a child's first sight of spun sugar. Who wouldn't want in on this warbling of plenty?

"CLOSER TO ALLAH"

When we moved to the new flat three flights above Canin's Tire Co. on the corner of Bay Parkway and 65th Street, Mom said that living on the top floor would bring us "closer to Allah."

Not then, but now I'm aware of how, when either blessing or cursing, the name of God my parents most often invoked was not the Hebrew *Ha-shem* (The Name) or *Eloheem* (Lord), but the Muslim *Allah:* open-breath vowels before and after the tongue drops "lah" down hard, a firm mandate, eternal edict laid on the obedient heart. In this invoking of God's name, like other Arabic Jews, they sounded more Muslim than Jewish. Of the two names, hearing or saying *Allah* also held the greater authoritative weight for me. Given her sly sense of irony, I can now appreciate how literally my mother must have meant we were indeed closer to God . . . by three winding flights of stairs.

Her name in English was Grace, in Arabic, *Garaz*. To this day I still prefer hearing it that way: two warm *a*'s glowing apple-red between the consonants, with the *z*'s final flash.

Perhaps I ascribe more meaning to her words than she intended, but even a platitude or stock phrase is a way of indicating what adults realize they face the moment they know they will one day die.

HE LOOKED LIKE THE SHAH

My father, Albert, looked like the shah of Iran—minus the imperial blue and gold peacock uniform.

Born in Baghdad in 1888, his early immigration photo on his original passport showed a look of deep wariness on a dark-complexioned, clean-shaven face, prominent cheekbones, and thin cheeks that the course of time would make even thinner.

Some time ago I received a manila envelope of letters and old family photos sent by my brother Nat. In it were early photos of my pre-married mother with her elderly mother taken either in their hometown of Aleppo, Syria, or later on, after they emigrated, in Brooklyn. There was also a photo of me that I hadn't seen in more than five decades, and several letters written to me by my father near the end of his life, though he never sent them, in which he relates more details than he ever did when he was alive, about his family and their emigration from Baghdad to

Manchester, England, in the early part of the twentieth century. Nat found all this among our sister Renee's belongings after she died from breast cancer several years ago, aged fifty-nine.

My brother and I live on opposite coasts: he on the East and I on the West Coast. We Marshalls are slow movers; over the years, I've come so far West I'm East. Nat, however, referring to California's noted tendency toward liberal politics, calls it the "Left Coast."

There are many details about my father's family and his early life before emigrating to America contained in one of these letters; details of which I was unaware until I received them from my brother.

DEAD LETTER 1

From a letter to me (I was thirty-nine, living in San Francisco) dated August 21, 1975, my father (age eighty-five) wrote:

My Dear son Jack,

I hope you will soon or late find a job as respectable as you can, and you will, if you use perseverance and courage. Not like when young, you didn't like work. I will cite to you in this letter how we came to America pennyless, less than $250.00 in our pocket, that was in 1928 here in America the worst business depression. Before that, we came from Baghdad. Can you imagine we lived in the land of our ancestors, the bible, the oldest richest culture, where the law was born. I was to go to school to study, but everything fell. The family lost the business, so my brothers went to England to make a living in textiles but it was worse and worse in England, and that was why we left for America.

We lost our flourishing wholesale business, lost our customers all because they couldn't pay us their debts. Can you imagine a business man sitting nearly all day in his office and came to America looking for a job, any job, not used to hard work? but thank God I had courage and patience. So here we started ready to face the hardship and the adversity and rough change to make a living.

Before we left England to come over here, my brother David and myself, I decided to sell the house after my mother died in 1920; the house was for the whole family, mother, young brothers 4 of them, and young sister Annie now in California. The house was sold to provide money for my sister to enable her to get married with a dowry of 5,000 pounds ($15,000 dollars), we did so, as my mother begged us on her death bed. After my sister married, we then lived in France, so we applied for visa to come to America; what a change! But we faced the consequences and started looking for a job. We were not young; your uncle David was 36, and I was nearly 40 years of age, but we used very young spirit and our good health helped us, mostly our perseverance and patience.

Listen very carefully. When we started to look for a job, it was end of autumn at the end of October 1928, in the worst depression year. I said to my brother, let us start with Madison Avenue where they sell wholesale silk & rayon material by yard to retailers to make ladies top and underwear dresses, and I specially urged my brother David to call on those Madison offices, where most manufacturers are Jewish Ashkenazim, and I insisted on him to call on Jewish offices, leave alone the Christian offices, of course as we both are Jewish.

And so I ordered him to call on one side of Madison Avenue, as he did not have the courage as an organiser (but he was very hard worker), and I started on the other side of the street, and I begged of him that when he find a big office that the boss is religious (I said he must be the boss or director, and if they ask him what message to take, he must politely say on private personal matter on business, the only way not to say he is looking for a job, and at that time we came over well dressed in hand made tailored suits & overcoats, we had used them in business in England, and so we kept calling and before the first day was over I picked a big fish (the real boss as I always do), and the big boss called the manager to give me a job in the mail room and it happened the man operating the mail room was sick (after 3 weeks he died and I took the job lasted 3 years where I made a fairly good salary and put money on the side to open a store in silk business.

I insisted on my brother David to eat well, to keeping dressing well, we had expensive material by yard all virgin wool from England. We called on English tailor on Lexington Avenue; he made us 2 suits each which would have cost us here very dear, but knowing us being English he charged us half price for his services.

You know English people are humble in nature and in their dealing and honest above board and we reared to the same attitude and used the English custom and politeness here in America.

My brother and myself worked for over 3 years continually in the same places, put money in the bank, then took leave and opened a small store on our own, did fairly well cutting expenses, but the store was very small on Lexington Avenue facing Gimble.

We lost our store as it was belonging to a bank, and they used the first floor to expand their business. It took us nearly a month to find another store on 51st Street, Bway, the store belong to car dealers and we couldn't get a lease, so we lost another store and started looking for another. Meantime in 1933 I got married to a Syrian girl your mother Grace your mother who thank God was and is homely, courageous, home builder up till today, but proud she was and arguing when she is not right, and I don't argue when she is right; all husbands and wifes argue but not force a divorce.

Time came when my luck change to the bad after I lost my business and 4 years after my marriage. My wife your mother had the courage to mention to me to try her uncle Sitt who had business on 5th Avenue; she didn't care, any job (you were 2 years old); so I started in the beginning to deliver packages of goods to their customers, after driving a hand cart in the morning to mail the packages of goods ordered by the customers, and in the afternoon I watched the salesmen selling on the floor of the store on 5th Avenue, I pushed myself to sell they saw I was capable and they let me; sometime I handle rich customers and in that case I introduce them (after I sell them 30, 40, 50, 75 dollars) to the manager so he sells them $100 to $5000 with very very big profit. Sitt Brothers I am talking about that I worked in their 5th Avenue store for 11 years, not big salary but I learnt their business, after I opened a store in Elizabeth New Jersey for 9 years; time came I lost the store in a good location; the landlord made a fire, in doing so the fire destroyed the store with the goods (landlord did so to get very big fire insurance from the Fire Insurance Co.). I took my insurance money that I insured my goods with and paid half of the credit I owe to all my creditors, then I bought a house the one now we live in. The time I bought the house in the year 1955, found a job in a mail room working half day delivering letters and packages to the Banks and the other half taking care of the mail. I was then 72 years of age, worked in that place 8 years continually till 1974; then I had to lose the job because business stocks and shares brokerage big house had to close up, because losing in millions, and closed up. So now I am not working too old and too weak I am retired forcibly, but to retire is very trying, one get bored.

Listen and read carefully to what I am writing to you; a man lose his business is a loss, losing partly his health is a big loss, but losing courage when he lose his job has to have patience and perseverance; losing courage is the greatest loss in life. These precious notes will carry you through to a respectable life. Read very carefully how I put up with all adverse circumstances and I won my life battle, otherwise I would have sunk and either gone for good or lose my <u>mind</u>. They would have taken me to a mental hospital; so I warn you; it is better for you to keep calling on Jewish houses of business, or other big decent business houses till you find a job, not continuing following your career of poetries and other miserable career that will drive you to poverty and sickness and loss of mind; what will be left to you only mental hospital. Keep these notes and letters of mine as a bible. I say again use these notes as you would read a bible.

Your loving father,
Albert

THE USES THE DEAD MAKE OF THE LIVING

Only while working on this memoir did it occur to me that during the years I lived at home and in these last letters of his, my father never made mention of his own father: no bit of memory, not a single reference or passing remark, not a word. There was no image of what his mother or father or any other family member looked like anywhere in the house. Why? Because of his innate reticence; or his fear that his parents might be disparaged; or his wariness of my mother whenever the subject of the social disparity of their families came up and she would not let him forget about the superiority of her family over his in the hierarchy of Aleppoans versus Baghdadians? How, she often needled him, she had married low and he, up! Though I remember once, during a heated exchange, with that sting to her tongue, my mother, in her arch humiliating tone, snapping: "If it wasn't for me getting you a job with my relatives, you'd be out on the street!" And he countering, reasonably, "And you with me." Either way, from motives of pride or prudence, we knew little of his past and nothing of his parents.

When I try to imagine the pressures at work on him and the sacrifices he would be forced to make in that promise to his dying mother, it dawns on me in the always late twilight of recognition what the psychic cost in the years to come would be in making such a vow. The dying do not care, being beyond caring, and cannot conceive of the straits they will put their surviving heirs through in the future, since they are free of that future and therefore can ask everything of it.

Extracting such a deathbed vow can, I imagine, create conditions that amount to a curse; the dying no more sparing their survivors than starving survivors will spare the corpses of their dead.

As he grew older, shedding that furtive look in his passport photo, my father's expression took on a more temperate aspect, his long hours working in retail stores turned his dark complexion lighter, domesticated. He dressed unobtrusively in conservative double-breasted gray or brown business suits, white shirt, and dark tie. One concession to him that my mother regularly—if not happily—made, aware as she was of the need to appear acceptable in the business world, was to send us kids on regular errands to the cleaner, to drop off or deliver his shirts for starching and suits for pressing. I liked the cardboard inserts—white on one side, gray on the other—and the soft crinkled tissue paper wrapped around a shirt's stiff white collar, regally new, when I'd pick them up again. His graying hair (which, in his attempts to restore its original dark brown shade, turned a dull yellow from the cheap dyes and lotions he used) was cut close, accenting the slim line from cheek to jaw to throat clasped by a starched white collar.

Usually he was clean-shaven. If he skipped a day, a gritty gray stubble appeared, rough as a wire brush on my face when he'd hug me. On cold winter Sundays, when he had the luxury of going about unshaven for the day, if I was out with him on the street, or when he'd return from a walk, with his hat-brim turned down and his coat collar raised, his spiky salt-and-pepper stubble gave him, the mildest of men, the instant look of a menacing derelict. He closely resembled those gaunt, raw-boned men standing in bread lines I'd see years later in grainy black-and-white news footage of the Depression years; hatchet-faced men, all with the same hollow look of anonymous doomed dirt-farmers and migrant workers lining up for handouts. Today, he'd no doubt find himself as one of those shadowy "Middle-Eastern-looking" men who'd be picked up as a suspect and held for questioning.

When his suit cuffs and shirt collars would begin to show signs of fraying, he'd ask my mother to take them to the tailor for repair. Uncannily, he seemed able to wear his suits year in and year out without having them wear out. Preserving and prolonging key materials essential for survival seemed a deeply innate quality in him, and probably were learned in his earlier years in the textile business. With my mother, who didn't seem particularly fond of mending, it was a matter of necessity. The weekly allowance my father gave her had to cover all household expenses. Any repairs to our clothing that she could manage doing herself, she did. One of the most characteristic gestures I recall her making was, when about to sew on a button, to bunch her lips together like a bud and lick the end of a thread she'd then—taking aim, one eye squinting—try, literally, to *pierce* the eye of the needle. She did a lot of mending and sewing; over the fraying years, a lot of spittle went into threading the needle's eye, about as much as went into the all-purpose handkerchief she carried and would spit into when she thought our faces were dirty and needed wiping.

The dark-stained walnut dresser that stood in a corner of the front sitting room, across from my parents' bedroom, held his neatly stacked shirts in its drawers. Its top was flanked by curved lids that slid backwards, opening on an interior stuffed with language-lesson clippings of French, Spanish, and Italian that he'd cut from the *Daily Herald-Tribune* and dutifully tied together with string and kept for further study. Do I only imagine him telling me that, as a young man growing up in Baghdad, he had considered studying to become a lawyer (which, given his interests and temperament, he would have been better suited for than a salesman)? But, at age sixteen, he was sent by his family to join his older brothers in Manchester, where they had preceded him and opened a fabric store for men's clothing. Some years ago, traveling in England, I was curious to see where my father had lived as a young man. As I passed through Manchester, my heart sank at its buildings still coated with the black soot's permanent shadow of coal-pits strip-mined in the early Industrial Age. Years spent measuring and fitting yards of fabric through a cold, acrid, coal-blackened mist would not stimulate a shy, retiring temperament. I was glad he had not stayed, but how difficult it must have been to lose his business and be uprooted into a new country and start over again, having to scrounge for menial jobs.

There were a few times I'd see him smile, but rarely laugh; when he did, it was more of an amused chuckle. It wasn't until years after most families in the neighborhood owned a TV, and after much "hounding and howling" from us kids, that he bought a set and, watching for the first time the slapstick antics and manic mayhem of Milton Berle, Dean Martin, and Jerry Lewis, and especially the sly, insinuating, killer timing of Bob Hope's needle jibes, was turned into a "howling" fan as well. I suspect that his reaction was less from his actually getting a joke's punch line than a visceral reaction to Hope's impeccably confident rhythm, timing, and delivery, triggering the audience's laughter.

Unintentionally and unknowingly, the biggest favor my father did for me was to instill a lifelong aversion to smoking by his example: he chain-smoked, lighting one cigarette with the stub of the first, indoors and out, windows open or closed, so that his fingers became stained a sickly yellowish-brown and the suits he wore and took such fastidious care of were permanently saturated with that nicotine reek that nauseated me whenever he came close. It left a foul acridness in the air I had to hold my breath against. First, you caught the whiff of cigarette paper catching the flame, then the sickening smoke of burning tobacco. Though, to his credit, after a lifetime of the habit, my father, warned by a doctor, was able in a short time to quit in his early seventies and lived to eighty-eight.

IF YOU LOOK ARABIC, SPEAK ARABIC, COOK ARABIC, DOES THAT MAKE YOU ARABIC?

I never knew my grandparents on my mother's side. The closest I came was the photograph of them that hung in an antique frame high on the dining room wall of our apartment. In order to see them now I have to let my eyes adjust to the waning light of memory into which they have long since been absorbed.

The photo shows a long-faced, hollow-cheeked, sturdy-looking elderly man with a handlebar mustache, wearing a vest and a collarless shirt, tieless, looking older than his actual years. His drooping mustache has an imposing curve at each end, which, to a child, resembled a walrus-tusked portal at the sides of his mouth. Though my mother had told me that her father had been a rabbi in Aleppo, I didn't notice on the sparse hair on his head any sign of a yarmulke or a turban, nor was he bearded like the portrait gallery of rabbis I found in a historical photo album of Aleppoan rabbis. Each aged, bearded patriarch wore the cloak, robes, and high felt turbans traditional in Arabic countries, and could easily be taken for Muslim clerics.

My grandfather (odd to call "grandfather" someone I never knew, who could have been any elderly stranger on the street) stands, looking more like a peasant workman than a rabbi. Bare of Judaic traces, he resembles the elderly Italian and Sicilian men of our neighborhood streets, or looking out from family photos on dresser tops and mantelpieces in their immigrant descendants' homes. In the photo, he appears neither curious nor interested in the instrument about to reproduce his image and pass it on to his descendants.

My mother's mother, posed beside her husband, is smaller than him and looks wearied, shrunken. In a plain black dress, squinting, her wrinkled features have been caught in a faint, forbearing smile.

She looks some years older than her husband, but, my mother said, she was not. Many laboring decades must have gone into constricting her gaze and thin lips into bemused, strained slits. Her gray hair, in a bun, is tied in a knot. She appears much the same in photos where she stands beside my mother who, not tall in fact, appears so as she stands alongside her diminutive mother. In one photo, my mother, a fashionable looking flapper in a black dress with lace top, shows off spit curls pressed so closely to her ears that they resembled tattooed hoops, above which her dark hair is piled high, bound with a Spanish comb. In another photo from that period, her hair is cut short, combed out full and straight, just below her ears; a blousy white shirt is tucked in at her waist with a wide belt, below which her hips appear spread out in the wing-shaped flare of jodhpurs tucked into the tops of leather riding boots. In another photo taken slightly earlier, she stands, her luxuriant hair flowing down her right shoulder to her waist, holding a tall broom, its long straw bristles jutting toward the camera.

Over time, the two figures of my grandparents have taken on the aspect of generic, universal ancestors. What life must have been like in such a remote, barren landscape I would later glimpse upon reading a Berber tribesman's quote in an illustrated historical book titled *Africa Aeterna:* "Raids are our agriculture."

From this distance, the features of those two ancestors—cavernous cheeks and shadowed depth around the eyes, faded even then—have bleached even more, receded, incised into stone, blended with it, the very nature of the stone and the weather it survives, like scars of time.

CHAPTER TWO

BABYLON/BAGHDAD ("DARK LAND")

Ard Al-Aswad, which can be translated as either dark or fertile land, is the name the Arabs gave to Babylonia (now Iraq) when they conquered it in 651 A.D. The dual meaning of the name is attributed to the fact that it was dusk when the Arab armies arrived and their first sight of the land was of the shadows cast by the thousands of palm trees spread before them. Another source for the name is from the fertility of the Iraqi soil irrigated by the two rivers Tigris and Euphrates, which supply the rich nourishment of crops in that ancient "cradle of civilization."

Abraham, the father of the Jewish people, was born in Ur of the Chaldees, in Babylonia (southern Iraq), around 2,000 B.C.E. After Nebuchadnezzar conquered Judea, destroyed the First Temple, and sent most of the population into exile in Babylonia, Jews lived there for 1,200 years, prompting that archetypal lament of ancient homesickness: "By the waters of Babylon, there we hung our harps." Yet many of them began to prosper there, even preferring to remain in exile rather than return to their homeland when offered their freedom two generations later by the Persian conquest of the Babylonians by King Cyrus. It is possible that my father's ancestors were among those original Jewish exiles who chose to stay and settle in their adopted land, where their descendants grew and prospered.

By its third century, Babylonia became the center of Jewish scholarship, its high point the compilation of the authoritative Babylonian Talmud. Beginning in the seventh century, under tolerant Muslim rule, many Jews held high diplomatic positions in government, and prospered in commerce and foreign trade from the caravans along the Silk Road, while others were esteemed for their contributions to astronomy, medicine, mathematics, agriculture, literature, and the practice of law. This benign tolerance was terminated in the ninth century when, whether from envy or religious fanaticism, new restrictions were imposed on Jews, such as the requirement to wear a yellow patch, pay a heavy head tax amounting to the expropriation of assets, and residence constraints. On the heels of persecution by the Muslims, in 1258, came slaughter by Hulaga, the grandson of Genghis Khan, who plundered and sacked Baghdad. In 1401, Tamerlane conquered Baghdad again and brought about the downfall of Babylonian Jewry as a major force in the Jewish world.

It is possible that my father's ancestors may have been among those who, originally dispersed into the Iberian Peninsula (Spain, Portugal, Turkey, Greece, Italy)—*Sepharad,* in Hebrew, hence *Sephardic*—were later expelled by Ferdinand and Isabella from Spain in 1492 and emigrated, like many Sephardeem, into the relatively more tolerant Muslim countries of the Middle East and North Africa, ending up in Baghdad, Iraq.

The origin of the name Baghdad is in dispute. Some claim it comes from an Aramaic phrase that means "sheep enclosure." Though this attribute may be accurate, others, preferring a more poetic source, contend that the word comes from ancient Persian: *bagh,* meaning God, and *dad,* meaning gift. The gift of God. During one point in history this was certainly true. From the eighth to the thirteenth century, while Europe was sunk in the Dark Ages, Baghdad was the capital and heart of the vast Muslim world's "Golden Age," its center of education and culture. A famous institution of scholarship, *Bayt al-Hikmah* (the House of Wisdom), attracted, among others, the great mathematician of the time, Al-Khawarizmi, the "father" of algebra (which is named after his book *Kitab al-Jabr).*

After the First World War, Turkey having been a German ally, the Ottoman Empire collapsed and the Sultan was deposed when British forces invaded what was still called Mesopotamia (part of the Ottoman Empire) in 1917 and occupied Baghdad. The country became a British mandate, because of British interest in the oil fields, and in 1918 an armistice was signed with Turkey. After an Arab uprising in 1920, the British government drew up a new plan to establish the state of Iraq, but independence was not gained until 1932.

By then, my father's family had left Baghdad and emigrated to England. Historical travails like these would seem to lend credence to the idea that survival genes are made tougher, more durable, the more they are stained with blood.

SHIFTING SANDS

In the early part of the twentieth century, when many Jews from Arabic countries emigrated to America, their traditional occupations had been as merchants and tradesmen in fabrics and precious metals. In the new country, since they could speak neither English nor the Yiddish of their fellow Jews from Europe (making them a minority within a minority), the trade these new immigrants took up, requiring no special skills or education, was peddling. Its relatively flexible day allowed them to work as many hours as they wanted, and, without a boss over them, they could observe the Sabbath, which forbids the exchange of money. Another major reason was that peddling did not require a large layout of capital. The peddler would buy his merchandise for the day from Christian Syrian-Lebanese wholesalers on Orchard and Washington Streets and sell the items he carried in a *chantayah* (satchel) from door to door. A couple of these large valises were found by my sister many years later in a bottom drawer set in the wall of our parents' bedroom. Tied with a hemp cord, peeled and with torn corners, their original black shiny surfaces had dulled over time. They'd been left with my father by his brother Dave, and were empty; either long forgotten, or kept handy in case of the need for yet another flight.

In previous centuries, when faced with imminent danger and when escape was impossible, many Jews had used the age-old survival technique of public conversion while continuing to secretly practice their own religion. In the fifteenth century, Marranos escaped the tortures of the Inquisition by publicly proclaiming adherence to the Christian faith of King Ferdinand and Queen Isabella of Spain, while in hidden chambers of their homes they wrapped themselves in the prayer shawls of their forefathers and whispered their desperate appeals and prayers to a God whom Rabbi Gideon in the Talmud could both entreat and reproach at once in the phrase: "Who is like You among the mute?"

When they could afford to, many Jews emigrated to Aleppo, Syria, earning their living as craftsmen in precious metals and as shopkeepers in the bazaar. Late in the nineteenth century, some Aleppoans emigrated to Manchester, England, as traders in cloth and fine fabrics, just as earlier in the seventeenth and eighteenth centuries other European Jews had come to Aleppo temporarily, intending only to trade in the bazaar, but stayed, at first establishing shops and then larger companies, bringing up families, and becoming integral parts of the city's Jewish community.

Finally reaching America, the Jewish immigrants from Arabic countries who passed the often humiliating physical examinations on Ellis Island were helped by Jewish social organizations and put up as boarders in, usually, Ashkenazic homes. Small, cramped, dingy, these single rooms usually held whole families of new immigrants.

As soon as a Syrian (S.Y., an abbreviated in-group term) could earn enough by peddling, he'd rent a room that held fewer boarders. If he did well, he could earn enough to rent a small flat on his own, and then start saving for a steerage ticket for his next family member in line for passage. Lower East Side streets teemed with swiping, jabbing hands and loud voices in tumultuous activity in the pressing interest of cash exchanges: sidewalks congested with piled produce and household furnishings, stacks of unfinished men's clothes, carpets, used valises, men's shirts and women's dresses on hangers making a patchwork quilt against shop windows crowded with old coats, trousers, and pots and pans. Pushcarts sat side by side with their vendors hawking, in summer, iced drinks, in winter, sweet potatoes with their sugars bubbling through charred black skins plucked by fingers wearing gloves with the fingertips cut off, out of the makeshift oven in the cart's interiors. Porters lugged sacks, furniture, and stacks of piece-goods, trolleys ceaselessly clanged their bells, horse-drawn wagons dripped with large blocks of ice melting through the floorboards. Topping it all off—literally—was the roaring, numbing clamor of the Second and Third Avenue elevated trains that thundered by the brick walls of those immigrant families and single roomers who, from a second-story window could have reached out and nearly touched the screeching steel rail cars whizzing by just a few feet away.

More so than even now, New York (and especially the Lower East Side's teeming Allen Street, the earlier red-light district) packed more volume of commercial activity moving at a velocity spurred by a freewheeling profit incentive than any other American city. Though there were department stores further uptown, they were considered "high-class," "overpriced," and certainly didn't have the new immigrants' interests at heart. *Fran'sah'wee* (Frenchy, fancy, folly), my mother would call such expensive places, her one-word summary of a wasteful, dandified culture.

This only strengthened the old adage: "Never buy retail."

From peddling to opening a shop was a growth in economic status; from shopkeeping to wholesaling was a growth even more positively ambitious.

Early in the century, several new, relatively successful Syrian Jewish peddlers soon hit upon the idea of creating a partnership, combining their resources and allowing them to establish a larger retail-wholesale business dealing in such household dry goods as tablecloths, towels, curtains, pillowcases, bedsheets, and men and women's underwear. They called themselves "Oriental Jobbers," located on Allen Street, and provided the necessary capital for their fellow Syrian peddlers, whom they usually knew through family or earlier business ties in the old country. This familiarity and trust fortunately made credit easy for the peddler to obtain, while the wholesaler, in turn, had family-related outlets for his merchandise. How better to maximize a partnership, imposed by restrictions, for the benefit of all members.

Oriental Jobbers served also as a meeting place for community news and gossip (as well as addresses of particularly friendly and attractive customers), a post office, an exchange bank, and as a prayer hall when the time for evening prayer approached and the men assembled a *minyan* service, after which they returned to their business.

Arabic Jews, unlike their European counterparts, had no tradition of workers organizing into labor unions. At that time, the Arabs were predominantly a mercantile and agrarian culture in a century avid for industry. And since there were no factories in the desert, there were no factory workers to organize into labor unions. The underlying reality of shifting sands, turned into a condition of existence and a motive for behavior, to this day, makes every foundation suspect and tenuous, and every political alliance liable to sudden alteration and betrayal. Coming from that tradition and trusting nothing beyond family—if that—as merchants, wholesalers, retailers, or freelance salesmen, the new immigrants saw no reason to entrust their financial future to a union of workers with whom they shared no intimate family ties. An innate wariness of large organized official groups—no matter how public their claim of good intentions—made them keep their welfare close at hand.

HEADLINES

From the *New York Times* on the day I was born, February 25, 1936:

- Anthony Eden, Declaring He Wants Britain Strong to Prevent European War, Finds Today's Problems Dreadfully Like Those Before 1914;
- Rome Hints of Signing Reich Deal; Reports Link Germany, Italy, Austria, Hungary; Threat to France Seen;
- Nazis Insist Duels Be Legal for All, Ending the Ban on the Swallow-Tail Coat and on Rouge and Smoking for Women, and Declare Oiled Workman's Boots No Longer Au Faut;
- Radcliffe Girl Throws (Silver) Dollar Across Charles River;
- Jaffa Arabs Stone Jewish Laborers but Later Accept 50% Representation on Job Contract Awarded to Jews;
- Professor Pavlov, the Foe of Soviets, Called "The One Free Man in Russia," is Ill in his Leningrad Home, Stalin's Regime had Furthered His Research;
- Reich Sues a French Newspaper on Story of Hitler Loves;
- Massachusetts Governor Curly Spent $115,000 To Aid Roosevelt, but Not One Job Resulted, He Tells Democrat Leaders;
- Man Gulps a Racket's Bookmaking Evidence, Forgets Carbons, and is Fined;
- Independence for Syria is Proposed by France, Britain to Follow Suit with Iraq;
- Soviet Bids Army Be Alert in East, to Crush Any Who Dare Fall on the Fatherland;
- Ethiopian Chief Reports 412 Italian Foe Slain at Adowa-Asmara Road;
- Militarists Attempt Coup in Japan; China Policy an Issue;
- Italy's 'Wool Made from Milk' is Belittled in Britain.

CHAPTER THREE

BROOMSTICK OR RIDING BOOTS?

I never saw my mother on a horse, or even near one. The only horses we knew were the old nags pulling the rickety wagons of peddlers in the street; their sore, fly-bitten hides twitching and tensing, their ragged tails sweeping their hindquarters that, when smoothed, looked like rippling wet velvet as they hauled wagons of old clothes and beat-up furniture. The driver would shout, in a long, drawn-out wail ballooned into a yodel of plaintive appeal and whose sound could reach a poignancy almost like yearning, while making clear the commercial value of his offer to his audience by enunciating the vowels, "Iy-buyy-yold clothes!" The open back-ends of wagons displayed sliced round halves of red-ripe, black-pitted watermelons in summer ("Waw-dee-melohhn!"). Or, meant for our dark, dank-smelling icebox, the driver would chip a chunk of ice from a large block on his truck with an icepick, shooting sparks that melted on the tarmac street like wet mirrors, then sling it onto a hemp sack on his shoulder and carry it, dripping, up three twisting flights of stairs to our flat.

Those were pre-freezer/refrigerator/television/telephone World War II days. Besides, everything then from foodstuffs to fuel was rationed. No grown-ups we knew could even drive a car, much less own one. Cars, for us kids, were the enemy.

DOOMSDAY

After her citizenship papers were granted, my mother put pen and paper down for good, having no further use for them, and made no attempts to study even the most common words of the language of the country in which she would live the rest of her life.

With stubborn finality, a last assertion of will in the face of an alien, even hostile world, like other immigrants without formal education, she could at least assert her full power to say "No!" Her decision to remain illiterate ensured as well that she would remain immobile in the new world, but not in the old: she became even more intimately bound with her sister and brothers who often visited and reminisced and consoled each other in their shared language.

Like all children, present but unseen, I'd listen to the flow of throaty, slurring, coughing tones and consonants of Arabic hawked up from far back in the throat, coughed up from the lungs and viscera. Praise often sounded as vehement as curses. Often, it was difficult to tell the difference between the fervor of a rebuke and the ardor of a compliment, unlike spoken English, whose clipped words are formed more politely, civilly, with the tip of the tongue playing close behind the lips.

Through repetitive osmosis, Arabic words and phrases that I heard every day, all day, needed no translation: *Lachh-meh* (emphatic, drawn out *"lachh!"*) in its sound-mass held the density of raw meat (a sound, which for a native English speaker, would evoke a sense-response similar to the word "beef"), *heh'wah* moved like air, and *ard* felt firm as ground underfoot.

In one photo of them together, my smiling mother's left arm is draped over her mother's stooped shoulder. A brick wall and trimmed hedges stand behind them, from which formal neatness I'd guess the photo must have been taken in Brooklyn, not Aleppo, after her family arrived. They crossed the Atlantic in steerage (so close to hullside, my mother said, you could hear a shark scavenging for garbage being ground up in the propeller) during the Depression. I can't say whether or not she was already married to my father at the time of the picture. Their arranged marriage was common then among new immigrants seeking to mate with their own kind, and which fact my sister discovered only by chance while going through my father's papers after his death. This, finally, explained the utter mismatch of two such opposite natures.

One day, made curious by some friends my age in grade school when their birthdays were announced in class (since at home we never celebrated ours), I asked my mother her birthday. "Doomsday," she answered.

And only now does it occur to me to wonder if she had in fact rehearsed that "Doomsday" answer. When would she have had the opportunity? Her family and Syrian women friends never discussed such *Fran'sah'wee* social commemorations as birthdays or anniversaries. Among new immigrants beset by harsh economic anxieties, celebrating birthdays was not a priority, therefore not important enough to take note of. I never went to an S.Y. kid's birthday party, since no one I knew ever had one. The social hardships and religious intolerance, if not persecution, in "the old country" where our parents were born and grew up, did not foster a mood to celebrate one's birth. My mother's response was as clear as it was concise: why commemorate one's bad luck with a date?

Besides, no one in our community wanted to be considered an assimilator into goyish culture. It was well known, though, that Ashkenazic kids were given not only birthday parties but received gifts on Jewish holidays—Purim, Shabu-ot, Sim-hah Torah, etc. . . . Gifts, to us, were an alien concept: they spoke of a generosity on the part of the giver toward a deserving recipient, which we were not given, nor gave each other, any reason to feel.

Our family and friends didn't discuss or mention birthdays or anniversaries. My mother wouldn't have had a chance to prepare for my question before I'd asked it. Her response had to have been off the top of her head, or more accurately from her gut. This innate ability to compress the gist of one's experience and immediately express it concisely speaks to an inborn talent for quickness, however much turned against itself. And perhaps, from my mother's milk, I too inherited a weakness for quickness, the effect of which takes for granted that time is not on our side and so it is to one's advantage to summarize the perceptual data of experience as swiftly and concisely as possible; the most meaning carried by the least means in taking the next step; agile, abbreviated. When no step is taken, the gist of one's realization rankles and cripples: Arabized.

Another time, after she had expressed some comparable damning appraisal of a situation and the dire consequences that would follow, I asked her why she always expected the worst, to which she answered, "I don't expect the worst; I expect the expected." These were her terms of engagement with a not-too-friendly future.

Unschooled, unable to read or write a word in either Arabic or English, only after much tedious practice did she manage to scratch pen across paper in what resembled a spastic scrawl, barely adequate as a signature for her American citizenship papers: a crooked, spider-web of hooked letters, quasi-spelling her name, in lower case, minus capitals (a forerunner to my introduction to the poetry of e. e. cummings). On her third try, she proudly told me, she was accepted by the judge.

After her initial failure on the written test, she then took the next step: refusing even to attempt to learn English when offered a free class. She would not allow any chances for further failure. The few phrases she did learn and use at home or at the market were her mimicking of other people she'd heard, which regular usage made automatic for her, almost second nature; to be used when strategically necessary. Among her family and close women friends, though, Arabic was my mother's mother tongue. Seeing and hearing her regularly speak her native Arabic was to be immersed in an atmosphere of living audible tones that opened to an ancient and universal past.

Over time, what little English she needed she picked up in fragmented bits and pieces that she remixed and matched: "the World Series" became "the World Serious"; my father's plea "Don't give me a lecture" was turned to mockery by her transposition: "Don't give me a rupture." At times, she could switch from flowing Arabic to broken English in the same sentence, especially when she was angry and bawling out us kids.

I wonder if those instants of her posing with a broom and in riding boots were not stages for her to mock the disparity of what, given her pride and independence, she must have suspected would be her life after marriage, when a matchmaker would soon arrange an engagement to my father. What would marriage and motherhood bring—given the sight of her own mother in the photo, stooped and shrunken beside her: broomstick or riding boots?

If our hidden intentions often disclose themselves when we least intend to reveal them because we are at ease enough in the moment to let go of guarding them, it would appear from this photo that my mother had already chosen the broom she held out toward the camera, and would henceforth bewail it. Who knows the immediate pressures—family, friends, finances (after all, it was during the worst years of the Depression)—that led her to be paired with a man so opposite in nature? What convinced her to accept my father? What choices did she have? Was that image of spit-curl sassiness and fashionable independence, or smiling, snug in riding boots, only a wishful masquerade, or was it once real, only to be erased for good?

FIRST FUNERAL

I have an early memory of a hot day, with the punky reek of white privet hedges, that pervasive flowering summer smell that on first breathing enlarges one's sense of space. I was following my mother on foot in a funeral procession from our house down a Brooklyn street. From the intensity of her inconsolable wailing, it must have been for one of her parents, but I am not certain which one.

She wore black, as did everyone in the procession, and followed a black hearse moving so solemnly that time seemed to slow down. With one hand she held onto the closed rear door of the hearse, while the other tore at her hair and dress. It must have been for the last of her surviving parents that she was so bereft. The sheer power of her ululations, customary among Arabic women both in times of celebration and mourning, resemble the cries of joy at a birth as they do in lamenting a death. Her whole body shook, and I shook with her. While the men in the procession recited prayers, the women followed, sounding as though they had reached a peak of bereavement that no words could express, as their wailing cut the air like darting serrated knives, took flight, and carried beyond grief for the deceased individual toward a vaster space of universal grieving.

(Years later I would learn that it was no secret at such funerals, that among the genuine bereavement expressed, some of the cries were often ceremonial gestures, as in Muslim countries where it is customary to hire professional mourners; no secret either that wives who were commonly known to have loathed their husbands were often shrillest in their display of grief.)

But at that funeral, I had never seen my mother taken over by such a powerful emotion. And from the mass of people solemnly following her, the high-pitched cries actually rippled the leaves on the nearby trees and the surrounding hedges and made the air shimmer with lament that seemed drawn from further than the human mourners present, and grew like a keening wind foretelling a natural disaster.

In later years, on hearing these communal cries up close or at a distance, I can never tell if they rise from joy or anguish. Nevertheless, once such ancient cries of human extremity are heard, they imprint their tremors permanently into one's nerve endings. Their origin is the desert, and since there are no echoes in the desert, this din, propelled either by jubilation or despair, is hurled outward beyond hope or appeal, and whether in delight or defeat, finds its direction aimed into endless, unanswering space.

CHAPTER FOUR

DEAD LETTER 2

From another of my father's unsent letters I received thirty years after it was written:

> April 17, 1972
> My Dear Son Jack,
>   I trust that you are fine and busy in your enterprise, which I hope will bring you good results. We are anxious to hear from you.
>   I lost my brother Morris a year ago or so and this brother left no means at all of support for his family. His son Joseph I am writing to you about cannot support his mother, only left the daughter to help the mother, and the mother can't work, so you understand the situation, not even social security, and if you can help him in any way I will appreciate it, it is a very worthy cause, so what you can do, help him verbally, advisedly and morally, for he will be a worthy man later on. So my darling Jack do what you can, communicate with him and <u>let me know what do you think of him</u>. . . .
>   I am still working, and thinking to retire by the beginning of 1973. We have paid for our house, now it is our own and we get social security monthly. I worked very hard to own the house and hope to live in peace. I will be 82 by October 1972.
>   Your father Albert

THEIR MARRIAGE PHOTO

In those days, couples in studio-posed wedding photographs were made to resemble royalty. In theirs, my parents smile so easefully from so far in the past, it seems not to have happened yet. I can hardly believe how youthful they look. I peer into, and through, the clear, direct look in their eyes, and follow my father's look of regal calm as he stands confidently behind my seated mother; his already graying hair (he is forty-five years old) is combed high in front in a fashionable pompadour; a carnation, big as a monarch butterfly, is pinned on his lapel; his right hand is tucked into his rented tux's trouser pocket from which a black silk stripe unrolls nearly to the floor, a yard of good luck he'll use up just in staying alive.

My mother-to-be sits on a straight-backed chair in front of him, turned sideways to the camera. She wears a white lace mantilla on her upright head and a glossy wedding dress whose long train is spread out on the floor before her like an expanse of foam; with a resolute, almost imperious expression on her unsmiling face, she holds in her arms a dozen white calla lilies in full bloom.

This photo is the only instance I can recall them ever appearing equal to each other. As I grow older, I find myself repeatedly looking at my father's face for . . . what?—a reflection of my own? But I am already twenty years older than he was then. And as I was growing up, did that curious gaze of his search mine for the reflection of his own as a young boy?

On the wall behind them, a customary soft-lit shadow-screen casts a hazy portal's aura of lacy romance, the only suggestion of it, I believe, that touched them in their life together afterwards.

DEAD LETTER 3

Often at night, after we'd gone to bed and were about to drop off to sleep, a sudden rumble of heavy furniture being shoved around, muffled, like thunder indoors, could be heard from their bedroom (with its two separate single beds), and would grow into a frightening clamor, keeping me in a state of constant anxiety. We never knew what those arguments were about. Such things were not discussed openly by parents, and certainly not among the children.

Not until after my father's death did we learn the likely cause for those regular nocturnal upheavals.

A letter from our father to my brother Nat dated February 1976 in part reads:

> When I married your aunt [sic] Grace, I got puzzled the first month, she showed me that she is arrogant, pride, and never give and take. I kept patient and hoped time will change her, and till now she is

worse, arguing with a loud voice. I didn't wish relatives or strangers to know, but the more I kept quiet she takes advantage on me, this behavior have been going on, it is a problem with no solution.

Lately she behave much worse than usual and I don't understand her, she doesn't say what on her mind, not living as husband and wife. She is cruel to me when sick no sympathy. I only guess that she want to live in Ocean Parkway with her sister <u>or what</u>? I live with her so miserably I lost my patience, I said to her you acting so strange, may God not bless you with good health. When I returned home from the Hospital, I told her the doctor told me to have change in my diet, no greasy meals etc., she jumped at me you better buy yourself, cook yourself. I told her I will give her $5 more over the $40 I give her weekly food expenses.

I said to her I am not working, it is very hard on me to give you more. I said I am using for house taxes, heat, realty taxes the money I or both get from social security, the bills are more and more every 3, 6, or a year's time. I said we have a house of our own paid in full, let us be thankful, as most people are not lucky as we are, so now I want to live in peace, but you are always kicking, don't be nagging, no use with her. I never divulged our private affair with relatives or strangers, and I am not asking you to mediate as husband and wife have to reconciliate. What the hell she is kicking for. If the house was in her name only, she would have thrown me out, and the house was in her name only, but since 1978 seeing her treating me so harshly I found a way by hook or by crook, I made her sign that the house belong to her and myself through a lawyer. I am now living in the house like as a tenant, absolute stranger. Since you were born and before I couldn't join her bed peacefully not even once in 3 or 4 months, and then for good, she seems allergic to that. However I want peace, and so I decided to sell the house and let her get the half of the sale, the money to spend on her food etc., and I do the same. If she jeopardise the sale, I will stop paying her weekly expense. Now I don't want to be subjected to take care of the house, I am very old and I am <u>finally</u> decided to sell the house for I cannot live peacefully with my wife. When we sell the house we must both live separately.

He wouldn't live long enough to sell the house or live separately. He would succumb to prostate cancer at age eighty-eight after refusing to undergo surgery that would have removed his testicles.

Divorce, for my immigrant parents' generation, was unheard of, never discussed, and not an option. None of our relatives or family friends were divorced. Among our small, tightly-knit community, blood-ties were so intricately bound together, marriage often between one cousin and another, one distant family relation to another, it created not two but one larger, intimate, extended family, which, in effect, was an entire interrelated community. At that time, marriage was less a personal choice than a social obligation to produce children and larger families. Love was considered an indulgence, an excess of private emotion no more enduring than a whim, a momentary fleeting excitation to be restrained, if not wholly repressed, for the stability of a suitable, arranged union. The creation of family was the politics practiced by the community; any affiliation beyond its confines was suspect. Socialism, Communism, Liberalism, were abstractions to those whose families not long ago were nomads scraping a bare subsistence from desert sand, and whose experience of organized groups was witnessing them raid their villages, make off with their meager possessions, and plunder their caravans. Life in the desert does not instill optimism in progressive social causes or historical justice.

Later, in my teens, when I'd think of dating a Syrian girl, my awareness of the complex interwoven lines that cross-fertilized even distant family ties composed of aunts, nieces, first and second cousins, made it frustratingly difficult to sort out if or how a girl I felt attracted to—slender, dark-eyed, olive complexioned—might in some way be related to me, since they more often than not appeared to closely resemble my sister and first cousins. For all I knew, anywhere I turned for female companionship within the community, at any social gathering sponsored for young people my age, my sexual attraction to any particular girl might eventually result in such an impasse. So much so that in my pubescent brain, a blanket ban prevented any such possibility, and I did not, until much later, date at all.

As for the onus of divorce, isolated even from their Ashkenazic counterparts whose traditions and antecedents were alien to them, for these new immigrant Orthodox Jews from Arabic countries, who comprised a minority within a larger minority, the shame of divorce was both a religious and social stigma and, in practice, if the community were to survive and flourish, would be more difficult to bear than the more ordinary unhappiness of marriage. Divorce would practically put one into a state of *hae'raem* (excommunication, in Hebrew), with its echo in Arabic, *ha'rahm* (forbidden), from which "harem" is derived. So insulated were we from mingling with the "outside world" that marriage even to an Ashkenazic Jew was considered virtually like marrying a goy.

(Recently my brother-in-law Ike told of how, on first meeting my family at his and my sister Renee's engagement party, mingling with our relatives [I was not present, having left home years before], he overheard one of them say to another, "But he's *Jewish!*" [meaning Ashkenazic], and he suddenly thought, *Oh gee, did I make a mistake? Are they* not *Jewish?* Until he learned, as he said, "the S.Y. ways.")

Instead of divorce, you'd hear whisperings about a husband who left for work one morning and never returned. Like a few men on our street, the father of my best friend, Marty, disappeared one day and was never heard from again. For such desperate men, families were to flee from.

My father's resigned, uncomplaining nature, however, forbade him the recourse of flight, and made him accept difficult circumstances as givens, which he felt bound to tolerate as well as he could. Judging by the sentiments in his letters, staying in a marriage, however unhappily, was for him a test of character, a matter of honor. Much as once, in my teens, after I had told him that I wanted to write poetry, showing real concern for my future well-being, he chided me: "You won't take advice; you want things easy and want to find things out for yourself." Both true. And I never had the chance to tell him how right he was, and that what I came to find out for myself is that things are not easy.

As my brother put it after our father died, "At least he never left us."

DEAD LETTERS 4 AND 5

The next letter to Nat, dated April 1976, when my father was eighty-six, reads:

My Dear Son Nat,
   I am returning to you the Will pertaining to your mother and myself. I finally accept it and abide by its contents as dictated by the lawyer and will sign it. Tell him please I am sorry I asked him twice

by letter and in person to change it, that was a long time ago. I have not changed it.

Rest assured Nat, I did not see a lawyer about the will, your mother's name joined me in owning the house. What you thought and you heard, it was to scare your mother. Threatening her by mouth only so as to let me live in peace. It is and it was her mood to argue with me. I have nothing to say to you, and said nothing to strangers, and it absolutely undescrible to have been and still is how miserable she treats me as a stranger. She has been rough and tough, and lately I don't give her the chance to argue. I beg of you that whenever you see her don't say to her you did this and that, it is much better to talk to her privately to treat me nicely and let me live in peace. If it was someone else being treated like she has treated and still treats me, he would have left her nothing, no house no nothing. The last job I worked for eight years and times changed, where I worked they gave up the business and that was 15 months ago—and so I had to retire. I worked very hard in my life not to let your mother be dependent on nobody, bought a house and since I retired up till now I give her . . . (No page follows.)

The last letter he wrote was to the manager of his bank, dated January 27, 1977, at age eighty-seven, which in part reads:

I beg you to know that in case I pass away, leaving this dear country America, kindly look over my saving account and distribute half of the amount to Red Cross and half to Magen David Synagogue of 67th Street facing the Public school and nothing to others, not even my wife as she will have the house of above address to get income from.

Kindly note I don't wish outside people to know, I owe no debt to nobody.

He willed nothing to his children. He must have anticipated, near the end, when he was in the hospital with prostate cancer, almost what would take place.

CHAPTER FIVE

CANIN TIRE CO.

There we would live three flights above the street for the next fifteen years, breathing in rubber tire smells, synthetics, lubricating oil, and gasoline fumes from Canin Tire Company. The landlord, Mr. Canin, his wife, and three grown sons who worked with him, lived above their gasoline and car repair station, and our apartment was one floor above theirs. Old Man Joe and his sons worked on cars that pulled up to the curb, and often blocked the busy street. Car service and repair in those days during World War II was a thriving business, and after a while so good it had to expand, which increased the Canins' workload. Sometimes they hired mechanics to help, but the labor was so intensive and conditions so crowded, they tended not to stay long. Work elsewhere, in other shops or factories for men exempt from military service was plentiful and profitable.

The service station—which they hardly spent any time in—was more a sturdy shed made of wood and steel; just the bare bones of a shop holding massed piles of tires, batteries, and spare parts hanging overhead. Summer and winter, fair weather and foul, they always worked out in the open, pumping gas, lugging tires on their shoulders, wheeling car jacks underneath carriages and engines they'd then crawl under, or slide beneath on a low, wheeled platform called a "creeper," or sometimes in a pinch, simply on a sheet of greasy cardboard. Surely, during those years they must have spent as much time on their backs beneath cars as they did standing upright.

To pump gas, they used several large, hand-cranked orange gas tanks that they wheeled over to cars parked at curbside. The vertical gauge-shaft atop the tank measured the gas flow in its slow rise and dip. Over the years it accumulated a thick black viscous coating, like a gushing oil drill in slow motion, as I'd watch it rise, the slick black surface flashing rainbow streaks and whiffs of benzene, a sweet stinging chemical smell that I grew to like getting whiffs of. At closing time, these gas tanks were herded side by side, chained together, and stored alongside the front of our building. It seemed not to have occurred to anyone to point out that this was potentially explosive: I never heard anyone—not my family, the Canins, their customers, passing policemen, visiting friends or relatives—ever mention it as a danger that any errant match could ignite.

Morris, Sol (Solly), Jerry, in descending chronological order, were muscular boys. Morris, the oldest, was the biggest in size; we kids called him Mighty Mo. With dark hair and a dark cast to his skin, his abiding look was a scowl; his day started in a bad humor. Large as he was, his sour expression and aura of distaste took up most of the mood-space in the station whenever I was there, usually sent by my mother in winter to ask for heat to be sent up. Winter and summer, wearing a short-sleeved shirt, his arms and torso stood out and rippled like cedar bark as he'd lean over any engine, look under any hood, crawl beneath any underside of any car that pulled up curbside. Some core distaste and anger in him, as of being pestered by the unceasing calls upon his attention, made him impatient, though as a mechanic, whatever the job he'd perform it quickly and efficiently, in order to be rid of it as well as any questions about his ability.

Sol, medium-height, with bright red curly hair, usually went about looking harrassed and irritated, not single-minded and dismissive like his older brother. At times his mood would brighten, he'd smile at a remark, his face suffused with the sunny aura of his red hair.

Jerry, the youngest, who, still shielded in his late teens, was of slighter build than his brothers, not having put much time in physical labor, and not appearing eager to start. I never saw him with a tool in his hand. Empty-handed, he managed his way around having to grapple with the rough greasy edges and hefty weight of car repair. Bookkeeping seemed the most he did for the family business.

From Old Man Canin's solid, stern build, it was clear he had also once been as compact and muscular as his sons. He could, and did, perform the same work as they, when things got busy. But his bulk lay heavier on him, slowing him down, making him more dependent on them, and therefore tougher, more demanding, and often openly resentful of his sons. With shoulders stooped, his face was dragged down in prolonged bitterness and complaint. His two older sons, in their twenties, were locked in feuds and recrimination with each other and their father; accusations and reproach could be heard shouted on the street or inside the station, with customers around or not. Practically the only times they didn't yell and curse at one another was when they were absorbed in the details of their work, too exhausted to argue.

In cold winter months we'd bang on the steam pipes for some heat that rarely (and if so, miserly) came up. When it did, you hardly felt any warmth; and if so, briefly, and only if you stood against the accordion-shaped radiator. After the initial gurgling and pipe-clearing clanking, the peeling silver-painted metal folds might warm a bit, but if no pipes below could be heard reassuringly punched with pounding steam, no hissing of heat was on the way, and we could forget it. Steam heat, to us, was precious; to them, a waste. After all, they worked outdoors, pounding hammers, pumping gas, changing tires, removing or installing engines; stretching, bent over, oil-stained, lying on their backs underneath cars. Since they were plenty warm from body heat, why should they imagine what freezing temperatures felt like three flights above their own ceaseless labor?

Living one flight above their shop, they must have figured, why spend on heat when their work outdoors provided it for them? In the evenings, after work, in their flat below us, if they sent up any heat at all, it didn't travel any higher than their radiators. Even Mrs. Canin, a mild-mannered woman, who worked as her husband's secretary, didn't see any need for expensive heating bills. We'd steadily bang and bang, and they'd ignore us, later pretending not to have heard it, busy working so far below. After all, they were in the midst of their own loud pounding hammers, crowbars, engines, drills.

I remember at times being feverish, lying in one of the two beds in my parents' bedroom. Thin from birth, we later learned I was anemic, prone to fever and infections. I've since wondered if, in such conditions, the body can induce fever as compensation for the lack of heat: fever as self-generated warmth in winter emergency.

Early on, whenever I went down to the crowded, cluttered station, I'd have a tough time getting anyone's attention. Mo would give that "Oh no, not you again" look; "I've got more important things to do."

"Yeah, yeah, kid, we'll get to it," Solly would nod, both of them on their way out the door with a hammer or mallet or tire in hand or over the shoulder, out to repair a motor or change a tire. I never had the nerve to approach the old man, his bad temper was so forbidding I didn't want him to even notice me.

They worked hard, long hours in that greasy, gassy, carbon monoxide cavern whose wooden walls fairly reeked with the noxious fumes imbedded over the years. Their arms, faces, and clothes were always covered in gasoline and motor oil. The curb was their garage. We'd hear the banging of metal on metal, the clang of iron tools dropped on cement, the loud rumble of ball-bearings rolled on the low-wheeled creepers on which they'd lay on their backs to check underneath a car's frame; rubber mallet on tire-rims, the whole works dragged out and dumped onto the street.

Some years later Old Man Canin suffered a stroke, leaving his face fixed in a grimace, and his sons took over running the business. Soon after, they told my father they needed our flat for storage, and we'd have to move. A short time after that the fire in the building that housed my father's store occurred, which he refers to in one of his letters. With the insurance money, he put a down payment on a house two blocks away from Canin's, which we moved to when I was about seventeen, and just about to leave home for good.

HER KITCHEN

The kitchen was the hub of the household; all the adjacent rooms were spokes of the wheel. I still hold its cooking smells, warmth, and human closeness as in a second stomach digesting a cud steadily accumulated over decades.

It was a constant worry of my mother's that I was so thin and ate so little. That didn't seem so strange, since I felt so insubstantial to myself, so much so that at times I wondered if I tried hard enough I could become transparent. This recoil of shyness most likely originated from a sense of shame. In children, that sense, if excessively felt, seems to anticipate an acute embarrassment far in excess of any circumstances that engender it, avoiding humiliation's full effect by preempting a measure of it in advance.

From as early on as I can recall, she would try to feed me with a spoon held up to, prodding open, my closed mouth. A doctor later prescribed a small glass of wine before dinner to help my appetite. A few sips of kosher Manishevitz concord grape wine before a meal did help my appetite somewhat, but not until years later when I lived in Paris and had my first taste of French vintages, did I discover the rare savor of even vin ordinnaire.

Small and thin, all three of us—my sister, brother, and I—each morning, in a repellent ritual, were given a nauseating spoonful of cod liver oil for anemia. We'd line up in the kitchen, hold our nose, gag at the viscous smell of concentrated rotten fish, as our mother precariously held out the oil in a large soup spoon, cajoling, cautioning, and finally exasperated, threatening us into opening our mouths.

Since Jewish kosher laws mandate that all red meat be soaked in salt and leached of all blood before cooking, my mother spent a great deal of time at this activity, pouring large coarse flakes of Crystal kosher salt out of the cardboard box onto meat and letting it sit until all the blood had drained, so that we never tasted anything approaching rare meat. Before any meat was put into a pot to be simmered, stewed, fried, or skewered, it had to look pale, almost blanched from my mother's koshering, then was cooked slowly on a low flame she kept her eye on for hours.

Substitutes for certain staples were used because they were inexpensive and easy to purchase at local stores and markets.

Sunday mornings, when we'd usually have pancakes for breakfast, the amber bottle of Karo was brought out: a cheap, sweet, all-purpose substitute for richer-flavored pancake syrups, its chief ingredient being sugar thickened with cane syrup.

Mom always made her *kaa-iik* (round, bracelet-like cookies) with smooth round edges; Aunt Becky's had crimped edges, like castle walls and the slit-spaces between. Mom's were generic and practical; Aunt Becky's were elaborate and decorative, designer *kaa-iik* you might say. Each woman had her distinctive trademark *kaa-iik*—with or without sprinkled sesame seeds, with or without slits, baked dark brown or light—which we could identify at a glance.

Mom spent most of her waking life in the confines of the kitchen, and as she cooked, she'd regularly dip into the pot and sample this, snack on that, so that by the time she had finished cooking the family meal, she'd already sampled enough spoonfuls for a meal before eating again with us. Mom took food steadily, secretly, like an addict; or she noshed her way through the tedium of days that would stretch into old age, taking on weight, arthritis, glaucoma, diabetes, blindness, and, finally, stroke.

More than any husband, the oven in the kitchen was her true constant life-mate: it treated her well and gave her what she most craved: meat, chicken, fish: gutting, cleaning, salting, cutting, stuffing, spicing, stewing, baking, frying, prodding, stirring, tasting. (Arabic cooking, extremely time-consuming, is a sure way of keeping women tied to the kitchen.) Despite all her efforts, I didn't partake much of the meals she had worked all day to prepare; I would nibble "like a bird," she'd complain. Passive resistance was my method. Her counter-move was to force-feed me, which made me even more tight-lipped, and thinner.

Those times (and they were often) when our father came home late from work and our mother and we kids were finishing dinner—or as much dinner as we could be cajoled to finish—whatever was left on our plates (and there was plenty!) she would scrape onto his, calling it "the gar-bahj pail," with brusque swipes of the spoon to clearly indicate that this was intended to make up for the meals she would in the future *not* cook for him; that each spoonful on his plate was serving notice of one *less* she would provide him. Watching this, he'd sit, elbows raised from the table to give her more space, with knife and fork in each hand, a bemused mild smile of tolerant surprise at such largesse cascading down before him all at once, and dig in. He knew it wouldn't last.

Although my father was what used to be called "a good eater," his lean, muscular frame didn't show it. He walked off extra weight during his several messenger, courier, and delivery jobs; even when working in a store, he did the menial, hauling, cleaning up, and moving work. Though a natural for such work, he'd come home every evening tired and dispirited. But if he could, he'd walk wherever he needed to go. Owning a car was nothing he wanted and, thanks to the rapid subway system, didn't need: a contraption whose expensive maintenance he didn't want. Wasn't it enough that he had to put up daily with the incessant hammering of iron and wooden tools below us and spilling out onto the street in front; the gaseous, rubberized smell of old and new tires piled in the hallway; the chaotic honking of horns; the rumble and grinding of the gas pumps' metal wheels dragged on the asphalt to service double-parked cars off the curb; the yelling and cursing that passes for human interchange at the busy intersection of a major commercial avenue that happened to coincide with our address?

If his destination was farther than walking could take him (a few miles) he'd take the subway, as he did to his jobs in Manhattan. But like most others in the close community, his family (two married brothers and their families) lived nearby, within walking distance, in different directions. As far as eating habits went, he could eat heartily and enjoy my mother's cooking (when, as on the Sabbath, it was available), he drank no beer or soda (having lived in England, tea was his preferred drink). Even his gluttony was kept in check: "moderation" was a favorite word of his. What effort had it taken and how much had he given up along the way to arrive at such "moderation"?

HER SPECIAL DISHES

- *Kibbeh:* meat-filled, fried bulgar side dish we called "torpedos" because of its shape;
- *Lacham 'ahjeen:* round, flat, baked dough topped with ground lamb, chopped onion, and spices we called "Syrian pizza";
- *Mih'shee:* cabbage leaves stuffed with rice and ground meat, baked slowly in a tomato sauce my mother often sweetened with raisins;
- *Koosah jibahn:* squash stuffed with cheese, cooked in the oven;
- *Shrob 'il' loz:* literally "drink of almonds"—almonds boiled and distilled, from which their fragrant liquid is pressed and sweetened with sugar, brewing an intoxicating beverage served at weddings and feasts; my favorite drink;
- *Maah-muul:* ground walnuts and pistachios stuffed in a thick baked pastry shell sprinkled with rose water;
- *Ruh-buh:* a ribbed veal breast stuffed with ground meat, rice, and spices, baked for hours in its own juices that, if left out, would coagulate into a dense, fatty solid.

With a steady diet of these and other such vein-clogging, plaque-packed fats and starches, one could literally stuff oneself to death—and from the looks of many overweight, sluggish, middle-aged, and elderly immigrant parents and grandparents, quite a few did. Among them, I remember a corpulent rabbi who used to drill us in reciting the weekly *perashah* (portions) of the Five Books of Moses. Hacham Bokai-ee was at least three hundred pounds, bloated as a sumo wrestler, barely able to get up out of a chair.

From the seat beside his desk, he'd wield a long stick to prod us out of our torpor or smack us with it for whispering to a neighbor, then settle his massive bulk back in his chair and, visibly sweating from the effort of breathing, between our monotoned recitation, he'd push forward on the desk the empty water glass he had drained at least a half a dozen times already, and point, calling out to one of us, *"Yabbo, ruuh jiblee muh-yeah* (You, go bring me water)." Eagerly jumping up for the chance to take a break from the monotony of rote recitation, the lucky one would grab the glass and dash out the door into the hallway and down the circular stairs to the basement where, beside the men's room, we'd stand there an idle moment, smelling the ammonia disinfectant, and leisurely fill the glass at the fountain. As soon as we'd return, he'd drain it, then place it on the desk until time for the next fill-up, which always came soon. In the three hours we'd spend each day under his tutelage, Hacham Bokai-ee drank an average of twelve to fifteen glasses of water. At that rate, each of us was called on at least once. I don't recall seeing him ever get up out of his chair, even to relieve himself. Then, one day when he hadn't appeared for class, on my way home, as I was passing a house, I saw several men clutching the sides of a canvas stretcher as they unsteadily carried the rabbi's voluminous bulk out to the waiting ambulance at the curb, slid him in, and closed the doors. We never saw him again.

I remember one July that even the usual high heat and humidity of a Brooklyn summer had never (at least in our memory) matched. We were able to convince our mother to let us buy bottled seltzer water (not really expensive, but considered a needless luxury). It was like having our own in-house soda fountain to experiment with: a quick spritz of the highly oxygenated fizzy water into a splash of milk over some chocolate syrup and you had yourself your own egg cream, topped by a luxurious overflow of foam spilling over the edge of the glass. Other fruit-flavored sodas such as cherry or root beer were made straight: a dollop of syrup shot with foaming seltzer filled to the bubbly top of the glass, which tickled my throat to rapid, repeated hiccups. This soda-making apparatus—the creative highlight of our early summers—would come in handy when I got a job in my mid-teens at a soda fountain shop adjacent to the Seabeach subway. Both the station and soda fountain shop shared the same warm, rumbling wall in common.

MICE IN THE TRAP, ROACHES IN THE WALL

One day, following a trail of roaches back to their hole in the wall behind the kitchen sink, I grew increasingly incensed with the creepy crawly feeling in my flesh that, thinking to stanch the flow, I sprayed DDT into the opening only to see the reverse happen: more roaches streamed out, waves upon waves of scattering antennas came pouring out like raw spillage in what became an unstoppable flow—pooling insects spreading across the white wall. The more vigorously I sprayed, frenziedly pumping the Flit cannister, sloshing the noxious spray onto my hands and rolling down my arms, the larger the careening stain of swarming roaches grew, some so heavily coated with shiny droplets of poisonous mist they fell dripping to the floor, while the rest scattered, till I was caught up in a blood lust that, making me light-headed, only increased my urge to pump even harder. I had to annihilate them, or they would overwhelm me. Their sheer numbers at first surprised, then frightened, then outraged me. Such small insects, massed, became one enormous, unstoppable creature, self-generating, spreading like fire.

By the time the DDT gave out and my arms grew too tired to keep on, the diminished horde had scattered to every crack and hole in the wall and floor and was making its escape in tatters. I stopped; the wall dripped like a mirror; the acid fumes still lit my sinuses with a stinging buzz. I used some newspaper to wipe the wall and the pool of fallen insects, knowing they'd appear again, but hoping not in such numbers.

Another time my mother baited a mousetrap with cheese and placed it under the kitchen sink. Finding a mouse caught in the wire cage the next morning, she placed the closed trap in the bathroom tub and turned on the hot water jet full blast as the matted rodent flung itself repeatedly at the wire door until it fell, a gluey mass. Both her hands gripping the tub's rim, I watched how hidden fear merged with fascination in her face as it often did: protecting herself against a feeling of deep repugnance by countering it with a relished revenge.

DIVING FOR AIR . . .

Of our first years in the flat above Canin's on 65th Street, I remember, I try to remember, as if having to dive for air . . .

My brother Nat told me recently that he had just visited the old place on Bay Parkway. It's now a storage warehouse for Canin Tire Co. "Get this: I got *floos* (money), two grand in a satchel in my hand. I tell the guy I used to live upstairs. Can I go up and see it? He looks me over and I'm practically ready to give him the bag, and he says O.K. I go up and, Jackie, you won't believe it. The walls are torn down, there's piles of tires and crap all over. The ceiling feels lower, and the whole place smaller, but I still get the old feeling of what it was like, down to the cracks in the wall. It's weird, I'm telling you. Tears nearly came. Remember the hallway? As ever, dark as a rat's ass. Used to give me the creeps. Still does."

I asked him what he remembers of that time: "It's on the tip of your tongue," I goaded him.

"On the tip of my tongue? You mean like truth serum?" he asked. "To remember what you tried to forget? O.K., how about this: Remember the black shoe-shine guy near the Seabeach station who couldn't hear or speak?"

"Didn't he have slicked-down hair and a thin Adolph Menjou mustache?" I added.

"Yea, slicked-down hair and an exact replica of Monjou's mustache. Very good," Nat said.

"Put anything on tape yet?" I had asked him to record any memories he could recall of those days on a tape recorder while driving in his car.

"Nothing on tape yet," he told me. "This is all flowing real fast. I could have a collision. Imagine if I was writing this?"

"Well, in a way, you are, Nat."

"O.K., here's one. Mr. Zerah, Zerah's paint store. Remember the old man used to hunker down and paint his window close to his nose?"

"Yeah," I chimed in, "he'd rest his right hand on his left arm like a ruler, and hold the thin brush like a tweezer in his fingers. Ugly man; lovely script. Remember his dog Queenie, always pregnant?"

"Yeah," he says, "I once saw a dog mount her and go at it; suddenly it started to rain, one of those quickie summer showers, and they got stuck together. She ran for cover, both of them yipping and yowling like mad. Gave everyone looking out from the bar a laugh. O.K., I'm tired. Can I go out and play now?"

CHAPTER SIX

NEARLY DONE IN BY SWEETS

During the years of World War II, you would see many front doors and windows of homes hung with a placard with a gold star at the center, indicating a son or a husband killed in uniform. One day, returning home from grade school, I found my mother sitting with her women friends in the living room that overlooked the busy shopping thoroughfare of Bay Parkway. They were seated on stuffed chairs and the one couch, and on the floor beside them were bags of groceries they'd bought with their green ration-book coupons. They were listening attentively as Aunt Sophie peered into a demitasse cup of Turkish coffee, turning it this way and that, slowly deciphering their futures from the dark grounds streaking the cup's inner edge in rippling veils and seismic ridges. Once, after they had left, I took a sip from a cup left behind; it tasted like filtered mud.

A cloud of cigarette smoke hung, rank and musty, a noxious mist that filled the front room when my mother's friends dropped in after shopping to *shrob cigarah* (in Arabic, literally, to "drink a cigarette"). The literal meaning was derived from the custom of smoking tobacco in "the old country" through the Arabic pipe called a *nargheelah,* with its long flexible tube and mouthpiece attached to a glass bowl that filtered indrawn puffs of smoke through the increasingly cloudy water within.

Such a gathering of my mother's friends felt like shifting cloud formations emanating from the couch they sat on that held their collective effluvia, perfumes and body lotions exhaled with each movement, as though exhaled by the couch itself after they left.

I felt this about my mother's women friends and relatives except for Aunt Rose, the youngest, whose vivacity was a true embodiment of a woman's name perfectly matched to her sunny nature. She was as tall and beautiful as Rita Hayworth, and buoyant—in or out of water—as Esther Williams. No doubt, the fact that of all the women present, she was the only one born in America and her marriage to my uncle Al, my mother's youngest brother, was a rarity in that time—a love match—in large measure contributed to her obvious happiness, which she gladly shared with all those around.

Despite her American origin, Aunt Rose was also a model of traditional female Arabic accouterment: large hoop earrings, jangling jewelry, gold and silver bracelets, bold makeup, exotic perfumes: what other women would have considered "overdressed" were Arabic women's daily accessories. Dress was not only practical garb but a lure for attention: unguents exhaling attar of roses, almond, rich floral bouquets; hair, by appointment, teased, curled, fried and frizzed, encapsulated inside those hair dryers whose cones resembled the helmets of space suits in salons, hair rolled up in large curlers that held them immobile, looking impassively straight ahead or staring at magazines, or having their nails done for hours. While their husbands worked all day in offices, stores, shipping rooms, the work of women who could afford it was to look as good as money could buy, as much for each other as for their husbands. This self-enhancement did not interest my mother.

Alluring as their perfumes could be, their scents were cloying in the nicotine haze. The room, the largest in the flat, overlooked the wide open expanse of Bay Parkway, and through its two front windows one could see far out above the roofs of the low stores and houses to where the sky spread unbrokenly vast, enlarging the room with the space it looked out on flooding in.

Directly across the street stood a large billboard ad of a larger-than-life, rosy-cheeked young woman's satisfied smile showing the largesse of her beaming eyes and immaculate teeth as she exhaled a halo of white smoke from a giant-sized Camel cigarette poised between her pink fingertips. Mornings when I'd get up too late to go to the synagogue, I'd put on my yarmulke and *tah-let* (prayer shawl) and stand at that window, facing east toward Jerusalem, and as I intoned the traditional morning service, part of me was aware that, while praying, I was facing the image of a seductive woman taking a pleasured puff from a cigarette six feet tall across the street.

Tilting the gold-rimmed cup toward the afternoon light coming in through the window, Aunt Sophie was intoning words in Arabic I didn't understand. I looked at my mother for a sign and saw her leaning toward Aunt Sophie with an expression of such eager anticipation, she seemed to have projected herself farther than the physical space between us. I didn't know if Aunt Sophie was reading my mother's fortune or someone else's as they all appeared held in the same mesmerized spell. As I stood there, I too was held by the stillness of a silent attention in which I could follow motes of dust, hook-tailed like amoebas, in a shaft of sunlight as they swayed and floated, much as in a liquid medium, which a slightest breath would stir. The stagnant smells in the room, which perfumes and colognes were meant to cover, drove me outside for air.

In the street, with no destination in mind, I began walking and was soon headed toward Gavot's candy store, three blocks away. Other candy stores were closer but, without thinking, I was drawn to Gavot's because it was more brightly lit and, as I entered, had a more spacious, mirrored interior. On the far wall a Swiss Air poster of the Alps' pristine snow-whiteness with a small chateau on a distant mountaintop hung overhead, emblem of an unsullied Shangri-la of fabled purity.

Mr. Gavot, a slender, silver-haired gentleman in a neat gray suit and tie, sat behind the register. He nodded, a kindly smile of invitation, and I wandered up the aisle, my nose reaching to the top of the showcase lids, and my eyes scanned what there was to look over.

Mrs. Gavot, a diminutive version of her husband, sat beside him. Both, uncharacteristically mild-mannered and natively elegant for this working class neighborhood, were to henceforth color my associations with that proverbially neutral country's spotless reputation, as would the shop's white walls and white-tiled floor's ideal surroundings—as pure as the poster—for the multicolored candies on display. The sugary cloud saturating the air I inhaled transported me instantly as on a magic carpet to a continent whose air was the sweetness I breathed even before I tasted its flavor.

Sugar buttons in dotted rows stuck on their bands of white paper; spirals of cherry-flavored and black licorice twists; individual cellophane-wrapped butterscotch drops burnished as copper; assortments of vanilla-streaked and coconut-sprinkles like snowflakes atop drops of dark chocolate; tinfoil-wrapped Hershey's kisses each topped with its tiny flag; jellied fruit slices, their edges outlined in black like miniature chinaware; red-and-white coiled peppermint canes resembling barber poles; all more desirable than the actual gems they resembled. This aroma of concentrated confection made my mouth water in a tingling uprush of saliva from below the gums of my back teeth; in no time, it was sure to eat through my enamel.

There were many candies I would have liked, but, limited by the pennies in my pocket, I pointed to the butterscotch drops. Mr. Gavot lifted the glass lid and, after closing it, placed one on top. I picked it up and felt the pleasure of holding what a moment before had been out of reach.

Outside, the late afternoon light caught the flowerbud wrapper in buttery glints as I untwisted it and placed the dark honey-colored disk on my tongue. My entire mouth was suddenly a waterworks, secreting a thick sap of honey and butter and a silken undertone of—was that the flavor of scotch on my tongue? I walked toward the rock-strewn baseball infield behind Saint Athnasius Church three blocks away; there I could concentrate without being disturbed. In the company of others I would be distracted.

On the corner, I paused at Romberg's window to check for any new stamps on display that I might add to my collection. In my stamp album, countries were arranged in alphabetical order, each page containing rows of small squares blankly waiting for their designated stamps to be glued on with tabs you'd lick and press onto their backs.

Displayed prominently on the top shelf was the prized one I hadn't been able to afford yet: the classic two-dollar Abraham Lincoln stamp with the famous jut-bearded profile in silver silhouette on a gray field.

I was drawn to the large colorful triangles showing leaping gazelles and plumed birds from exotic-sounding places like Mauritania, Malaysia, Sudan. The more distant and unfamiliar the country, the larger and more vivid the stamp. Displayed on tiers of felt-lined shelves were zebras from Zanzibar leaping toward the Archduke of Austria, and pink, stick-legged cranes nestled along the green Nile bent their plumed crowns toward heaped stacks of oranges from Madagascar.

As I scanned and calculated how much more I'd need to save up in order to buy any one of them, the butterscotch drop I'd been absently sucking had been dissolving into a slick paste thicker than I could swallow, and just as I sensed not to let it near my throat, it was pulled there by a suction that landed it like a plug in a drain. I gasped for air, shocked by a dread that gripped me in a series of shocks gulping my breath away. I jumped in place, trying to dislodge the plug in my throat, but it was stuck.

A woman pushing a baby carriage approached. I ran toward her, jumping, wheezing, jabbing a finger to my throat. She became bewildered, then frightened. Head averted, she pushed the carriage past me, then from a distance looked back. I again ran toward her. As I neared, I saw she was ready to knock me aside, so I kept running past her and out into steady traffic as I speedily calculated the distance to my house, kicking against gravity for lift-off as my footfalls on the pavement jolted my whole body, but the lozenge didn't loosen. I had never run this fast before, my heels not touching the ground, only the tips of my toes, just barely, as if at any second my weight would fall behind and just my eye continue on, flying. Fly! I commanded my skimming strides, but they touched down, only to spring back up in automatic reflex, lurching for another level. Later, thinking back on this moment, I would wonder if—to all worldly purposes—I'd actually died.

Reaching the house, arms outstretched pushing open the building's front door, I bounded up two, three stairs at a time and banged into the apartment door, racing to the far end of the flat where my mother looked up as I raced in, jabbing my throat. She grabbed me in mid-run and turned me facedown on her lap and smacked me hard with her open palm several times on my back. I gagged, coughed, gasped, and a miniature drop suspended by a thread of saliva stretched and, lazily, landed on the floor. Gulping air as a thirst-crazed man gulps handfuls of water, I stared at the pebble-sized dot a moment, amazed at how so small a thing could bring on so great a terror. Shaken with fright at my helplessness, I lay still, subsiding, on my mother's lap.

"How are you, dear," asked my Aunt Becky, her face transforming concern into reassurance.

My mother looked down at me. Her mouth made an effort to smile, but the lump of wrinkled skin between her eyebrows gave her away: that look I'd often seen on her and my sister Renee's faces when they'd nervously chew their inner cheeks out of apprehension.

Her face unusually pale, my mother said to me reassuringly, "*Laht chaff* (Don't be frightened)." To her friends she said, "It's just a scare. He'll be all right." Turning back, talking with her friends who took up her expression of feigned unconcern at just-missed disaster, the color returned to her cheeks and I let myself be reassured. Their attention returned to the demitasse cup into which Aunt Sophie was intently gazing. She rolled the slender curved handle between her fingers this way and that, shifting the muddy grounds that formed peaks and valleys along the white cup's inner rim.

She peered into it for a moment, then, not taking her eyes away, said, "Good news, Mabel, you will soon get a letter from Abe. He is in France. He is all right. He will send a picture of himself in uniform, with some friends. He will get a furlough soon."

"*Allah ma-ohh* (God be with him)!" Mabel exclaimed. "Is he coming home? Soon?"

Aunt Sophie, studying like a text the cupped depth in her hand, replied, "It's not clear."

"Look again," pled Mabel. "Look hard." She brought a small handkerchief to her lips and bit the exquisite lace trim.

"It's possible," Aunt Sophie replied as she turned the cup edge toward the light, then put it down. "Let it rest now. *Inshallah* (God willing)."

She picked up another cup. "*Beh'hee-yeah* (Becky), you will get flowers next week."

"Flowers?" Aunt Becky cried, mock-seriously. "Allah is joking, no? From who?"

"A secret admirer," my mother put in, and they all laughed. "I wish someone would send *me* flowers. Like the doctor in the hospital when Cheerah's son was born. He was examining someone and I thought, 'Examine *me, yah' kway'yehs* (handsome). Examine *me!*'" They all laughed again.

Aunt Sophie replied "It's not clear, *Beh'hee-yeah*. You'll find out then."

Aunt Becky sighed. "More waiting . . . Sophie, *dah-chee'lehk* (please), can't you do something about all this waiting. It's like waiting for the Messiah. *Bess ba-aa* (Enough already)! It's killing me."

Putting the cup down, Aunt Sophie began to get up. "No more now," she said. "It's getting late. I have to start supper. 'Brahim doesn't like to wait when he gets home."

Slowly rising, she picked up her grocery bag and asked me, "Feeling better now? You're lucky to have your mother."

The other women, gathering up their purses and grocery bags, murmured their sympathy as their movements stirred a jangle of bracelets and musty odors from the couch cushions that would retain their imprints after they left.

While my mother saw them to the door, I sat, looking out the window. The quietness in the room settled into me. Across the street, the grocery stalls and open-air markets were covered with green tarpaulin. Somewhere farther on, in countries called France and Germany, there was an ongoing war we heard news about every day on the radio; the front pages of newspapers showed thick curved arrows crisscrossing borders in circling motions, poised to strike.

My mother, returned from seeing off her friends, gathered the cups and saucers and wiped out the ashtrays. Watching her, I couldn't quite recall my connection to her. Who she was receded, almost dwindling away, and then, in an aching glimpse of just how far my separateness had yet to go, her immediacy rushed back and I clung to her housedress smelling of smoky cooking odors and sweat.

A BEAUTIFUL FAMILY

I recall being dressed as the page boy at the wedding of my Uncle Al and Aunt Rose. She, of whom people remarked, "She's a gem," "she's a peach," "she's a rose," and deservedly so; and my Uncle Al, handsome as a movie star. I couldn't have been more than three or four years old; dressed in a snug red velvet suit, carrying a ring on a silken white cushion down a long carpeted aisle.

Later, their honeymoon photo on our wall showed them strolling along the Atlantic City boardwalk, arm-in-arm, both lit up, smiling (in a lovers' smile that can't be faked), the photographer's camera having caught a breeze that billows the cuff of my uncle's trousers, ballooning a puff of momentary bliss. It seemed that all their later happiness (at least what I saw of it) was prefigured and permanently held in that honeymoon photo's expansive hoop of air. My mother would say of Aunt Rose: *"Dah'ka mittle shemis* (Her laughter is like sunshine), so open and full, it lights you up." And their children were beautiful as well.

AUNT BECKY

Of my mother's family, my favorite was Aunt Becky (her Biblical name, Rebecca). Older by a few years than my mother, Aunt Becky, usually practical and a peacemaker, could be tough and blunt, even ferocious, when she felt someone's selfishness or injustice needed to be read the riot act. And she felt it often, especially when she saw my mother openly disrespectful of our father in our presence, or when she'd put herself between one of us kids and my mother who was about to punish us for some minor infraction, or when she thought my mother was about to say words she would regret. In a husky, quavering voice, Aunt Becky would bark out her no-nonsense indignation that, because just, prompted no argument. In such moments, the sound from her throat was like a gear being stripped from its lining.

Lean and lanky, she was the physical and emotional opposite of my mother, stocky, and given to sneers and sarcasm. Aunt Becky, even-handed until in her last years—blind, diabetic, riddled with cancer—when her indignation at injustice grew mute. Her husband, Uncle Joe—heavyset, gruffly loud when not overbearing—was her opposite. When I think of it now, I see them as my parents' opposites. Their pairing, too, an arranged marriage, produced my cousins: two sons and two daughters.

Aunt Becky's kindness and compassion reached further than her own immediate family. During World War II she volunteered as a nurse and served in several Army hospitals in Brooklyn. I remember her in her triangular nurse's cap, crisp white uniform and stockings; in photos taken at the time she looks happy in the company of her sister-nurses standing beside the rows of beds of convalescing soldiers.

Those photos bring to mind a scene that returns when I think of Aunt Becky living a block away from Seth Low Park: I must have been around four years old, as America was about to enter the war, in 1940. Just outside the gates of the park, in the wide avenue, a military parade was passing: soldiers, sailors, blue-jacketed cadets with white spats topping, like milky-white cozies, their shiny black boots. A mass of humanity—more than I'd ever seen—marching in tidal lock-step to rumbling drumbeats, blaring bugles, tingling xylophones; hundreds of cresting, colorful rows, perfectly synchronized formations: uniforms, helmets, rifles, jouncing bayonets; young men's heads held high in the hot summer air steaming with crowds of onlookers pressed together on the streets. I was small enough to perch on someone's shoulders (my father's, I think), held high so I could get a good look—above the milling, sweltering crush of people that were a huge breathing body—of wave on wave of passing soldiers and cadets, sweating in their uniforms, proud, swelling, then subsiding, heads and shoulders rising and dipping, led by twirling batons in blaring flourishes and fanfares. Before a war there's always a show put on before the slaughter starts and young bodies return in pieces, if at all. A summer's glare throwing such blinding light-points off helmets, rifles, and bayonets, and more than sixty years later I'm still squinting.

Aunt Becky was as ardently loving as she could be fiercely outraged, and I felt gladly received by her. Before we had a TV set, I'd happily walk the eight blocks to her house to watch the original Captain Video. She was one of that new space TV program's appreciative fans. Watching a single character wearing a large v on the front of his tunic while seated in front of a keyboard of dials and talking into it, was all it took to hold her attention and keep her enthralled, as I watched lying on the floor.

Walking through the neighborhood streets, seeing the same familiar faces every day hanging out their windows, or lounging on their porches, sitting on their stoops, or promenading on the avenue like a fashion runway, gave a sense of inhabiting a safe, privileged zone. My eight-block walk to Aunt Becky's apartment gave me a fore-sense of awaiting welcome.

I'd go around the corner to Bay Parkway and pass the greasy, pungent odors from the Chinese Mandarin restaurant above where my best friend Marty Lowy and his family lived, and glance into Zerah's paint store with its exquisitely hand-lettered sign on the front window in which paint catalogues lay opened to cube-shaped colored tabs graduated in hue and intensity from pale to intense primaries; and passing Pellagrino's Bar, always dark inside, its regular clientele of bookies and bettors shrouded in murky whiffs of tobacco and a fermenting beery brew you'd smell wafting out its front window; past the cavernous entrance to the Sea Beach train station and the soda fountain next door in which, years later, I'd work the night shift, squirting sodas, whipping malts, cherrying banana splits, a dream job for a sweet-tooth like mine; past the bank whose sidewalk flashed with eye-catching glints of mica.

Inhaling the fragrance from the bakery, then the spices mixed with pickled brine wafting through the open door of the adjacent kosher deli, I'd pass the Marlboro Theater, glancing at the marquee to see if my favorites—blond, Asian-eyed Virginia Mayo or bathing-suited Esther Williams—were featured; and (getting close now) across the street, the vista of Seth Low Park opened nearly as far as the eye could see to the spacious black tarmac of the outfield and beyond; there we'd play handball inside the gated courts unprotected overhead from home run bombs that regularly came dropping in; the player's cry of "Heads up!" always seeming the opposite of what should have been called for, but we all instinctively knew what it meant; and turning onto her street lined on both sides with tall citadel-like cedar and oak trees, their great arched shady branches cast a carpet of continuous interlaced shadow on the pavement ushering me toward her cool, welcoming door.

CHAPTER SEVEN

JOSEPHINE DESTIFANO IN P.S. 205

She sat in the row in front of mine; her open oval face—olive complexion, large eyes black as the prized marbles we called "purees," with arched eyebrows and a bow of plump purple lips like a swimmer out of water, her dark glossy hair brushing my desktop—was a symmetry of features that held hypnotic power. I was smitten; taken up with wanting her attention, which soon grew to obsession. Her smile lit up the space around; you felt rare delight in its presence. Of course this made her popular with the other kids, girls as well as boys, and I would be jealous of her too-easily-given gift to others.

Even more than goy, Josephine was Sicilian. True, her family emigrated here long before World War II broke out, but still—Sicily, Mussolini (Hitler's barrel-chested, plumed parrot), and on top of that, Catholic—she was *assuur* (forbidden), and yet she looked somehow familiar, even familial. How could such beauty be forbidden? Was this a test? If so, how unfair was God!

Seeing her in homeroom class each day was a religious experience; the closest to a living incarnation of the divine spirit housed directly across the street in the Magen David synagogue, but nowhere in sight.

Outside, punky-smelling privet bushes whitening in clusters were beginning to give a provocative sourish-sweet aroma to the passing air.

One morning in early April, with sunshine spread down to the honeywood floor from the high windows of the classroom, I felt a physical stirring, a nerve-tingling impulse aching to be released. The clear mild weather, after a cold confining winter drew stimuli and sensations close.

Sometimes you'd sense a light-headed giddiness nag your nerves like an itch; it'd yank like some unknown marine life caught at the end of a line, gasping its first full mouthfuls of oxygen before lifting, airborne. "Like mad"—the overwhelming physical urge to burst out of one's skin!

I FOLLOW

One day I followed Josephine home through a neighborhood unfamiliar to me, five blocks from school into the lower-numbered avenues, with broken patches of cement in the sidewalk and patched potholes in the streets. The weathered wood frame homes, faded red-brick storehouses and garages looked like they had, over time, absorbed the deep hues of summer sunsets in their pitted surfaces. Lying low to the ground, nearly at the horizon line, they had that run-down, abandoned look like the edges of prairie towns put up by settlers who had moved on—making it doubly deserted—and underneath the broken concrete of the streets a vast emptiness would someday take back what still stood and, in time, scatter it.

As I followed about a half-block behind Josephine, the suspended air smelled of sharp parmesan cheese and pepper; thick lengths of salami crowded the ceilings of butcher shops along the way, and pigs hung snout-down on metal hooks, their cloven hooves suspended, caught as if in mid-run behind parted checkerboard-curtained windows.

When she reached her house, a two-story apartment building, her grandmother, slight and suspicious in her eternal widow's black, who'd been waiting behind the front door, stepped out to meet her and, spotting me (Josephine hadn't), though I was still a distance up the street, gave me a full dose of the Sicilian evil eye: that directed, condemning beam aimed at you, singling you out, was a feature I had noticed among elderly Italian men and women on the streets and in shops in my neighborhood. The dark-shadowed half-moons under their eyes conveyed an aggrieved look of having unjustly suffered and wishing that suffering on you. It seemed that the older they were, the more they looked as if their faces were sinking into those shadows beneath their eyes, the look of the grave stamped in them. It worked. Feeling the threat of that woman's look, with such a vindictive force, as if it had all of time to be carried out, I stood still, frozen in her gaze, and didn't come any closer, that day or any other.

MR. LIPPMAN, PRINCIPAL

Since I tended to have little appetite in those days, my mother would try to force-feed me, afraid, I suppose, that I would otherwise not eat at all, which turned me nearly anorexic. No doubt my thin, under-nourished look one day, when I was in third or fourth grade, prompted the school principal, Mr. Lippman, to ask me to bring my mother in for a meeting with him.

When we arrived and were shown into his office, Mr. Lippman, a tall, courtly man who (though beardless) reminded me of photos of Abraham Lincoln, came out from behind his large desk and took a few steps toward us on the shiny parquet tiles. With real concern in his voice, he asked my mother why I was so pale, and did I ever play outside after school let out. I could sense my mother gather herself to try to explain in a language that was alien to her.

In broken, heavily accented English, and pointing out the window, she indicated that we went to "Magen Daveed Talmud Torah across street."

"Every day?" asked Mr. Lippman.

"Yes," she said.

"How long for?"

My mother paused, searching her memory.

"Two year," she answered.

The usual composure on Mr. Lippman's face looked disquieted. He thought, then said, "I mean each day, Mrs. Marshall. How long each day?"

My mother raised the first three fingers of her right hand.

"Treee hour," she said.

"You mean, every day after school the boy spends three hours in religious training?" he asked, surprised.

"Talmud Torah," she corrected him. "Our religion."

"My religion, too," said Mr. Lippman, "but the child's so thin and pale. When does he have time to play outdoors? Children need that."

"My chillen play pleny," my mother reassured him.

This didn't seem to convince Mr. Lippman, but he didn't press the issue.

Instead, he had me assigned to health class.

HEALTH CLASS

"Health class" turned out to be an odd title, since health was exactly what we lacked. It was, in effect, a day care, or kiddy sanatorium/rest-home-away-from-home, for the under- and overweight, and variously handicapped kids. No difference was made between physical and psychological "challenges" as the current parlance has it. Weirdos and nose-pickers, catatonics and jabberers, fat and skinny—we were all lumped together in a large sunny room and left, as if at sea. A crutch here, a leg brace there; an always-smiling girl's face, who in a permanent mask of surprise never seemed to blink; a boy whose body odor and breath always stank from neglected hygiene; the tubby kid who let his fingernails grow long and fanged, like Fu Manchu, and whose parents apparently saw no reason to do anything about; the underweight bony kids, like me, who each ate "like a bird." Excused from strenuous activity, such as gym class, and from most of the prescribed curriculum of regular students, we were allowed to pass the time mostly as we pleased: drawing, doodling, chatting, napping, or simply gazing into space.

And the best part was that instead of desks, we each had a deck chair to lounge on for the school day's duration. As though permanently on a cruise, stretched out on polished honeywood slats, with lots of legroom, though lying prone most of the day was hard on the butt and backbone, especially for skinny kids like me. Except for an occasional lesson in spelling or math, we hardly had any schoolwork to do.

Mrs. Daley, our all-purpose teacher, spoke with a faint Irish accent, a melodious break from hearing flat, standard English. She went over basic writing and spelling on the blackboard, pulled down large maps, and covered elementary math lessons to which, having little interest in, I paid less attention. But being of a spirit as capacious as her physical bulk, Mrs. Daley didn't press lessons on us, as long as quiet was kept in the room. No tests were given, homework was rarely assigned. In a way, we inhabited the enviable splendid realm of being left to our own interests.

Perhaps looking older than her actual age, and thus called in the common term of those days, an "old maid," Mrs. Daily wore her coiled gray hair in a bun and dressed in conservative gray suits and flounce-collared white blouses, always with a fresh green shamrock in her lapel buttonhole. She gave one pause about believing that all women called "Mrs." were, in fact, married. The title, "Mrs.," was given to any woman reaching a certain advanced age, a respected dignitary who'd earned her honorific through longevity, or by turning gray.

From home she'd often bring in a record of Irish folk songs and play it for us, always the same, featuring "When Irish Eyes Are Smiling." She'd play it over and over, singing in a surprisingly sheer contralto voice that she seemed to keep in reserve for just this particular beloved song.

When Irish eyes are smiling,
Sure, 'tis like the morn in spring.
In the lilt of Irish laughter
You can hear the angels sing.
When Irish hearts are happy,
All the world seems bright and gay.
And when Irish eyes are smiling,
Sure, they steal your heart away.

It was her anthem, love ballad, courtship song, and lament for a lost world, all in one. When she'd play the record, she'd face it as if facing the singer, and croon and lull along, hardly concerned with us, her voice following the singer's lead, just slightly behind, out of deference, touching on the sad and sweet memories from so long ago and far away.

With a yearning grown sadder over time in realizing the impossibility of attaining its lost home, her nostalgia attained a kind of pure state, affirming the desire to go on desiring all the more. It was the poignancy of hopeless longing, pure because impossible, and kept pure by the everlasting impossibility.

The room was the largest and sunniest in the school, with the tallest windows letting in the most light. Lounging most of the day on the deck chairs, doing an assignment, or taking daily naps after lunch, all were part of the curriculum. Sometimes I felt shame at being in the company of kids whose progress together through the schoolyard to our small play area in a corner to ourselves looked like a zany, crooked-legged circus to the rest of the student body. They'd yell, "Hey, boogie class!" as we crossed their games, most of us uncaring, if at all aware.

One day when I couldn't read the words she had written on the blackboard, Mrs. Daley noticed me squinting and notified my mother to have my eyes examined. Sure enough, when she took me to a local optometrist who checked my eyes with several magnified lenses, to my surprise I could see what until then had been fuzzy shapes on the screen instantly sharpened to peaked A and lightning-flash z, and from then on I could see objects in more finely edged detail.

MRS. RILEY'S KITCHEN

Matronly, stocky, white-haired, always in a clean apron, good-natured Mrs. Riley kept her kitchen as clean as could be expected in the school's lunchroom, which never saw daylight.

My memory is of an artificially lit basement, and her heavy figure moving agilely back and forth to the large stove and grill backed by the smoky cinder-block wall. Despite being busy and having to spend her working day below ground, Mrs. Riley was pleased when you liked her food; her appreciative smile added its small light to the place. Even with my usual lack of appetite, now and then I'd ask Mrs. Riley for another helping of her thick green pea and onion soup. How she could make the odious onion taste so sweet!

Above her, on a long rail, hung large-bellied, scoured utensils, stocked like a ship's galley. A flame-blackened cauldron simmered, giving off a burnt tomato smell that seared itself into the walls. The food was basic institutional cooking presented with no frills. She'd put out a tray of plentiful peanut butter sandwiches on white bread or plain margarine spread on whole wheat, each cut diagonally and stacked on one end of the long counter; at the other stood the trays she'd washed by hand, before the days of washing machines. I never saw Mrs. Riley with an assistant. She prepared, cooked, and served all meals by herself, then cleaned and washed up afterwards.

I leave her with her pots and pans and steaming cauldron, like a ship's stoker, in her underground kitchen where the small, passing kindnesses of memory hold still.

MAPMAKING

After lunch, we'd file back to our sanctum for another rest period on our deck chairs during which you could read or draw or doze, whatever happened to be your pleasure. This period was my favorite; undisturbed, I began the habit of copying (no longer merely tracing) maps from history and geography books. Carefully following the jagged, multi-inlet outline of an island or continent made me feel kinetically linked to the topographic details of the land mass that trailed from the lead of my pencil. I felt my first stirrings for foreign places begin as those craggy continental shapes took form on paper. Using crayons, I'd color in the green landscapes and the ocean's blue.

In copying the squiggles, outcrops, and indentations shown on the maps, I suppose I was trying to get a feel for the exact formation of coastlines, coves, and inlets, which in time turned out to resemble the route of an actual voyage I would take to Africa at age nineteen when I signed on as a deckhand on a Norwegian freighter.

I became fairly skillful at reproducing these maps, so that when our class was assigned homework to copy a map from a textbook, several classmates, knowing what I had been doing for fun, asked me to make copies for them, and thus I turned my fun into my first (and rarely repeated afterwards) financial profit when I sold them for a penny apiece. It was this fascination with the actual physiognomy of the earth that led to my seeking out biographies of cartographers and geographical explorers with exotic names like Vasco de Gama, Magellan, De Soto, Ponce de Leon.

It must have been those first intricate in-and-out indentations and convolutions of coastline that led me to the interwoven networks I discovered in the surgically detailed illustrations of the human body. The tributaries of nerves and veins; the lacing systems of blood vessels; the taut, layered sheets of muscle were maps of a layered interior geography, no less intricate and fascinating than the Earth's and, literally, closer at hand than islands and continents I might never get to see.

BEARINGS

That map
I crayoned over and over as a boy
trying to get it right   the greens and blues

74

then having to slog through on foot
was my body

More transient of the two
I make my light
take in   disappear into
giving back   world for world

PUNCHBALL

After public school let out at 3:00 p.m., in the narrow, one-way street
that ran between the two schools, we kids would play punchball for
the half hour before Hebrew class started.

Often, a car would approach and we'd have to stop our game to let
it pass, then start again. Later, after we'd tired of the stop-and-start
intrusions and the drivers' dirty looks, we'd roll a round cement-
based DO NOT ENTER sign from its stand across the street and set it
down at the entrance to ours, and continue playing undisturbed by
traffic until 3:30, when we'd roll it back.

This play in the street between the two schools, limited to a half
hour, was more focused than our usual play, being so brief.

A player would cover each base at the side of the curb while a lone
outfielder's job was to cut a ball off and cover the long distances
between sewers. Hitting "grass-cutters" ranked high in our strategy. It
was something of a practical science: backspinning the Spalding
Pinkie with your middle finger's mid-knuckle jammed into the hard
rubber, backwards off your fingers it would spin in front of you so
that, when it bounced, then stopped in midair, still backspinning,
waiting for you, the momentum of your rising body from its crouch
as you were beginning your run, let you swing and punch the ball at
your shoetop just before it touched the ground. Skimming the tarmac's smooth surface, the ball hugged it without a bounce, and so fast
that the nearest baseman had barely a chance to reach down before it
shot past him. Or, to surprise the distracted outfielder, you'd lob the
ball above your head, like a tennis serve, and, while still high in its
arc, punch it as far as you could over their heads; if you were lucky,
the ball would keep rolling down the street and out into the wide-
open avenue, and while the scurrying outfielder now had to contend
for the ball with passing cars, you could round the bases forever.

We were always running; it seemed our most natural rhythm, our limbs free, airborne; sprinting on tiptoe for minimum drag—the higher you leapt the less gravity held you—and made for maximum drive; a running that was more like levitation—your heels hardly ever touching the ground. All this half-hour's working up of speed would soon have three and a half hours of imposed piety and prohibitions to slow it down.

MAGEN DAVID HEBREW SCHOOL

A child's ability for total absorption will make what he learns by age four or five a permanent reservoir of memory. Practice without distraction, complete concentration, total immersion. That's how they get you and keep you.

From early on, I absorbed Arabic first, hearing it between my parents in the charged atmosphere between them, a thundercloud massed in their throats. Hebrew came soon after. Spoken Arabic and Hebrew are similar in their thick, throat-scraping enunciation. You didn't want to be cursed in Arabic, a jet like a flamethrower burning through the scrotum's genetic channel, back through time, through parents, ancestors, origin, and God; it annihilates all trace of past lineage and any future, voiding all evidence of your existence as surely as the desert erases all signs of passage. The purpose is to instill a sense of omnivorous peril, undermining resistance, eating away emotional reserves, and to pulverize enemies into a pinch of snuff you'd see old Arab men stick up their noses.

Since our father couldn't (or wouldn't) pay for tuition to Hebrew school (about five dollars per week for five classes), my mother managed to have us enrolled by badgering and shaming the board of directors. The case she brought was simple and irrefutable: if they truly wanted the children of their community to learn and practice their religion, how could they turn away any whose parents didn't earn enough to pay for their primary Hebrew education? She pointed out to them (though they already knew) that English public school was free. The members, wealthy owners of wholesale businesses and uptown retail stores, who prided themselves on their philanthropic good deeds, couldn't argue with that bit of Talmudic reasoning, and had to accept its conclusive logic. Thus was our Hebrew education acquired.

I started attending Hebrew school at about four years old, around the time I was enrolled in public kindergarten. The two schools were located directly across the street from each other. My mother would walk me there each weekday, drop me off at public school, and return that evening at 7:00 p.m. to pick me up from Hebrew school.

Seated on wooden benches at desks for hours, we read and learned the Torah in Hebrew; if our attention strayed and we lost track of the text droned and slurred in rapid mumbling monotone by successive readers, we'd suddenly get smacked on the head or on the knuckles with a stick by the rabbi. Elders know it's through this manner of directed repetition and boredom enforced through fear, that the student's resistance is broken down: boredom, your bride; repetition, your reward.

After innumerable repetitions, there was another reward: for us kids who weren't as yet privy to the caffeine habit, *ahh'wae* (Arabic, "coffee") was a secret weapon in the arsenal of fragrance our rabbis used: catering to our sweet tooth, it also kept us from nodding off during the hours of study: a dollop of finely ground Turkish coffee mixed with powdered sugar spooned into your open palm when you gave a correct answer. Bringing your cupped palm to your mouth for a lick, your nose first got a whiff of the rich, slightly bitter aroma. Then, like mixed night and day, the powdery white and dark granules on the tongue bit deep, causing a rush of saliva to burst in your mouth like a waterworks.

Rewards like this, literally on the tongue, made us eager subjects. I haven't seen one of my favorites—the crispy, toasted, six-sided kosher cracker, Tam-Tam, more flavorful than most—in decades, and wonder if it has survived those years.

As much as the classrooms of our elementary p.s. 205 were large and brightly lit, the rooms in Hebrew school were small, bare, dim (especially late afternoons during the brief, waning light of winter), with dark-brown hardwood seats and desks, and smelling of mildew and faulty plumbing. Besides my own, how many other pairs of eyes grew weak from all that reading and reciting from the standard Hebrew texts of the Bible chapters, with our fingers flying along the encrypted letters resembling claws and wing tips, pronged clubs, and tapering lances with their phonetic dots and dashes underneath like a visual Morse code, all revolving enmeshed in gears of running fire; all to keep up with the reader in case the rabbi, prowling among us with a stick, asked us to point to the spot the reader had just paused at, or flown by.

Sometime after we had learned and grew well-practiced in reading Torah, we were taught to decipher the tiny, unpunctuated script of Rashi's commentary at the bottom of each page, a lexicon of rigorous annotations on practically every phrase and word of the Five Books of Moses and the Babylonian Talmud. Rashi's interpretations were intricate, ingenious, and as legalistically exacting as a law brief.

We plowed by rote through our recitation in the light gradually dimming, the afternoon waning into evening. Just before sunset, the rabbi would announce it was time for *Shah-reet,* the evening prayer, and we'd rise with our prayer books and, facing east toward Jerusalem (just as for morning prayer, facing east, we faced sunrise and the start of day), we recited the *ameedah* prayer as fast as we could, most of us out of impatience and boredom, with others showing their piety through the proficiency with which they had committed the complete multipage prayer to memory. The rapid mumbling of the Hebrew words, manic and monotonous, riffled by like cards. Finally, in practice, the communal act of prayer amounted to a horse race: whoever came in first was assured of being counted in God's good favors. Here too, as above so below, numbers counted most.

THE DEATH OF ROOSEVELT

One late afternoon when I was nine years old, seated at my desk in Hebrew class at Magen David, as one of the other boys was reciting aloud a Biblical passage, without a knock the door opened and there stood Rabbi Silverman, our principal, holding his glasses and wiping his eyes with a large handkerchief. He was sobbing, openly, unashamedly.

Our rabbi looked up from the text he'd been following, and watched, stunned, like us, and didn't bother to raise his hand to stop the reading. The split in behavior between Rabbi Silverman's shameless grief in public and his usual officious manner in the privacy of the principal's office, was surprising. My first thought was that a family member had been in an accident. He blew his nose and walked in, and facing us, in a trembling voice said that President Roosevelt had just died. We were shocked. How could a president die? Sure, we'd read in school about Lincoln's assassination, but that was long ago, we weren't around; there *was* no "being around" then: it was history. And though "history," as it plays out, often doesn't feel like history being made, this grown man's unashamed grief was living proof that history *was* being made.

Death of a leader: How could it happen, I wondered, during a war still going on? Besides, President Roosevelt was a hero to Jews, especially those immigrants who arrived during the Depression and, like my mother, came to consider him a savior for instituting the social reforms of the New Deal. He was the closest to a savior this side of the Messiah who was promised but had never materialized. We were urged to say prayers for him. My mother, on hearing the news, was devastated. For her and her friends, Roosevelt—with his long aristocratic cigarette holder, braided cape, and pince-nez glasses—was royalty.

The next day, my mother's favorite singer, the square-shouldered Amazonian Kate Smith, in a radio memorial to F.D.R., performed her rousing rendition of "God Bless America," like a pugilist of sound. Over the years, her imposing size and bulk, as much as her powerful lung capacity, so impressed my mother that she soon began to physically resemble her patriotic singing idol.

HACHAM SHLOMO

Our class rabbi was Hacham (Rabbi) Shlomo, eldest son of the community's chief rabbi, Hacham Jacob Kahleel, and heir apparent to his father's title.

The elder Kahleel, tall and regal in his titled rabbinical bearing, used to jam a wad of snuff into one nostril, then the other, and in his black domed homburg (under which he wore the perpetual yarmulke*)* and penguin-tailed frock coat with the velvet collar over a white wing-tipped shirt, was a strikingly commanding figure who gave off the sweet scent of rose water. Wherever we were, whatever else we might be doing, we'd rush up to kiss that fragrant hand magisterially extended to us as he approached. So pure and tonic was the fragrance wafting from him, we could believe that, having attained such a spiritual level, his body had taken on the aroma of holiness that he exuded: heaven must smell this sweet. All of us wanted to be in its presence.

Smell sweet enough, and the flock comes running. And not only us, but men would rush toward that outstretched hand to feel the comforting touch of the smooth, scented fabric of his sleeve brushing your face as he lifted his hand to be kissed, then placed it on your head in blessing. Whenever he entered a room, each man present got up out of respect, offering his seat, as if this eminent rabbi were followed by a line of ancient *zaddikim*.

In fact, he was: Rabbi Kahleel, descended from a family of rabbis in Aleppo since the sixteenth century, had been chief rabbi of the Sephardic community there before his services were engaged by the Magen David congregation of Brooklyn in 1934.

His son Shlomo was something else: wiry, tightly wound, agitated by inner unease and dissatisfaction that rocked him like a chronic palsy, he was not revered like his father. Standing at prayer, his torso would nervously rock back and forth in a steady rhythm. In class, as he followed our reading seated at his desk, one leg crossed over the other, his foot, as though strung tight, would continuously, abrasively tap-tap the air—and at such a pace! His tense frame seemed wrapped in a tight cocoon about to burst. When he spoke to you, he'd fold one arm around his chest and with his other hand twist the ends of his trim mustache; he'd rise from his chair, repeatedly buttoning and unbuttoning the double-breasted suit jacket he had earlier unbuttoned to sit down. Wary, touchy, an air of agitated secrecy in his glances, his face turned aside from you in petulant impatience.

Young *mujahadeen* rocking in *madrassahs* all over the Islamic world had nothing on him! He rocked with the most zealous of them.

Rocked, but not rolled. And for years in Magen David *madrassah* we too rocked . . . but not rolled. That would come later, the first time we heard Elvis in the house.

In an e-mail, my brother reminds me:

"Remember the shul's Annex, & the pool to throw your sins away on Yom Kippur, not that you had any! How about the time I chased you around the house with a quarter and you wouldn't touch it because it was Shabbat!"

"I know," I answer. "I could be such a dork."

MAGEN DAVID SYNAGOGUE

The facade of our shul, Magen David, had the shape of a tightly wound Torah, its two central poles jutting up in the middle, corresponding to the Holy Scroll wrapped and stored in the synagogue's inner sanctuary. The concave dome at the center of the synagogue's roof was tinted the palest blue, no matter what weather dimmed or clouded the sky outside. Beneath that heavenly "wink of eternity" (the image I'd later discover in Hart Crane's poem "Voyages"), an ancient order reigned. Under its protective hood, a harmony of traditional practice, prayer, and gesture was determined by the season, the month, the week—all held together by the constancy of Shabbat. Because of business necessities, a man might neglect performing, in private, the three required daily prayers, but attending weekly Shabbat services with the congregation was mandatory.

Located directly across the one-way street from P.S. 205, and in clear contrast to its practical, cereal-box shape, Magen David synagogue was constructed in 1922 on a plot of land bought by donations from wealthy members of the Syrian community. Shortly thereafter, a Hebrew school (Talmud Torah) was erected across the synagogue's courtyard.

In the center of the synagogue's facade of red brick stood the tall dark-wood front doors with several stained glass panels above, and flanked by a pair of narrow turret-shaped windows through which sunlight was refracted into the building's interior. Opening the heavy doors, you stepped onto a red carpet extending past rows of polished honey-wood benches on either side and reaching all the way to the elaborately carved, four-poster *beemah* (raised dais) covered with a burgundy velvet cloth. From there, a cantor conducted prayer services, facing the podium in front on which the chief rabbi sat near the closed tabernacle where the Torah scroll was kept. High above, the celestial blue eyeball cast a spacious glow on all beneath who worshipped together. Out of a pervasive sense of order issuing from individual adherence flowed a communal tranquility.

After more than five decades of use, and after most of its original members and their descendants moved to the farther outskirts of New Jersey (where they built other synagogues), it still stands on its original site on 67th Street, off 20th Avenue, but is now used mainly for funeral services.

FIRST MINYAN

Though I was winter-born (late February), in December the onset of frost and snow felt like a punishing alien power that moved in, occupying the outer world and my inner body, setting down inflexible laws, restricting movement and freezing access.

Thinking about it now, I can understand how the sense of isolation in adolescence can make us seek out a group of like-minded individuals. The individuals, in my case, decades older than myself, were men in their eighties and nineties. They seemed ancient, Biblical. I must have wanted to stand out from the kids my own age, and be admired by these elderly sages for my knowledge and religious observance, reflecting theirs, if not yet in such a long lifetime of comparable tenacity, then perhaps in fervor and devotion; wanting to be part of a living tradition that drew deep sources from the remote past. I doubt whether the question of belief or disbelief ever entered the minds of these living patriarchs, or if they even gave it any thought. *Ha-shem* (The Holy Name) had always been with them, their most ancient inheritance.

When I was about twelve, I began to attend their early morning penitential prayer services during winter: I had to rise at 4:30 a.m., long before the required first morning service of the day.

This extra-early *minyan* began in the dark, as close to midnight as to dawn, making of night and day an ongoing uninterrupted prayer service. On my way, in the dark, I would stop at the house of Abu Abraheem (in his nineties) to help him to the synagogue.

After the jarring of the alarm clock, out of which I'd try to squeeze the last few drops of sleep, wakening out of the dark *into* the dark was like spilling from a brief nap into an arduous haul. My eyes felt scoured with sand, and my limbs ached as if they'd been snatched from the distant realm of dreams. And I was awakening to the same darkness, it seemed, that only moments before I had fallen asleep in.

Getting out of bed and, prohibited from bathing or eating before prayer, after no more than the allowed drop of water on a dish towel to wipe my eyes of sleep, I'd put on my boots and a winter coat whose lamb's wool lining had cracked in the freezing cold, to make my way through the snowdrifts to pick up Abu Abraheem at his door four blocks away and lead him to the synagogue for first *minyan*.

When my Uncle Abood had first asked if I'd help Abu Abraheem— oldest of the old men—from his house (since all the other men were so elderly themselves) and I accepted, I felt appreciated in my uncle's eyes. It has since occurred to me I was trying to anticipate (or bypass?) the process of aging by prematurely taking on the ways of the elderly and sharing their traditional ancient world with them.

How many years had Abu Abraheem followed this regimen, harsh even for a much younger man, scorning comfort, trudging through biting, bone-aching, penetrating cold, deep in snow, without missing a morning? So feeble was he, having to take such agonizingly slow, doddering steps, I wondered how he managed to rise out of bed, and so early? Maybe he didn't need much sleep. How did he put his clothes on? Did he sleep in them? Is there perhaps a certain perversity in piety? Does submission also have its pleasures?

On the snow-blanketed pavement, without a visible division between curb and street, and with no trace of any other footprints on the snow-crust, the crunch and squeak of my boots made the only sounds and the sharp cold stung my teary eyes nearly frozen shut. The whiteness all around was like waking on the moon. It gave me an eerie, otherworldly sense, as though I were still asleep, dreaming.

For the practice of penance, conditions couldn't have been more favorable: bitter cold, heavy snowfall on already deep drifts and packed ice underneath on which I'd step carefully, then shuffle more than step, slide more than shuffle, using the sides of my boots as snowplows until I'd hit a bump or a snowbank and trip; all of which further roused me awake.

Even so, I felt a sense of pride as the first one out this early in the still-dark, hushed morning. I had recently read Admiral Byrd's *Alone,* his account of his solitary ordeal in the Antarctic, and could well understand the appeal of giving oneself up to the cold in stages: first inertia, then lulling numbness, then the slippage into unconsciousness and the sleep of death.

Taking deep aching lungfulls of breath, I'd feel the air freeze the moisture to the hairs in my nostrils and, snorting out, my breath leaped into vapory animal shapes whipping around me.

When I'd reach Abu Abraheem's house and ring the bell, I'd wait, knowing that I would not hear his footsteps on the other side of the door; it would slowly open and he would be standing there, stooped forward, head bent, ready to go; a faint squeak, without moving his lips, was his greeting. He was hunched in a long black overcoat and felt hat, his cheeks a slack, papery gray, and his lips drooling saliva he slowly dabbed with a handkerchief in his shaking fist. Decades of strict piety had hollowed his cheeks, made his watery eyes rimmed red, and bent him from all that sacrifice and self-abnegation. Yet I never heard him complain.

Then began the most trying part of our trek, which comprised the length of only a single block. Gripping my arm surprisingly more tightly than I'd expect of such a frail man, Abu Abraheem could manage no more than a tottering step or two at a time, gasping, and we'd have to pause for him to catch his breath, before taking the next. The pauses between his breaths took up more time than the steps forward. In the icy blowing air, his breath smelled of the sharpness of vinegar and flesh in the process of decomposing. At this pace, we had to factor in almost half an hour to reach the synagogue. He didn't communicate in words, but with looks and nods and sighs and shakes of his head.

One morning when I went to pick him up, I noticed a light on in his house. That was strange; there had never been a light on at this early hour before. When I knocked and waited, there was no response, which wasn't unusual. But this time I did hear footsteps and when the door opened, an elderly man slowly rolling down his shirtsleeves and wiping his hands on them, stood behind it; wearily looking at me, he said nothing. I was about to tell him why I had come, but before I could he told me that his father had died earlier that morning in his sleep and, in accordance with Jewish law, his body was being washed in preparation for burial that day.

Since then, I've noted how, frequently, those who seem to enjoy life's physical pleasures the least live the longest.

Shortly before my Bar Mitzvah, my Uncle Abood presented me with a new velvet pouch that contained a shiny blue-and-white *tah'let,* a prayer book, and a pair of *tefileen* (phylacteries, one box to tie with the leather thong around your forehead, and the other around your left arm, close to the heart). It was his gift to mark my entry into manhood, as well as his recognition that my voluntary attendance at the early *minyan* proved my steadfastness.

CHAPTER EIGHT

CANTOR; THE LOVELIEST VOICE
I HEARD AS A BOY

The loveliest voice I heard as a boy belonged to the ugliest man. His name was Benyameen.

Squat, bald, toad-faced, small-pox-pitted, bullet-neck swollen with exertion, he stood at the podium facing east in the prayer he led each morning before first light. With the silver pointer in his hand, he'd follow the text; his steady arabesque of a voice coiling like a *muezzin* from a minaret, all keening velocity and voltage near the dim glow of the "eternal flame" on its wick in the lantern the sexton, Sion, always kept filled with oil. All the keener for coming from such a stern, stocky man, the voice seemed threaded through the finest of needles, driving and darting among these shrunken elders wrapped in prayer shawls, drawn huddled together, like the last bees still in the hive. Nowhere had I seen living faces as old as these: as though already buried in the afterlife, all breathing moldering earth-smells, their flesh withered parchment.

I wanted to be one of the Kohaneem, the priestly clan, like my Uncle Abood who, unlike my mother, retained his family name, Cohen, and thereby his priestly status. On festivals and fast days, when the time came in the service for the special benediction and the cantor would call in that sweet, drawn-out summons, *"Ko-ha-nee-eem,"* I wished I could answer it and step forward to the front of the assembled *minyan* and stand beside my uncle with the others, lift the prayer shawl over my head and with my eyes closed and arms outstretched spread my fingers apart, creating a space between them like a cloven hoof (the signal made popular as the "Spock salute" by the faun-eared extraterrestrial in *Star Trek* who, in turn, modeled his gesture from just this ritual). Beneath this hovering tent of a *tah'let*, swaying in place, I could bless the congregation members who, in this calling forth of the Holy Spirit's presence, are not allowed to look and must close their eyes. But this was not to be. Since my mother had forfeited her family name by marrying a "commoner," I had lost that claim.

One day Benyameen, unaccountably, did not show for the morning service. I missed him and was disappointed in the way his last-minute stand-in droned on in tame, pedestrian tones, methodical as the merchant he, in fact, was. Afterwards, walking home on the empty street, I heard a cry, a woman wailing, and turned my eyes to the sound from the large front window I was approaching when I saw the familiar round head and neck puffed like a cobra as the hand that had held the silver pointer had become a fist brought down in grunting fury on the woman's head.

RABBI HECHT: REBELLION

Though Hacham Shlomo was apparently his father's heir, a rival candidate soon arrived: Rabbi Abraham Hecht, contracted for one year in 1942, when I was six. Alhough Ashkenazic (and therefore in "old world" Sephardic eyes "not one of us"), he came to be accepted as a more liberal alternative to the more inflexible Hacham Shlomo's inheriting of his father's role as chief rabbi.

This move was initiated by a dissenting group of younger men who felt they had outgrown the traditional shul of their fathers, where the Shabbat sermons delivered by Rabbi Kahleel were always in Arabic, the language of the elder members, their fathers, but not all that accessible to them.

These first-generation, American-born young men wanted to form their own congregation and hold services in their own separate shul, as well as having English the language spoken by a "modern" rabbi of their own choosing. And Shlomo was not their first choice. He was seen as too "old world," too strictly prohibitive of the ways of the new world in which they wanted to marry and raise children and benefit from the opportunities offered by the new America.

Shlomo's demeanor—withdrawn, secretive, evasive—were qualities deemed unsuited for such a prominent role. Rabbi Hecht, on the other hand, was "modern," and more than fluent—in fact, quite eloquent and colorful—in English. Brisk, eager, and crisply cheerful, he larded his weekly sermons with examples of salty Jewish humor, and was open to opinions other than his own regarding traditional laws, their reasons and interpretations. He turned out to be a brilliant, engaging speaker, giving Shabbat sermons that seamlessly wove that week's *pae'rashah* (chapter recited from the Bible) with parables, proverbs, and ancient Jewish lore, all leading up, in meandering, delightful Talmudic byways, to addressing the needs of his young congregation's daily lives.

All this made his appeal that much more popular and winning. Anticipated with curious excitement among his new congregation, Rabbi Hecht's Sabbath speeches gave the impression of being improvised, though they were, in fact, carefully prepared. Rising from his seat on the synagogue dais, he would take hold of the two side-tassels of his *tah'let* in one hand, face his congregation, and, rocking side-to-side, tassels jiggling, would seem to free-associate legends, homilies, metaphors, and Talmudic speculation, bringing them all together into a unifying precept in a last inspired, digestible sentence.

Once, cautioning the congregation against arrogance, he gave an example from the Babylonian Talmud: "Adam was created last of all creatures, on the eve of the Shabbat. Why? So that if a person becomes too proud, he may be reminded, 'The mosquito was created before you.'" From the *Pirkeh Avot* (Sayings of the Fathers), he quoted, "Be humble in spirit, because in the end you will be eaten by worms." Another time, concerning the nature of fate, he cautioned, "Expecting the world to treat you fairly because you are a good person is like expecting a bull not to charge you because you're a vegetarian," which drew a laugh and knowing pokes in the ribs among the listeners.

Rabbi Hecht's religious zeal, however, years later would get him into trouble. When Israel's Prime Minister Rabin was working out what many thought might at last be a peace plan with President Clinton and Chairman Arafat at Camp David, Rabbi Hecht one day from the pulpit announced that according to Jewish law, anyone advocating surrendering land that had been won by Israel deserved the death penalty. When this extreme "penalty" was soon put into effect by the hand of a fellow Israeli, with Rabin's assassination, the directors of the congregation, in what some said was an effort to placate the worldwide liberal Jewish community, summarily dismissed Rabbi Hecht from the position he'd held with great popularity for nearly half a century.

And only a few years after he had been hired, his congregation of young first-generation sons were themselves rebelled against by their sons and younger brothers who, in turn, wanted to set up their own shul and create their own model of worship. Ari—the congregation's equivalent of "a loose cannon"—led the way, appealing to our adolescent sense of injustice and betrayed absolutes.

ARI'S SHUL

My brother Nat e-mailed me:

"o.k., here's one: Remember Ari's shul?"

"Do I *ever!* Don't get me started . . ." I wrote back, already recalling Ari (lion) in his early thirties, medium height, sinewy build; his entire compact body a fist in perpetual motion—lunging, pointing, exhorting, promising, proscribing, threatening. From some minor differences about religious custom, or from a sense of having been slighted by committee members of the synagogue, or whatever, Ari became a dynamo of resistance and defiance. He'd stop us kids in the hallway or out in the courtyard or wherever we were playing ball, and demand that we form our own congregation. It was understood that he would lead it.

He had faith that we would be "courageous," he said, calling us "Maccabees," the Jewish resistance heroes who rescued Judea from the Syrian rule of Antiochus Epiphanes in the second century, B.C.E., and made it independent for about a century. On hearing an adult call us that ennobling name, we took it to heart. Ari's genius was to enable us to feel like chosen cohorts in a plot for independence. In preparation, he had rented one of the unoccupied homes across the courtyard from the main synagogue. We knew he wasn't a rich man. He had a wife and children and worked as a salesman in a Syrian retail store on lower 5th Avenue. He couldn't afford to pay two rents. But, given his bracing, persuasive manner, one saw how he could convince some concerned, religious businessmen in the community that their young sons and brothers would be looked after and responsibly led by one such as himself, looking out for our social well-being (meaning keeping an eye on us, and out of trouble) and continuing our religious practice (meaning we'd not likely stray).

For firebrand fanatics, though, Ari took the cake—sponge cake, at that, the *glot kosher* (Yiddish for "most scrupulously kosher") Hebrew National kind in a box he gave out to us—another sweet inducement—when we attended his new shul.

Shrewd, convincing salesman that he was in his day job, he'd gotten the Magen David elders committee to contribute benches, a dais, and a new Torah scroll to us, plus renting the ground floor of the house across the courtyard for us to hold services in nearby, but not in their way. For a small donation, they had themselves a dependable babysitter, plus they had gotten a malcontent troublemaker out of their hair.

Ari's face, clean-shaven, showed his firm, defined features. You could instinctively tell there was no fat or "soft life" there and, for that, you could trust, even admire, the man. He made us feel heroic as the youthful vanguard of an ancient tradition.

With no mustache, beard, or Hasidic *pae-oht* (the long side-curls that Sephardic Jews, unlike their Ashkenazic counterparts, do not share the custom of wearing), his expression could be quickly read. He'd fix you with a steady, searching look in which—if he smiled with approval—you felt yourself chosen as one of an elite cadre; or, if with disapproval, the edge was always shaded with aggrieved disappointment. His glare could make you feel like a *koh'fer* (an apostate) who should be stoned, though you might be one of those who were *already* among his devoted followers! For those kids on the outs, he prescribed the eternal fires of *Gehenam* (hell). Talk about tyrants! He held that shul in his fist like a sultan gripping his empire, distributing sweets and praise and pats on the head, or else banishment. Kids he bawled out never came back. The ones he patted on the head and gave candy to loved it . . . at first. He made you feel like a freedom fighter, or like young cubs in the lion's den.

For a time, he was both father and father-killer. I'm sure he saw himself as a proto-Messiah. It was the zeal in his eye that picked you out, that set you apart.

He'd tell us not to engage our "enemies" in argument; that if you stayed around to explain your case, they'd have won by the plain fact of having held you back that much longer.

He'd exhort, "If people say you are going too far, tell them, 'Then too far is where I am going.'"

In our adolescent craving for certainty and independence, how could we help but be drawn by his passion and rebellion, especially against our elders?

He drew us away from the grown-ups' shul by insisting it was not enough to be an observant Jew; one must become fervent with ardor. Our fathers and older brothers weren't religious ENOUGH! They didn't sing *pizzmonim* (sacred songs) loud or long ENOUGH. They didn't fast ENOUGH. Often he'd dash out into the street, his *tah'let* fringes flying in the breeze, and yell at kids for playing ball instead of being inside, praying.

I remember the pained fervor of one of his Shabbat speeches: "The world is *tref* (unclean); without Torah, the world is filth. Without Torah, the world is *hah-za-rah!* And as we are learning about our brethren in Europe, the world kills us! And if it doesn't kill us, it tempts and poisons us! It will lead you astray if you don't study and keep the Torah! It seduces us to join in its ugliness, its greed, its disease. And not just in one place or one language, but in all places, in all languages. And all the sanctuaries that hold the Torah—the original language—weep in all the letters of all the alphabets. There is no place not weeping now; no language not grieving. So be on guard, like the Maccabees, and be strong and ward off evil."

I wrote another e-mail to Nat:

Ari could at times be a one-man Inquisition, remember? He'd humiliate you in front of all the other kids, then banish you, and forbid anyone from seeing you socially. And he had spies everywhere. For a blessing from him, a pat on your head, or sometimes even hard cash, friends would turn against one another and report some minor infraction as though it were a major abomination. Sweet-rewarded traitor-system he had going. The C.I.A. could've learned a thing or two.

Then, he'd turn the tables, praise us and make us feel important, treating us like grown-ups, and let us *hazzan* [be a cantor reciting the service], or read from the Torah, just like our fathers and elders did, across the courtyard.

Remember the silver pointer with the long tapering finger? Holding that holy heft of precious metal in your hand made you feel special. As for my not having any sins to throw away in the Annex pool—I had plenty, and have added a few more since then.

Nat wrote back:

> Reassuring to hear you've added more sins. Any you wanna share?
>
> As for Ari, we were scared shit of him. He was tough & needed to have control, but all in all, I made some great friends & had great times there. Some religion & free tuna fish sandwiches as well. That environment, playing stickball, friends & free food, kept me stable. Otherwise who knows? Your bro is not too stable, as you might think.
>
> He hooked up with Gene Autry when he sold him some chandeliers on 5th Ave. Talked him into donating stuff every once in a while, like six-shooters & holsters, with his autographed picture, of course. Guns in shul. That was good for us. Made us ready for the world.

DISCOVERING THE PUBLIC LIBRARY

There were no English-language books in our house. Other than *siddureem* (prayer books in Hebrew) and *Haggadahs* for Passover, I never saw any books at all. It was not until I learned, by chance, of the existence of that storehouse of potential explosives, the public library, that I discovered my first access to English-language books outside of school.

One summer day while playing running bases with my friends on the street, I spotted tall, bespectacled Eddie Strasser, down the block, walking toward us. A few years older than the rest of us (and not a ballplayer, although his younger brother and little blond sister were), I noticed him carrying an armful of books and asked where he'd gotten them. "The public library," he answered matter-of-factly, suggesting he'd been going there for some time. I asked him where it was. "18th Avenue and 60th Street," he said. That was four long avenues and five street blocks away. Wondering about the stack of books in his arms, I asked, "How much?"

"You can take out eight at a time," he said.

I had meant how much did it cost, but was at first shocked at the number of books allowed. "Eight books? What does it cost?" I asked.

"It's free," he said.

"Free?" Now I was suspicious; if I had learned anything by age ten it was that nothing was free. He assured me it was true, but my first impulse told me there was a trick. "How?" I asked. He explained that all I needed was a library card.

"How do I get it?"

"Just ask."

It sounded too easy, too good to be true. "That's all?" I asked.

Squinching his nose to keep his glasses from slipping down from perspiration, he nodded, swallowing his sharp Adam's apple in his long thin throat. "It's closed," he said, "but you can go tomorrow."

As we stood, with the game going on behind me, looking up at his face (he was at least a foot taller than me), my eyes turned skyward; the space behind and above his head enlarged, like a close-up drawn back from to reveal its subject within its larger background, and I remember having a premonition that the world was about to open: the street longer, the sky more spacious, time more full.

Before he left, with the books cradled in his arm, I noticed several had scientific titles on their spines. Eddie had earlier wanted to be a doctor and planned on attending Harvard Medical School, to which we all expected him, with his genius brain, to win a scholarship. Years later, on one of my trips back East, I asked about him and learned that he had married a woman whose wealthy father owned a mercantile business; Eddie was made a partner and that ended his medical career.

Next day, I set off to walk the nine blocks with a growing excitement, but prepared for disappointment. The library was located on the ground floor of a building off the corner of 18th Avenue, just as Eddie had said. When I opened the door, I faced row upon row and shelf upon shelf of books in the middle of a large room, as well as shelves filled with books lining the walls. Reading tables stood invitingly uncluttered in the center of the well-lit room. Wandering around in the children's section from one subject to another, I came upon a series of books titled *The Great Scientists, The Great Explorers, The Great Composers,* with an illustration of each famous man at the head of their biographical chapter (there wasn't a woman in the series, as I recall, except for Madame Curie paired with her husband, Pierre, the discoverers of radium). All this—was free? Why hadn't I heard about it before? And now that I did know, part of me wanted it kept secret. My excitement grew into an anticipatory joy when I was so easily granted a temporary card (to be followed in a few days, I was told by the librarian, by a permanent card) and proceeded to take out my first in a long series of free books. Despite the quietness of the place and the few silent browsers, this was no island of calm; I sensed I was about to discover, in the midst of the daily doldrums of living, an as-yet unnavigated sea of possibilities, an unrest I knew I wanted to spend my days exploring. Walking back home, sensing I was on the edge of a new, more adventurous world stranger and more unpredictable than the familiar world the twilight around was closing in on, I felt a hitherto unknown mood of tranquility in the atmosphere of that summer evening spread out, and I walked with more purposeful motion in the soft, buoyant weather.

The more widely I read in history, biology, and astronomy, the wider my perspective grew, affording a distance from which to look back and examine what increasingly seemed a narrow view of existence expounded by what I knew of religions, along with claims, tacit or declared, of their exclusive "truth." Was it anything more than sheer chance that I happened to be born a Jew? What, I'd wonder, if I had been born Chinese, Eskimo, or (closer to home) Italian? Would I therefore be denied God's favor? Why should one's fate be determined by haphazard genetics? Would we inherit heaven merely by happenstance? It was becoming unsettlingly clear that being born into a religious faith enfolded and suffused one with its history, laws, habits, and prejudices, giving pattern to one's days, purpose to one's years, and, supposedly, meaning to one's life—all in order to gain a reward after death. This made life a permanent holding cell. Like a culture in a petri dish, one was grown, nurtured, trained, and shaped by its laws and customs. But, to my mind, evidence was mounting, at first disturbing and confounding, then, by degrees, alarmingly incontrovertible that I needed to extricate myself or sink into practices that put prohibitions from the past before present reality. I could not continue practicing them even for the sake of appearance; *especially* for the sake of appearance, now that appearance itself had grown suspect.

I would have to give up practicing Judaism in much the same way as I would have to give up childhood.

One day not much later I would by chance come upon Emerson's essay "Self-Reliance," the potent grain that, in effect, tipped the scales.

CHAPTER NINE

OUR MOTHER HAD A SWEET TOOTH; WE WERE CANDY

She enjoyed us as much as she could, despite our loudness, wayward-ness, and attempts at independence which she tried her best to stifle early. I have no doubt that she loved us and would protect us as she would her own life—and that was the problem. For a woman with no career or interests outside her home, her total attention was fixed on her children. We, literally, were her life—and she had to fight us to have it, often erasing the border between child and adult. Holding us so close meant there was no chance, no space, for her personal freedom.

When we were out of her hands, out of her sight, she must have worried about the dreadful things that might happen, and those were days when reports of muggings, child abductions, and rape were uncommon, nearly unheard of.

As her firstborn, I was her first project: she had to shape me out of herself. How dare I disobey or defy her? I remember one day, I must have been about ten years old, I resisted her about something I don't recall. Exasperated (not the first time), she picked me up and, heaving me over her shoulder, declared she was taking me to "reform school," a term that, in those days, was every kid's worst fear. There was no question as to how "reform" would be meted out, the word itself brought penitential visions of cement walls and gray prison garb and the very Irish and Italian kids she'd warned us about. Thrown into their nest! I struggled and sobbed, but she held and swatted me hard, and headed for the door. I could smell the anger in her sour sweat.

"Why? What'd I do? " I cried.

"You stopped listening to me," she said in Arabic.

Confused, I couldn't comprehend the severity of the punishment for what seemed a minor infraction. "When?" I asked.

"A long time," she said. When did that start, I wondered; what did "stopped listening" mean? Then I knew: it was my growing (and to her, alarming) curiosity about the life around me. Previously dutiful and obedient, I'd somehow (through those books!—she knew it!) become obstinate and resistant. When she wanted me to get rid of my chemistry set after I'd left a piece of meat in a petri dish and, after a few days, its rotting smell fouled the air, I had refused. When she'd see me absorbed in reading a book, she'd threaten to throw it out. Her fear, no doubt, was that it would confuse and corrupt me. She must have felt frustrated at every turn. Now she would set me straight. I was in such a state of panic at the prospect of reform school, that I gave up: pleading, promising, wanting, striving; I swore never to repeat whatever I might have done or said or failed to do or say— until she was satisfied, and put me down.

But not for the last time. My will was not equal to hers; but hadn't I inherited it from her?

A relatively mild case of what might now be considered "child abuse" was how she handled us. At times, in a playful mood, she'd grab and knead us like the *feelah* dough she layered in *bak'la'wah;* other times, she'd paw and pound us like a brisket she was tenderizing. It was just this pawing and pounding, this maternal manhandling, that held us close, physically constrained.

As we'd run by, she'd reach out her arms, grab, caress, or cuff us, depending on her mood. When my father would protest on seeing her reach for my genitals, teasing, praising my *behdaht* (eggs, testicles) with sing-song laughter, she'd dismiss him with a scornful wave of her hand.

GOING FOR COFFEE

My mother often sent me shopping to 18th Avenue (not a far distance, but for a kid it was unfamiliar territory), the district of Middle Eastern groceries, whose shopkeepers were Christian or Muslim. Their shelves were fully stocked with the pita we called "Syrian bread" and canned *dolmas;* the floors were crowded with sacks of *bur'ghol* (barley), bags of lentils, and barrels of olives. Behind the glass counters were pastries, *kibbeh,* and other delicacies, among which were sheets of thin-pressed *amardeen* (dried apricot) we called "shoe leather" rolled out on wax paper. When chewed, the tart, sweet, dense texture would stick between your teeth so that you'd continue to taste the mouthwatering flavor after you left, as you probed the bits with your tongue, savoring them again, a mini-cud you could return to later on the walk back home.

I was to bring back the *feelah:* the papery dough pressed out into long sheets through which sunlight diffused as through a blurred window. My mother would layer these sheets and stuff them with pistachio nuts and honey; after baking them in the oven, she'd cut the flaky sheets into the dense, sticky quadrangles known as *bak'la'wah.*

In the shop's interior, as I waited for the elderly, slow-moving merchant to weigh and wrap my order as he spoke Arabic with a customer, I'd inhale the mingled smells of cumin, cinnamon, allspice, oregano; all of it infused with the burnt aroma of roasted Turkish *ahh'wae* (coffee). I'd eye the large wedge cut from a massive wheel of chocolate-marbled *hla-waeh* (halva) studded with bits of light-green pistachios set on a silver tray on top of the counter; just seeing the compacted slab of alabaster sweetness, and getting whiffs of the *mazah-har* (rose water) was enough to make my mouth salivate.

The shop's shaded, crowded interior made me think of the cavernous deep of some resinous, dappled bazaar—secret, hermetic, known only to initiates. The aroma—sweet, earthy—had an exotic savor I associated with the fragrances of my mother's cooking, and the finely ground Turkish coffee smelled like roasted earth, transformed into a taste of ancestors.

My mother had once told me how, as a young girl in Aleppo, she'd accompany her mother to shop at the local *souks,* the alleyways of bazaars covered by arched roofs built in the thirteenth century. Holding her mother's hand and closing her eyes, she could tell the trade of a particular *souk* they passed: one she recognized by its fragrance of herbs and spices; another, by the sound of the hammer, was the silversmith; while the rancid odor of the next told her it was animal hides and skins; and then the rich fresh brewed *aah'wae.*

In the shop on 18th Avenue, leaning against the piled sacks of coffee beans imported from Egypt, Yemen, Somalia, Madagascar, and other countries in the East, the names intrigued me and I wondered where these places were and what the people living there were like. Inhaling the aromas in the cramped shop, there was also the under-odor of the rough fiber and hemp of which the sacks I leaned on were woven, packed tight as ball-bearings, and I'd imagine following them back to their ports of origin across the ocean.

Before leaving, for a few cents I'd buy a sheet of the apricot shoe leather stacked on the counter in layered sheets, and with the wrapped *feelah* dough under one arm, I'd bite off a piece of the chewy, compacted dried fruit and in a burst of flavors, discover a deeper, darker tang, and work at it like a tough hide; its sticky burnt-orange hue as deep as the sunset toward which I was making my way home, as though the lowering sunlight had a corresponding flavor.

"THE DUMP" (METRO THEATER)

When I'd reach 65th Street and 20th Avenue, there stood the Metro. True to its underground name, entering its doors felt subterranean; though calling it a "theater" would be gross hyperbole. Kids in the neighborhood referred to it simply as "the dump." Rundown, seedy, rank-smelling, its interior was a cavern without air-conditioning; in summer, huge fans on either side of the screen roared, big as B-16 propellors, drowning out the dialogue on-screen that, considering the I.Q. level of the movies shown, was no great loss. What was not drowned out was the whooping and whistling and cackling mayhem of a renegade children's nursery gone wild, and the yelling of elderly matrons with only a flashlight to maintain order in a chamber of shadows and darkness. Kids had a great time leading these poor, panting hirelings on chases up and down and, more often, over the many empty rows that even the bargain nickel admission price couldn't fill.

There, before the advent of television, for the price of a candy bar, mothers could plant their kids for a couple of hours to watch Sinbad the Sailor, or dark-skinned Sabu in *Ali Baba and the 40 Thieves,* flying on magic carpets over domes and mosques and the needle-pointed minarets of ancient Baghdad. Was this where my father had come from? Did this that our eyes were seeing some-where exist?

Other features were cowboy cliffhangers and the latest episode of comic-book hero serials. But at the Metro, Superman, Batman and

Robin, in padded, ill-fitting costumes had nothing of the clean, sharp-edged angles and features of their comic strip prototypes.

Clean-cut Gene Autry and lean Bob Steele (how could a kid not be drawn to that name?) were the daredevils we went back for. And as for my favorite, Roy Rogers—neckerchief and shirt-fringes fluttering in hot pursuit—the weekly serials featuring him always ended with the suspense of wondering if the wagon holding Dale Evans—hands bound and in fringed boots—that was careening along the edge of a mountain pass could be reached in time; if his creamy sleek palomino Trigger could catch up and Roy rein in its wild team with a mighty tug on the lead horse's traces.

The chapter would invariably end with the wagon dangerously tilting, one side's upturned wheels spinning in the air, suspended as the final image on the screen blacked out. Certainly nothing could save them . . . and yet, if you paid your nickel the following week—which I usually did—you'd see the stagecoach favored by a more amenable law of gravity, this time not so precariously teetering on the edge, but fortuitously bouncing off a rock and back onto the road, and our fringe-flying Rider of the Purple Sage reaching out to rein in the runaways, to rescue his cowgirl queen.

Summer and winter, the fetid air in that cavern stank of kids' sweaty feet, unattended body odors, and stale popcorn. But I'd go anyway to see the loopy shenanigans of straight man Abbott and roly-poly (though surprisingly light on his toes for the timely punchline) Costello. In later years I read that they divided their salary sixty-forty: sixty percent (to my surprise) for the reputedly more difficult role of straight man Abbott, and forty percent for the clown, Costello, who looked to me as though he were taking all the physical punishment in punches and pratfalls. Other favorites I regularly came back for included the finger-pronged eye-jabs and frying-pan-conked heads of the irascible Three Stooges. The Metro's weekly flyers listing the coming attractions were printed on cardboard placards and handed out to local shop owners to place in their windows by an ingratiating small man, who had one leg shorter than the other. Despite this pronounced handicap, his friendly manner helped him perform his job more easily as he went about distributing his placards by hand.

Despite the stale seediness of the Metro, especially in the still suspended light of a summer evening's dusk, I remember the anxious desolation that would rise in my solar plexus when I'd leave the movies to re-enter the harsh, glaring streets of a world monotonously devoted to defeating magic. It was the same feeling I experienced toward the end of summer vacation: the sinking pang and anxiety of having to soon give up my freedom for autumn's summons to the confinement of school.

CHAPTER TEN

RUNNING BASES

If you had a bat, a ball, and a glove, you could play baseball with a few friends; if you had a broomstick and ball, you could play stickball; if only a ball and glove, you could play catch; and if you had only a ball you could still play: punchball, stoopball, boxball . . .

My favorite was running bases; as you ran, it seemed, you cut an evermore lengthening corridor in space, running against your own body's gravity. The speed of the ball between catchers was a challenge, not a fate. Your running created currents of air around you that, in turn, told you how fast you were moving and creating even faster currents around you as you upped the speed with your own momentum. We ran like those cowboys' horses we saw on screen: skipping in triple time, hitting our own horse's ass, sped to a gallop, then reigning in for the dismount. The more skipping, the more the air gave itself to ride through, a medium absorbed in your body through its pores, each pore a quivering sensor.

Summer was our high season. Even when, sometimes on a sunny day, in the middle of a game, the air would gather darkly and unexpectedly give off a chill in waves you could feel on your warm skin before it broke in a sudden shower. At first it misted the pavement like a smoky shadow and then coated the slick tarmac soon hissing with traffic, returning to objects the vividness that moisture brings. It was not much relief: your light shirt stuck in the humidity; dust erupted from the pavement and swirled in the hazy air. And just as suddenly it would subside; after a few minutes, the air would clear and the dried tarmac return to its duller shade of gray.

Summer days (into the evenings) were full of the sounds of balls being hit, wooden bats and sawed-off broomsticks clattering on the cement pavement, loud cheers and groans. There was always enough activity in the street to feed one's craving for speed. That, in memory, would last a lifetime.

LOCAL ABYSS

My sister Renee, a year younger than me, took part in our boys' games, eagerly, and as often as she could, as did several of the other girls who lived on our block. We never called them tomboys. Often they were as fast or faster than we were, and more adept at slipping through narrow spaces in walls and fences.

Thin and scrappy, Renee could shimmy and slither through most any tight space between a gate post and a wall. When playing hide-and-seek, she was small enough crouching behind parked cars to go undetected, or standing sideways behind a tree, inhaling and holding her breath to make herself even thinner, she was practically unnoticeable, wraithlike. In dodgeball, agiley ducking and spinning in midair away from the hard, basketball-sized ball thrown at her head, she was a premier dodger; in running bases, she'd throw herself into the fray in bursts of darting speed that made her a top choice of team captains.

One summer afternoon, while playing running bases, the pink rubber ball we called a "Spauldeen" (manufactured by Spalding) got loose, bounced away into the gutter, and fell down a nearby sewer grating. Gathering around, we peered down into what at first seemed a bottomless dark shaft that sent up the rotting smell of stagnant sewage, motor oil, and gasoline, and could see, just barely, the pink crown of the ball bobbing in the grease-streaked watery puddle below, within arm's reach. As traffic passed by not far out in the street, hunched over this local abyss, we boys were considering how to retrieve our lost ball when Renee spoke up.

"I'll get it," she said.

"How?" one of us asked.

"You'll see." She addressed her remark to us as to a single body and gestured with her head toward the grilled sewer lid. "You lift it," she said, "and I'll reach in." "Red" Dweck, the biggest and strongest moved close, at the ready. Slight myself, I was still bigger than the other kids; besides, being her brother, I felt I'd better be in on this and make sure it went right. I leaned forward, ready to lift one side of the sewer, looking up to see if Red was getting set, his soft, bright hair shining like orange filaments in the sunlight behind him. We reached down, grabbed the metal rim, pried it loose and slowly, carefully, each raised our side toward us so that the heavier-than-expected steel grate, propped tilting in its groove, leaned precariously open on one side; its surprisingly immense weight pulling, as if sucked by some core magnet at the center of the Earth, almost tipping me forward as I felt the straining muscles in my arms and back stiffen.

Renee, leaning forward, reached down into the hole. Just then, I felt Red's side loosen and suddenly all the forceful weight resisted like a flood, and surged forward as the steel cover threw its mass out of my hands and fell into its groove with a cavernous thud as Renee's hand shot back. She screamed, pulling her hand up to her face, her bleeding middle finger dangling by a thread of skin. Instinctively, as I glanced at her, I registered Red's face, sweating, redder than ever in the heat, looking baffled, chagrined.

That look of shame is my permanent memory of him, wherever he may be. Renee, jumping in place, was holding her finger tightly, her face contorted in pain. I took hold of her other hand and together we ran up the stairs to our flat; our mother wasn't home. I led Renee, who by now was moaning, into the bathroom, thrust her hand underneath the faucet and ran cold water on her finger that, looking oddly detached, barely hung from the second joint. I was afraid that the forceful jet of tap water might tear it loose. I lessened the pressure, then bound the finger tightly in a towel. After a few minutes our mother returned from shopping, and somehow gauging what had happened, sent me to tell the doctor, who lived a couple of blocks away, that she and Renee were on their way.

Renee's finger was stitched back in place and years later you could hardly tell by looking that it had suffered a trauma years before.

The one permanent loss that day was the ball. We never retrieved it.

"NOT HAVING CHILDREN IS SAD"

If summer was our high, bright time, it was also bright enough to let us see the dark. As one summer day, while we were playing running bases, the ball got loose and bounced into the street and Eddie's five-year-old sister ran out between two parked cars to retrieve it at the moment an ice cream truck, not speeding, approached, and slammed into her; she bounced off one of the parked cars and was wedged between it and the truck. The driver jumped out and, seeing the little girl motionless, began to wail. I had never seen a grown man so distraught, nor heard such despair from the deepest source of animal misery.

The girl died on impact. From that day on, Eddie's ten-year-old brother, Carl, was forbidden by his parents to play with us and would have to henceforth ask an adult to hold his hand before he crossed a street, no matter how narrow, even if no cars were in sight.

Years later, the wife of a friend of mine, childless herself, but whose sister had to recently bury her youngest son, sorrowfully told me, "Not having children is sad; having children is terrible." She spoke this as a passing thought, but the gravity of the words suggested she had spent a good deal of time thinking about it, and this was her summary judgment.

Besides being our playground, and treacherous at that, the street was our primary education in emergencies. For instance, one day while playing some game or other, I heard a loud cry coming closer. Suddenly the butcher, who I had seen only behind the display counter of his shop across the street, was hurrying in our direction, holding with his right hand the blood-soaked apron tied around his massive girth, his left hand lying in it, severed at the wrist, as he ran past.

Living as we did at a busy intersection, it was common to hear the continuous honking of horns and screeching of wheels followed by the sickening thud of steel crunching against steel. Once, as my sister and I were looking out from our window onto the traffic below, we saw an open-backed truck, with a family standing in the rear, slammed into by a car behind; several of the people fell out and were run over by a car that couldn't stop in time. At that intersection, accidents were to be expected.

THE WHITENESS OF THE WORMS

Playing out on the street I recall one day seeing a more familiar occurrence: a cat, struck by a passing car directly across the street from our flat, dragged itself to the curb to lie down in its last minutes, and when it reached the curb-edge, toppled onto the strip of grassy ground alongside the thoroughfare. A passing policeman, reacting to the screech of the car's brakes before the impact, walked over, not hurrying, and looked steadily at the panting cat, its black fur sopped in blood. As he stood near me and my playmates a moment, quietly deciding something, I noticed the tightly-woven fabric of his blue tunic was as coarse as the khaki uniforms of soldiers we saw in relatives' homes and in the streets, on furlough for brief visits.

Backing us away with one outstretched arm, with the other the policeman drew his revolver from its holster, aimed, and fired. The explosion was deafening, and left a dull ringing in my ears. More than a sound, it had a physical force whose impact shattered the equilibrium that held things steady, as if a protective layer in the air, thin as onionskin, had broken, and with it, space torn open. In the silent aftermath, the usual noise of traffic was stilled a moment in a prolonged hush, and time stalled without direction or purpose. Soon enough then, traffic sounds, even the stir of maple leaves nearby, resumed, at first distinct, then as usual, grew slurred, disarrayed.

That night I left our apartment and using some cardboard I found nearby, I scooped up the cat's body and carried it to some nearby bushes, dug a shallow hole beside them, and slid the body in and covered it with dirt. I don't recall whether several days or weeks passed before I grew curious about what would happen next, or if there even was a "next" for something dead.

One night I returned to the site, and under the dim streetlight on the corner, when I brushed away the dirt, worms crowded in and out of the corpse, coiling like knotted rope where the innards had been. In the near-blackness of the street, they were their own ghastly spotlight. I felt a dropping away in my center at realizing I had interrupted a process of decomposition that the earth kept hidden. The more closely I looked, the more drawn I became to the stark whiteness and feverish activity, beginning to sense what they would be doing inside of me when the time came, if they weren't already.

Was this death? So furiously alive—more alive than the living?

CHAPTER ELEVEN

REFUGEES

About a year after the end of World War II, Mrs. Kaplinsky, the widow two houses down, had a family from Poland staying as new tenants in her upper flat. The little we saw of them was in the form of the slight, nearly emaciated boy who one day came out onto the sidewalk where we were playing running bases beside the house. He stood a moment, peering at us through squinting, dark-circled eyes; his thin legs stuck out like straw in short pants, and from his wrinkled shirt hung arms skinnier than any of ours. A thick tangle of brown hair matched his stare. He stammered sounds in a foreign tongue and made a zigzag motion with his hand that we took to mean he wanted to join in.

Apparently, he had been watching our games from the upstairs window and had a fair idea of how to play. I and a few other kids were standing on the base opposite to the one he now stood on, facing us. When the ball was thrown from one catcher to the other, he took off, scrambling, scurrying, like a rabbit, close to the ground. I stood still with the others, watching him approach in that frightened, gangly manner, and it wasn't until he got close and his right arm, like a T-square, swung into view that I saw a dotted pattern on his forearm. At closer range I could make out a series of blocked numbers, a little blurry, which I associated with the blue letters of the official seal of approval on government inspected meat at the butcher's. At one point, while running, he tripped and fell, skinning his knees, and his mother came rushing out of the house. She must have been watching him from behind the window. Her young face was dark with worry and summer heat as she picked him up, kneeling to dab at his minor cuts with a handkerchief she wet with her tongue. From her calling to him, we gathered his name was Hehshee. We had never heard such a name before.

Though it was summer, she wore a long-sleeved black dress that must have been as cumbersome as the woolen jacket and pants worn by her full-bearded husband when he came home from his job in the city. Those were clothes of constraint and inhibition. Among ourselves, we'd mimic and make fun of Hehshee's overprotective mother. Our mothers never did that for us.

News of what had happened in Europe had not been made public yet, and if any of our parents heard or knew, they were not telling us.

Growing up in Brooklyn during the 1940s before the creation of the state of Israel by the United Nations, I was unaware of the political conflicts between Jews and Arabs over the land of Palestine. We heard of no pogroms, no armed battles, not even confrontations between the two peoples. What little news seeped out was that the United Jewish Appeal (UJA) needed our help in collecting donations to purchase land from Arab landlords. We were given blue-and-white collection boxes to solicit contributions from passersby in the street, at train stations, bus stops, street corners, shop entrances, wherever people came and went to and from their jobs, their errands, their daily shopping. We'd stand, shaking the round boxes, turning the nickels, dimes, and quarters inside into a rhythmic clinking of coins that would be a *mitzvah* for a donor to make into a denser clatter, like applause. When the coin box was full, we'd return it to the office at our Hebrew school and were rewarded with candy, and given a new collection box to fill. Our neighborhood, predominantly populated by Ashkenazic Jews who were much concerned with Zionist causes, was a generous source of donations. This benefited not only kids, but, as it turned out, also the Arab sheiks and "leaders" who were selling parcels of land in Palestine out from under fellow peasant farmers who for generations had believed they were tilling the groves and orchards of their ancestral inheritance.

At that time, our greatest concern was to retrieve a ball that got away from the catcher and bounced far down the street or landed somewhere beside a curb or under a car. "Get the ball!" we'd call to any passerby to retrieve it. "Get-de-baw-ll!" we'd chant in a pleading yodel, as far as it took to catch a passing adult's ear who'd listen, hesitate, usually on their way home from work, and, heeding our cries, bend under a car or along the curb, and throw back our ball. In summer, from whatever neighborhood we played in, I'd make my way back home, my torso and legs cooling off, nearly numb with an inner humming, as the sky grew dimmer with a feeling of a deep-sunken uprooting in the heaviness of dusk.

YANKEES

My cousins—Aunt Becky's sons—Nat (younger) and Gilly (older by a year), personified what they taught me about playing, especially baseball. Their well-oiled gloves, plump bats with knobby ends, white sneakers, and cleated shoes were strewn in the closet of the bedroom they shared.

I'm sure it was at my mother's urging that Nat used to take a baseball and two gloves from his closet and have me accompany him out into the backyard where, from far less than sixty feet away, he'd throw to me at first with moderate speed, then accelerate the pace and velocity of his fastball into the cracked, unpadded glove he'd given me, until it nearly spun off my hand, or, if I managed to catch the ball, it smacked into the shallow pocket (in fact, my palm) with the blunt, bruising thud of the actual.

Both he and his brother were archetypal Yankee fans, so cocky about their team's unquestioned superiority, it was as if you were talking about royalty when DiMaggio was mentioned breaking another record; or how quickly "Scooter" Rizzuto cut off a bounder that had eyes going up the middle, ending a rally; or how Eddie Lopat finessed another squeaker; or, despite his short, stocky build, how agilely Yogi sprang up out of his crouch behind the plate, or how you could predict that he'd come through with a hit in the clutch again.

Throughout the six months of a baseball season neither of them showed the least concern about who would win the pennant: it was God-given, without question, and not even a matter of faith, but of statistics. Whatever extra largesse of interest remained, they might spend on the doings and dealings and certain collapse in the clutch of the Boston Red Sox and the incipient cellarhood of lowlier teams.

I remember (was it several occasions or only once?) Nat took me with him to Yankee Stadium when the Yankees were playing the Washington

Senators, a team whose play and standing in the league were as dull and dismal as the executive body that gave them their name.

Like other fans coming upon that mythic swath of a diamond when entering the stadium for the first time, I was enchanted by the lush green grass, smooth as a pool table, that stretched in an unbroken vista to the distant outfield. Upon entering the stands, you looked beyond the diamond and the shade cast by the upper deck, to the outfield that resembled a perfectly preserved emerald carpet more than a field of grass. When the players finally jogged from their dugout toward their positions, they at first looked like toy figures, so small in size, despite their large individual reputations. I remember most from that game the great Yankee reliever, Joe Page, called in from the bull pen late in the game and, with that high leg kick, firing fastballs I wouldn't see the likes of again until Sandy Koufax in his prime.

At home, after school, I'd follow the Dodger games on the radio with Red Barber, aptly named for his clipped, staccato delivery and his precise knowledge of baseball lore, but took greater pleasure in Mel Allen's mellow Southern drawl with its chortling delight in its play-by-play enactment of a drama in which time was banished, and which you didn't actually need to see in order to feel fully present. On radio, the sound of the crowd was close, electric, engulfing. Later on, with the advent of TV, the crowd would sound diluted and subdued, the announcers less engaged with describing the details of each play, and more with "color" commentary.

The prospect of playing ball, for me, was akin to recovering from an illness and, walking out on the street, leaner, headier, not only were your movements free of the ordinary, but when the ball flew, you flew to it—with it—were it—pure instinct, going, ongoing, gone.

PANTHERS

Another World Series in the record books,
and bereft now of baseball for the next six

winter months, I'm ready for grief counseling. Is this why
they come to mind, those sleek Young Turks (actually

Italians) who played as if they were royally born
to it? I see their jet-black T-shirts emblazoned

with PANTHERS in gold script on the back and black pants worn
loose that billowed in the summer air. On

weekends they were rumored to play, the benches along
the foul lines filled up long

before they appeared in Seth Low Park
where we kids used to choose up softball games in the black-

top outfield. Sandy Koufax, my classmate at Lafayette High,
and not yet the fireball hurler he'd soon be,

lived a few blocks away. Playing ball was our break-away
to the diamond where time held no sway

and we'd practice the magic of plucking a feather-
stitched sphere as from a flying stem in the air.

They promised a game made more seductive by the imminent
whiff of possible menace. For we'd seen them,

when behind in the score and their high-stakes bet
in danger of being lost, create a pretext—

a brushed-back batter, a bumped runner—for an all-
out bat-swinging assault on their rivals.

An umpire, calling balls and strikes, who called against them,
risked bodily harm. When, as usual, regally late, they came

through the gate at the far corner of left field, their black
outfits set against the outfield's flat black

asphalt top, they filed in, shimmering like heat waves raised
as if wraiths from a further dimension in the distant haze.

In a slow laze, blinking in bright sunlight, sorely hung-
over, they looked pissed already. And strung

out behind them, their gorgeous girlfriends seemed to thrive
being pregnant, though much too voluptuous to be wives

for the childbearing years of the rest of their lives.

Here came Paradise in pairs: two lips,
two eyes, two breasts, two hips.

We on the benches made room for them, but
it was on their lovers' laps they sat.

And we forgave them all their faults:
their arrogance, their tempers, their hangovers, and being late.

They'd shown up! And with such beauties, besides!
Nine innings . . . nine lives

in which to look forward to them, sleek
and sullen as their feline namesakes

in midday, moving with midnight reflexes
and fluid, arboreal grace.

Afterwards, we'd feel we could face
coming back into time for the sake

of being able to look forward to leaving again. Tall
blue sky. Bright sun overhead. The coin is tossed. Called. "Play ball!"

One afternoon, convincing me that he could teach me how to ride a
bike, Nat put me on his Schwinn, promising he'd follow and hold the
seat; I pedaled, slowly, glancing back to make sure he was holding on,
which he was. Gaining momentum, I began to pedal faster and could
hear Nat running behind. Then feeling the bike jerk free, I knew,
even before I looked, Nat was standing back almost from where we'd
started. Balanced—barely—on two spinning wheels, I saw his head
cocked teasingly sideways, eyes blinking closed, as was his way, to dissuade and thwart any protest with a dismissive grin sinking further
out of sight, just this side of a sneer.

Having come this far from that day, I wish his wry grin and mocking laugh, long dimmed and faded, were near.

SEYMOUR ABADI: WHAT'S A RABBI'S SON LIKE YOU DOING . . .

My cousin Nat had a close friend, Seymour (Cy) Abadi, a rabbi's son and a star in the softball league of the neighborhood. "Softball," though, seemed inaccurate to me, since a new softball was as rockhard as a baseball.

Cy kept his glove, sneakers, and play clothes at Nat's house. On Saturdays, after attending shul with his father, he'd return with Nat to his house, change out of his pressed suit and shined shoes into a pair of old pants and T-shirt, and hurry to the park to join his friends for a nine-inning game or two.

Playing ball was like oxygen to Cy, Nat, and their friends. Although he wore glasses (unusual then), Cy was a graceful, sure-handed shortstop, with the instinct to anticipate where a ball would be hit, and expert at backhanding a grounder about to shoot by on his right side, or at snagging a line drive, leaping, in midair, or cutting off sure hits up the middle. And he was as much of a threat with a bat, hitting balls like rockets over the left field fence, or in majestic towering arcs that often landed on the roof of the apartment building across the street, or through a window. When the occupant, an elderly woman, was approached and asked, sheepishly, by an outfielder for the ball, standing at the broken window, she'd curse and refuse to return it. Nevertheless, as soon as enough change was collected among the players to buy another at the soda stand, the game would go on. Over the years, the victimized woman must have collected enough new and scuffed balls to open her own supply shop.

After finishing playing for the day, Cy would go back with Nat to his house, shower, change into his dress clothes, and return home, his extracurricular Sabbath activity unsuspected, or at least unmentioned. If he did find out, his father must have known that Cy would continue to play out of his sight. After all, this was America, not Aleppo, where Cy's grandfather had at one time been chief rabbi. And it was common knowledge among his friends that he'd been approached in private by major league scouts as a minor league prospect, if he was interested. A commitment and contract would test how far he wanted to take his talent. He must have given the proposals serious consideration, though he finally declined. The old man had gotten wind of some of the appealing offers to his son, and invoking who knows what religious prohibitions or family interests, put a stop to it.

Why were the best players on these weekly choose-up teams, especially the hitters, the most religious? Was there some law of physics that compensated them with physical prowess for what they were denied in worldly pleasure? And being the son of an Orthodox rabbi was guaranteed to ensure that a talent like Cy's would be denied even the everyday secular pleasures. As far as I could learn, Cy later went into retail.

SAMSON AND DELILAH

One day my cousin Nat took me with him to the Paramount Theater in Manhattan to see *Samson and Delilah,* the Cecil B. DeMille epic that had just opened, starring Hedy Lamar and Victor Mature. Even before either of the two stars appeared, as the credits were rolling, the theme, composed by Dimitri Tiompkin, opened like folds of Oriental drapery drawing aside, the introductory horns trumpeted you back to an ancient time, both foreboding and bewitching; followed by the strings in a spiraling, silken phrase that I would later guess was, if not an outright borrowing, a deft retooling, of Rimsky-Korsakov's *Scheherazade* and later in the film visually echoed by Samson's ringleted locks of hair. From my viewings of other movies starring Mature, with his fixed smile and pampered leathery looks, this role suited him, while Lamar, in a bejewelled sarong and bare midriff, her sultry languor as she lounged on a divan, winding her long-haired paramour around her fingers like a cluster of grapes, was a beguiling presence. Her name, "Hedy Lamar," already radiated the double pleasures of Delight and Amour. Had the real Delilah looked like her, it would've been clear why Samson, with all his lordly locks and superhuman strength, wouldn't have had a chance.

CHAPTER TWELVE

CONEY ISLAND

In summer, Mom would often take us to Coney Island, to get herself and us out of the stifling apartment. She'd pack a lunch of our basic sandwich staple, baloney (cheaper than salami), its pale pink smooth slices tasting as bland as the coloring it was injected with. This she'd stuff into halved loaves of pita (we called it "Syrian") bread that we'd pick up regularly from the market. Traditional among desert Arabs, and made simply of flour and water, this pan-baked flat bread served as our staple. The pocket could be stuffed with scrambled eggs or tuna or cream cheese and jelly for school lunches and outings to the beach. For variety, as well as thrift and convenience, she sometimes used Wonder Bread. How many feather-weight, flavorless, spongy slices did we swallow—you hardly needed to chew!—and so white, it reflected light when you raised a slice to your mouth. Actually, mustard was the main ingredient in those sandwiches; so thickly did we slather on the bright Gulden's, the yellow would seep through even before we set out for the beach.

In the subway station, to avoid the nickel fare, she'd have us duck underneath the turnstile, telling the glaring attendant in his booth that we were all under the age of five; small as they were, my brother and sister looked it, though at eight and nine, I didn't. When I'd try to hold back, she'd push my head under the turnstile, all the while insisting to the attendant, shaking his head, that I was only five. We'd get away with it, as the families behind us were clamoring for change at the counter, and finally with a defeated shake of his head, he'd give up protesting as we ducked and dashed for the incoming train roaring toward the platform below.

It was always crowded on the train, especially on Sundays. You could forget about getting a seat. People were in various stages of undress, or already wearing their swimsuits, carrying baskets of food, holding inflated inner tubes, young couples rubbing one another with suntan lotion. As the train approached the beach, a sulphur stink rose from the black pool we passed, and as we did, people shouted, "Perfume Bay!" Even after the train had passed, the stink lingered until we reached the Coney Island station.

My earliest memory of Coney Island is of looking down from high above the boardwalk, held outward, like a ship's prow, over the crowded beach below. I was held by the hands of a policeman; he blew a whistle and held me tightly around my waist, exhibiting me to the mass of people below who, with a slow turn of heads, took a long curious look up at a lost kid found wandering alone on the boardwalk. But I wasn't *lost,* I was *loose*—among the games in the penny arcade, and gawking at rides like the Cyclone, the Hurricane, the Parachute, the Ferris wheel, the bumper cars, the Dipsy Doodle.

I was suspended, angled aloft in the air above the railing, over the staring crowd; I had a clear view of the ocean, and for a moment, I felt I was about to become airborne.

After several shrill attention-grabbing whistles, during which people had gotten a good long look and been reassured that I wasn't one of theirs, I was retrieved from my brush with outer space and brought back down to stand on the planks of the boardwalk and returned, holding the policeman's hand, to the station. Soon after, my mother arrived, showing concern, but not overly anxious, and claimed me.

A couple of years later, my sister and I were free to roam the beach, hotfooting over the sand as we'd nimbly mince on our toes and leap onto our heels or the sides of our feet to avoid the full burn of reflected sunlight. We collected as many empty soda bottles as we could carry and cashed them in at a stand under the boardwalk for the two-cent deposit. We'd pick them up near bathers lying on the beach who were not about to run the gauntlet of hot sand for two cents, but that for us, if we ventured far enough, was profit enough to treat ourselves to an outing of fun in the arcade. The miniature fighter plane attached to a wire you controlled by its handle, strafing a town below before anti-aircraft guns, signaled by a loud buzzer, shot you down, was one of my favorites. So enwrapped would I become, I lost track of my sister, off somewhere else in her own favorite games.

To "go under the boardwalk" with a girl meant "going all the way." Otherwise there was no need to leave the crowded beach where near-nakedness was already the norm. On weekends, fighting families and amorous couples spread out on blankets so close there were hardly any empty areas. With the sand heated practically to cinders underfoot, I'd run across the edges of a daisy chain of blankets, zipping past lovers knotted together like flesh-colored vines, oblivious to all those around, although everyone nearby was keenly interested in them, including, briefly, me, as I ran by, landing my toes on the edge of their blanket, careful not to disrupt their union on my dash to the water's edge, because you never knew what was going on underneath a spread, springy blanket.

To avoid the discomfort of putting on my swim trunks at home and having to wear them under my pants during the train ride, I'd opt for having my mother hold a towel around me as I slipped out of my pants and wriggled into my swim trunks guardedly, as if all the bathers on the beach had nothing better to do than stop and train a collective eye on my breeze-wraithed parts.

Beefy, operatic *paisans,* wearing the skimpiest of thongs, sang popular arias from *Pagliaci* and *Travatore,* projecting to the farthest ends of the beach, where surely they were appreciated by fellow *paisans,* and Sicilian matrons with thick unruly hair, in hoop earrings and ruffled swimsuits, looking like well-fed gypsies, belted out "La Forsa del Destino" with the lung power of honorary Sophie Tuckers, putting on a show for an audience larger than any theater could hold, fueled with jugs of vino, cooled with cans of beer, and stoked with meatballs the size and density of cannonballs, salami sliced from long sausage-cased tubes, and chunks of provolone cut from wheels nearly as big as tires.

At Coney Island, prudishness was not an issue; once you passed Perfume Bay, modesty was left behind. Lust ruled. Caressing, massaging, kissing, fondling were normal sights on the beach; those who wanted more would go under the boardwalk. There, in privacy under the slatted coolness of the boards, moaning soon led to sounds of thrashing and sighing, then a stillness in which the smell of sand stirred and the wooden planks thumped overhead.

Out on the hot sand, ice cream and soda pop vendors carried compact refrigeration units on their shoulders, walking barefoot from group to group, hawking their refreshments to thirsty sunbathers, sparing them having to cross the sand to the nearest concession stand underneath the boardwalk. When the vendor opened the lid of his case, wafts of dry ice billowed white puffs of refrigerated air if you were close enough.

RUNNING AWAY FROM HOME

One day my cousin Nat vanished. Each day I'd accompany my mother to my Aunt Becky's house and watch the worried looks and listen as the search was carried on. To facilitate matters, a telephone was installed and calls were made to police stations, hospitals, and morgues, but to no avail.

The anxiety felt by my Aunt Becky, Uncle Joe, and their two daughters, (Gilly was in the Army), was plain on their faces; hurried, hushed whispers were exchanged; now and then a moan of disappointment could be heard when the phone was put down, followed by accusations by Aunt Becky to Uncle Joe about his habitual harshness. She went from kitchen to phone, phone to bedroom where, from behind the closed door, I could hear her crying; then she emerged, ready to take up the search again. What, I wondered, was in store for the rest of us when the peacemaker couldn't solve the crisis at home?

After about a week (or was it several?), we learned that Nat had joined the Army, claiming he was of age when in fact he was not. On his return home, Aunt Becky was visibly relieved, whereas Uncle Joe showed no such relief, only anger, which must have been part of Nat's reasons for leaving in the first place. A year later, when he was of legal age, he again joined the Army.

WASHINGTON BATHS

When Nat was about to leave for basic training, he gave me his season pass to the Washington Baths in Coney Island. Located between Surf Avenue and the boardwalk, this bathhouse, one of several in the area, was favored by Jewish and Italian patrons, while Ravenhall and McLaughlin Baths were patronized by the Irish and Scandinavians.

In those pre-photo-i.d. days, just a card showing your name was enough to give you entry into these privately run bathhouses and swimming facilities; they featured large pools with several diving boards, showers, individual lockers, and, best of all, steam rooms. Washington Baths had two such steam rooms: one, kept fairly warm, was used by most of the young male patrons; I tended toward what was referred to as the "inferno," used by the elderly men.

On opening the door to this furnace, you had to breach the swirling gust of steam fired up by powerful jets to a thick skin-flaying intensity in order to step inside. There you had to sit still or else your slightest movement would scorch your skin; you even had to hold your breath against drawing the heat into your lungs. Only as you grew accustomed to the cooking temperature could you take brief, shallow breaths as the vapor was pumped into the room growing hotter the longer you stayed.

Seated on wooden planks in the misty corners of the room, you could barely make out the portly shapes of naked, slack-skinned elderly men with their bathing trunks soaked in cold water placed on their heads as improvised babushkas. If you moved, or the door opened to let someone in or out, you could see dancing droplets practically boiling on your skin, and could barely escape with a rush as you raced to the door and dashed to the nearest stall for a long cold shower.

One day, as I was about to leave the locker room, a middle-aged woman strolled into the men's shower area, looking confused, albeit interested in what was going on, muttering that she had lost her way to the women's section while she stood there, gazing around, open-mouthed, with a smile as if she had chanced upon a dream, until she was kindly escorted out even as she craned to look back.

CAMP SUSSEX

Summer camp for kids was among the best uses of Jewish philanthropy and among the most satisfying experiences I had as a boy. Three summers in a row, from age ten through twelve, thanks to the Jewish Federation and the ingenuity of my mother, who had an immigrant's canny antenna for such free social services, we went to a camp in Sussex, New Jersey. First my sister and I, then later my brother Nat, enjoyed those three-week respites from Brooklyn's sweltering summers in which, among other things, we learned to swim and canoe in a nearby tree-shaded lake.

Unlike the smell of sea-water, almost sweet, the odor that pervaded this shadow-enclosed lake was a stagnant sump-smell. Over the summer, though, I grew to associate that odor with the peaceful stillness of the place.

There, we sang "Hatikvah" around a campfire; in the large mess hall we ate three meals a day. With no prompting, my appetite grew with the activity and games in the fresh air. One afternoon, playing third base, as I knelt, glove touching the dirt, ready to field the sharp grounder coming straight at me, the ball caromed upward off a rock and slammed into my knee, sidelining me for a couple of days; but even that couldn't spoil my fun. At bedtime, when the stink of socks in the barracks holding twenty boys double-bunk-style felt like being enclosed in a sleeping bag never aired, forced me to take shallow breaths, I soon gave in, and breathed more normally, deeply, until blissfully asleep.

Girls had their own barracks on the other side of the camp, separated from the boys by a stand of hedges. After the day's activities, boys, girls, and counselors gathered around a campfire and sang patriotic Hebrew and American songs, which, in effect, were a warm-up for the head counselor to recount Jewish aphorisms and anecdotes:

"When a father gives to his son, both laugh. When a son gives to his father, both cry." Though the meaning's import was unsettling, the symmetry and turnabout surprise were like a punch line.

He told a story about an old Jewish peddler who arrived with his satchel of merchandise at a train station. The first official he saw, he asked: "Are you an anti-Semite?" "No, no!" the man replied. Next, he asked a well-dressed couple: "Are you anti-Semites?" "No," they both answered. He then approached an elderly poor couple. "Are you anti-Semites?" Without hesitating, they replied, "Yes." "Thank God, honest people. Would you please watch my valise?"

When the campfire was put out, the girls went back to their quarters behind the hedges, and we returned to our barracks through a mist of clover and crickets drilling into the thin fabric of our fatigue.

I grew to like the feeling of autonomy within the rituals of camp life: the morning raising of the American flag accompanied by reveille played on a bugle by a counselor before the assembled campers at attention, and the lowering of the flag at evening accompanied by suitably mournful taps; the orderly filing in to the mess hall for meals; the stories told around the outdoor fire; the songs we sang; the homilies we heard. . . . Here again, I was drawn to the semblance of order that these rituals provided, such as my first fulfilling "police" experience, when I was chosen as one of the camp monitors. Our job was to see that the other campers lined up, kept order, did not disrupt the morning and evening assemblies, and filed, in orderly fashion, into the mess hall. I prized the blue armband I wore, and felt the authority when I put it on.

Aware that the time spent in camp was privileged, I sensed that when I returned home I wouldn't be able to keep that feeling, which helped me enjoy it while it lasted.

One activity, though—my least favorite—was mandatory: the daily de-lousing by a muscular matron standing at the door of the boys' shower room with a large bucket of soapy disinfectant. As we waited in line, she'd dip a stiff bristle brush and vigorously scour the scalp of each naked boy as he inched forward. With the sting of ammonia in our tightly shut eyes, we'd scramble through the door, crashing into walls and shower stalls and one another as we raced toward a nozzle. But the water jet only spread the soap into our eyes and burned deeper—should we keep them open to rinse them more quickly, or keep them shut and ride out the burning sensation until it eased? Even this, after the first week, became a marker, part of an ordered sequence, to be expected, if not looked forward to.

One afternoon, while playing center field, I was motioned by my teammates to play deep for a batter on the opposing team. I moved back, closer to the edge of the field. Not too far behind was a border of knee-high grass, and behind that were tangled shrubs, before dense woods took over.

I barely saw the batter swing before the late crack of bat on ball sent me running, the ball arcing over my head.

Racing back, I was aware I wouldn't be running on grass when my feet landed, crunching on sticks and branches breaking underfoot. I spotted the ball in a clump of wood chips and ran to pick it up, but it was too late for a relay back to the infield. And I was no cannon-armed Carl Furillo.

As I reached for the ball, my eye caught sight of an object that stood out by contrast to the surroundings: a cow's skull. It startled me, lying there, intact, strangely whiter than the ball just a few feet away. No other bones were in sight. The elements had scoured the skull: scooped-out eye sockets, polished jawbone, and preserved rows of teeth gave it the look of ivory at permanent rest, almost as white as the sky. Yet from that spot hidden from view, its sockets stared out toward all the activity in the field, and I wondered how long it had been there. Was it before the camp was founded, the barracks built, a clearing cut for the field?

My last year there, age twelve, I won the Camper of the Year trophy—a palm-sized bronze globe with attached handles on a plastic stand that I brought home, and put on the dresser in my room. Before long, the globe began to rust, the plastic cracked, and sometime later the trophy got misplaced, or lost, or was thrown out by my mother in her annual housecleaning.

CHAPTER THIRTEEN

TERRITORY

After the war, in the late 1940s, while Europe was plucked and parceled into new power blocs, my friends and I would meet and bring out the switchblades and pocketknives we'd use to carve a slice of real estate only inches away from passing traffic off the corner of Bay Parkway, 65th Street, Brooklyn, and play Territory.

Snug-palmed, blade-first, with a rolling heave from the shoulder, in turn, we'd each fling our knives with a snapping twist of the wrist; the aim was to spear a rival's parcel and partition his marked ground; then, erasing their boundary lines, annex them to our own. Soon, the ground on which we stood was crisscrossed with crazy-quilt segments, and whoever ended up with the largest unified portion was the winner.

In summer, we'd ride on the makeshift scooters we rigged from an orange crate set upright on a plank to which we nailed the halves of a rollerskate at each end, one foot pedaling fast and faster just to keep from sinking into the softening blacktop.

As often as we could get away with it, we'd wage our own guerrilla war on the cars intruding on our games, and sling green grapes like buckshot at them, whole hard bunches we'd swipe from old widow Kaplinsky's fenced arbor, and drive her raving from her shaded room.

Pale, looking all the more haggard against her mourner's black, she'd rush onto her top step, eyes and mouth slackly askew cursing us into the hellish hereafter with her guttural Yiddish. Her tirade—even though we understood little of what she spewed—stung, but not as sharp as the hard grapes we'd thrown at the passing cars. Sputtering, shielding their eyes, angry drivers would stumble out and leave their cars open in midtraffic and, to our shock, come after us, especially the middle-aged ones for whom added insult injected an extra burst of speed; but, fortunately for us, not fast or far enough through the alley mazes whose every twist and turn we knew like the moods in our mothers' faces.

And even as those enraged men fumed, giving chase, and we fled, all about us the thick, thorny gardens that hid us quietly flourished.

MARTY LOWY

Marty's dog Rover, who he used to walk every day, twice a day, was bigger than either of us. A sleek, gray, short-haired hound, Rover would pull on the leash and Marty would go lurching after. This was the most exercise I ever saw Marty get.

Once, out with him and Rover on our daily walk around the block, we saw under some maples and cedars across the street a young woman walking a majestically maned collie, a Lassie look-alike with that long snout, elegant as a racehorse. Rover, sniffing the air, glanced up and stood still. So did we. Just then, a middle-aged neighborhood man walking by us stopped and looked across the street. After a moment, he turned and said, "You know, when I was younger and a pretty girl would pass me with her dog, I'd turn for another look at her; now I turn for another look," he paused, "at the dog! That's what'll grow on you. Don't believe me now. You'll see," he said, and continued on his way.

Marty, with a chunky build and slow bearing, wasn't much of a ballplayer, but was nevertheless a good friend. With his mother, older brother, and sister (his father, of whom he never spoke, had left for work one day and never returned), he lived one flight above the street, next door to the Chinese restaurant with the stink of rotting soybeans in its basement that wafted a foul breeze through our back window all summer; a cloying, fermented smell like decaying garbage. Even so, every Sunday night that we could afford it, Marty and I would treat ourselves to their specialty, sweet-and-sour pork ribs. For two Jewish kids—one brought up on bland gefilte fish and matzo-ball soup, the other on meats koshered nearly tasteless—these pork ribs were the most exotic dish we had tasted. We couldn't take in fast enough the crispy glazed fat we'd slather with sweet honey-orange sauce to fill our mouths without gagging. This was nectar; this was *tref* worth sneaking around for! *Tis-wah aavon* (worth a sin), as my brother Nat would say. Never mind your chintzy, run-of-the-mill breaking of the kosher law against ham or bacon. This was high on the list of no-no *esureem* (prohibitions). Sin number one.

As kids, when I first lived on the block, Marty was my only friend. We always played together: checkers in his hallway, making wooden pistols by attaching a rubber band from its nose to its cocked handle that, when thumb-flicked, could shoot a piece of linoleum or cardboard far, if not accurately; sharing and trading the whirring whistles, secret rings, and other prizes we sent away for with cereal box-tops; playing alternately Batman and Robin (with homemade capes and masks); all this besides our daily walk with Rover. At the time, I didn't have any other friends; I didn't need any. Marty lived right around the corner. I didn't much care what I was doing because whatever it was I was doing it with Marty.

One afternoon, after school, I remember this little kid stood next to Marty in the schoolyard, loud with stampeding kids, and said "Marty is not playing with you any more." I looked at Marty; he didn't say anything. After they and most of the other kids left the yard, I went over to the swings, sat in one, and just swung there awhile, slowly, and a thought occurred that never occurred to me before: What was I going to do next? Before, there was never any question of what to do next; I would be doing it with Marty; that filled up time. Now I would have to wonder, plan, figure out, what to do next. Later that day, then the next, what would I do without Marty? Whatever it was, it would have to fill up time the way being with Marty filled up time. Then I realized I'd have to start making plans and choices I never had to think about, and after they filled up a time, they also would give way to having to make new plans and other choices I couldn't begin to imagine just then. It was as if what I had taken to be firm and stable was shot through with pitfalls. What would I do the next day? What about the day after? Next week? All that uncertainty was beginning to expand and grow heavy, and with a wrong choice, would grow even heavier. Time, then, became real as a solid, and more unmanageable because invisible. I was in it now, the emptiness could fill me or leave me, either way, at a whim. I was beginning to feel a growing dread, then revulsion for that dread, and knew I would die and mourned in advance, and knowing would make no difference except that my revulsion would remain along with my dread because I would never be able to ignore it.

Some days after that, Marty and I made up, the misunderstanding or imagined slight repaired, reinterpreted and reconfigured, and we were friends again, but not exclusively. The problem was cleared up, but the dread it opened remained.

A related incident is worth recalling: thirty years ago, soon after he was married, my brother Nat was seriously injured in an auto accident. While driving from his store in Brooklyn another car hit him on the driver's side. The stop sign had been knocked down at the intersection, and evidently replacing it did not rate as a top priority with the city. The sign lay facedown near the curb. The other driver, seeing no sign, drove on and plowed into Nat's car as it passed, crushing the driver's side. From the hospital my sister Renee called me in San Francisco. Within the hour, I booked a direct flight to New York and arrived seven hours later, where Renee picked me up at the airport. Nat, at a nearby hospital, was already ten hours into a critical surgery that would last another hour.

The whole family was there in the waiting room: Mom, Pop, Nat's wife Vivian, and their first son, Adam. Mom, quietly tense, was holding back tears, while Vivian, her beauty blanched by worry, was silent. I heard Pop, his voice rising in alarm: "We're losing him . . ." But later in his room, after the "successful" surgery (eleven hours under the knife, with the visible scars to show for it), as we stood around Nat's bed, in walked this chunky, bald, bearded guy in a suit (it was summer!). He wore dark glasses, and there was an intern at his side who he told to take special care of this patient. I didn't recognize anything about him . . . except for a particular trait that identifies a voice as unmistakable, the way a familiar outline in the dark identifies its bearer before the light is turned on. Deep in the echo chamber of memory, sound can be retraced to its source, least affected by the passage of time.

That timbre in a voice I had once been so familiar with, I was hearing again in the same nasal bulkiness and street-inflected Brooklynese as on those daily walks together, and in the hallways we played in, and over the pork ribs we shared.

Later, in the hospital coffee shop, taking off his shades and with only a trace of his old shy smile, Marty told me he was the hospital's chief bursar. Always officious, thorough and responsible, years after his father abandoned the family, when his older brother joined the Navy, Marty was "the man" of the house, looking after his mother and sister. Good with numbers (he'd beaten me often at cards and checkers and tried to teach me to play chess, but I never could take to it), I was not surprised that he'd risen quickly in the hospital's administration. He assured me that Nat would get the best care and he would look over the bill.

I thanked him and we traded brief accounts of our past; old acquaintances whose first meeting after many years was overcast more by recent losses and illnesses than the nostalgia of boyhood memories. His mother was in a nursing home on Long Island, and he lived near her with his wife, herself in the late stages of cancer. The look on his face was of unremitting worry. After news like that, reminiscing seemed a callow indulgence; I think we both knew it, and mercifully refrained. We traded addresses; from New York City where we were at the moment, his living on Long Island didn't seem so far. But, back in San Francisco, Long Island seemed like a distant time and a long way off, and we never got back in touch.

CHAPTER FOURTEEN

JUDAIC QUICKSAND

In the Russian poet Osip Mandelstahm's memoir, usually translated as *The Noise of Time,* but which Vladimir Nabokov renders as *The Hum of Time* (capturing the sound time makes in its droning passage), he refers to the "Judaic chaos" in his boyhood home in St. Petersburg. At the time when my faith began to unravel, (long before I knew of Mandelstahm), observing codified religious practice felt like being submerged in a magma of solidified past, the act of breathing itself gagged with anxiety; more a predetermined acquiescence to sinking into quicksand than the chance hazards of chaos. Was I the only one? Why did no one else around seem to feel that dilemma, or even suggest questioning—let alone doubting—Biblical accounts of creation, or Joshua's stopping the sun from setting to complete the collapse of Jericho, or the genocide of rival peoples that the God of the Old Testament commanded the Israelites to perform?

Religion, with its legends, miracles, and pageantry, naturally appeals to children. Questioning or raising doubt wouldn't have occurred to my fellow students in Hebrew school, since faith and family were one and the same legacy. It would be like questioning the authenticity of one's parents and heritage: not a matter for speculation, but a given in the genes. One is orphaned by doubt into dread and confusion, as when two divergent thoughts occur at the same time and, trying to follow each on their course, we lose the thread of both. To lose one's faith is to lose one's bearings—up and down, right and wrong, everything topsy-turvy. It seems that only through defeat—exhausting all our inherited belief systems—do we finally come (inwardly kicking, quietly screaming), by default, to recognize that only in following our heart's conviction can we open a way, however precarious, for ourselves.

Tradition's thick shield felt protective-to-the-point-of-suffocation from birth, possessively, physically, engulfing—beginning with circumcision's proprietary notch. Further along, entering manhood, Bar-Mitzvahed at thirteen, you put on the fringed undershirt of *tzi-tseet* beneath your dress shirt and bind the black leather *tefileen* strap in seven mystical loops around your left arm, close to your heart, and place the small lacquered box containing the Holy Name on your brow and wrap the *ta'leht* (prayer shawl) around you. On your arms and neck you feel its scratchy woolen fabric smelling of mildew mingled with rose water; or else out of the communal cardboard carton at the synagogue door, you pick what's left: a rayon prayer shawl smelling of your elders' aftershave and sweat. Whether what to some was a habitual, mechanical series of motions having long ago lost their original meaning and significance, or to others the codified steps that brought them in daily prayer nearer to the Almighty, did not seem to be the issue. One's belief was not a theoretical matter to examine and question: belief was a given, along with birthright, tradition, and heritage; family and faith were the same interwoven fabric, interbred.

This became clear to me when my brother Nat phoned me recently and asked where I wanted to be buried: near our parents and family in the Syrian cemetery on Staten Island or in California, where I live. I told him I'd been thinking about cremation. "What?" he said, surprised. "But we've always done it that way!"

"I know, " I said. "I like the heat. Never got enough in winter when we were kids."

"Yeah, that cheap bastard landlord Canin . . ." he began to drift off, then caught himself. "No, seriously, I never thought of that: cremation." He sounded truly bewildered.

"I've been giving it some thought," I hedged.

"What's to think about? You wanna become a cinder? Some ashes blowing around until you get stuck to some asshole's shit-stained shoes, or worse?" he cried, cackling.

"They don't do it that way," I said, trying to sound reasonable. "It's in a sealed jar."

"Bullshit! Who's this 'they' and what makes you think *they*"—he emphasized, mocking—"give a shit where you end up? It's not bad enough with those scummy morticians who dump corpses in garbage bags while the family's paid for burial in an expensive casket? Is that how you want to end up? Oh, pardon me," he corrected himself, "there *is* no you. You wanna end up like the Heinz guy?"

"What do you mean," I asked, "what Heinz guy?"

"The guy who started Heinz ketchup. You never heard? In his will, he said he wanted to be cremated and his ashes scattered from the Golden Gate Bridge. So his family goes to San Francisco with his ashes in a jar and one of his sons holds it out over the water and shakes it. Nothing. He looks in, turns it upside down and shakes it again, and still nothing, then—" the sound I hear through the line is of clapped thuds, "Claap! Claap! Claap!" and Nat asking, "Get it?"

"What?"

"What do you do when the ketchup doesn't come out?" he made the universally recognized clapping sound against a ketchup bottle's bottom to unplug the air pocket, "Claap! Claap! Claap!" and I imagined him scrunched, cradling the phone between shoulder and ear and hitting one open palm against the closed, rounded rim of the other.

"Right," I said. "So, after cremation you turn into ketchup. That's not bad."

"*Cremation* means there's no you anymore, right?" he asked.

"Right," I said, trying to keep this short.

"But *our way,* at least there's bones left after the worms are through. You know why we bury in the ground? This is interesting, Jackie. Put away your books; you'll learn something. The Talmud says that on the Judgment Day, when everyone is called up to pay for his *aa-vohn* (sins), and, if he's lucky, to get his reward, *Inshallah* (God willing)!—all our bones—every lowlife rat bastard who's ever lived— will rise up out of the earth, except for those who got themselves crisped—like you, bad choice—since there's nothing left to put together again. There have to be bones that survive to rise, to take on flesh in *olahm-ha-bah* (the world to come)."

I could tell this wasn't going to be short.

"What about those who were cremated—against their will?" I asked, sensing, as in the old days, that I had him in the vise of his rigmarole reasoning. "You know, like Auschwitz."

Pause. "*Ha-shem* can do anything. He can create bones again. He could make anybody over again," he concluded.

"Exactly. And what about *my* bones? Or am I just chopped liver?"

"If you're lucky, if you're not dog food."

"o.k.," I admitted, "if not me, there has to be *somebody* who was burnt at the stake or torched in their sleep and ended up as ashes, you know, unintentionally, not exactly by choice."

"Yeah, yeah, I get it," he said. "You think you're pinning me with your cockamamy logic. *Ha-shem* can do anything; He can put flesh on our bones again and brains in our heads. Even yours. He can even give you the satisfaction of thinking that you can outsmart Him. But remember what Mom used to say when she'd catch us at something we thought we were sneaking by her?"

He didn't wait for me to recall, let alone reply. "Remember, she'd grab us by our *behdat* and with that sly knowing grin that owned you, remember, she'd whisper 'I'm trickier than you. *Bef-hemack* (I know you).' And boy, *did* she ever!"

"That would be called 'child abuse' these days," I said. "But I think she just liked to handle us. You know, the way I play with my cats; I grab them and cuff them around; it's loving; the way Mom used to play with us. We were her kittens." I stopped, beginning to feel I was getting too metaphorical.

"Oh yeah?" he crooned, his tone larded with a drawn-out mock pity at my naïveté, much like the tone our mother would use with us as kids when she thought we were being taken in. "She knew when I needed to take a crap before I did."

"That's because she'd given us our dose of cod liver oil for the day, remember?" I noted.

"Was it cod liver or castor oil? I don't remember. Just that taste . . . Jeez!" He gave a disgusted sound. "It was all the oily *fah'chem* (filth) scraped from the bottom of the ocean and squeezed into those spoon-fuls of shark farts. We had to hold our noses while she pried our mouths open. Ugh," he shuddered, *"Elbee haash* (My stomach's in an uproar)! Oooo-ooo-ooo-ooo!" He gave a shudder of revulsion from the old days: voice in a chilled shiver of loathing rippling in distinctly more repellent stages, down the disks in his throat and through his entire physical frame in waves of recoil against the viscous, vile after-taste that still coated his memory-cells. His, and now mine.

"You could hardly trust putting *anything* Mom gave you on a spoon into your mouth," I said.

"Yeah, I guess they figured if you could down that, you could stomach anything. Talking about *fah'chem,"* he continued, "I'm so glad that Pop isn't alive to see that bastard Hussein butcher his own people; who knows, maybe even our family. *"Haa-zee-tohn* (Poor wretches)!" he exclaimed. Then, lowering his voice a bit, he asked, "Do you think we might still have relatives there?"

"I doubt it," I said. "They would've had better sense than to stick around this long."

"Hope so," he said. "Think there are any shuls left there?"

"Shuls? I doubt there are any Jews left, except maybe for a few *khit'-yars* (old men)." I couldn't envision how they could have survived.

"If it was me," he continued, "I would've been on the first banana boat out of there when that *khaa-raah* (shit) took over. I guess that's what they meant in the old days, remember?—when they'd curse you?—'Fuck you and the boat that brought you!'"

"Yeah," I said. "Very specific, too; tells you the era."

"Yeah, immigrant humor." I heard him clearing his throat, trying to hawk up phlegm. "You want to know something, Jackie? When I do that, I hear Pop grunt: 'hunnnh!' (throat clearing). Remember?"

"The same thing happens with me. I can taste what Pop must've tasted."

"We're turning into the *haa-zeet* cases we tried to ix-nay," he said, slipping into the Arabic-pig-Latin commonly used by S.Y. salesmen telegraphing to one another in code in the presence of a customer. *"Khallasnah* (We're finished)."

"Not exactly," I held out; actually, it was more like a hope. *"Ya'ruhbee decheelak* (Lord please)," I heard myself say before I could think it.

We both paused, to allow things stirred up to settle down.

With a change of tone, Nat went on: "I see things are getting hot out West. It's not enough you got nutcases blowing up shuls and shooting civilians, you got park rangers setting forests on fire!" he exclaimed, with more than outrage: exasperated to wit's end. *"Bess-ba-aa* (Enough already)! *Khuh'rab il din'yeah* (The world's falling apart)!"

"Doesn't go away," I said, and sounded to myself like my mother's voice in one of her fatalistic "expecting the expected" moments (which, in fact, was usually what came), as if she and I both drew the substance of what we said from the same source.

"There *is* no *away,"* Nat said, and in his simple summary I was taken aback by the deep low-note of marrow-weary resignation infusing his voice, yet at the same time I felt a surprised satisfaction, even admiration, for the concise finality of the expression—an experienced conviction—and hearing it from him I realized that he too drew from the same source.

"It's poetry," I said, and meant it.

"Yeah?" he asked, only semi-kidding, "you mean it's never too late?"

"There *is* no late," I reminded him.

"Oh yes there is," he laughed. "And you just reminded me. I have to go. My help is robbing me blind . . . as we speak. You know all those illegals who sneak over the border? They're all here, working in my store."

"Are you still coming out to San Francisco?" I asked.

After a pause, "I'll get back to you on that."

My mother, probably before her marriage

My father and mother's wedding picture

My grandmother with my mother

My mother shortly before her marriage

My mother in a riding outfit

My cousin Renee Shemis
and my sister Renee ("the little Ethiopian")

My sister Renee and my brother Nat

My father in his eighties

CHAPTER FIFTEEN

DARWIN, THE FIRST CRACK IN THE EGG

Steadily taking books out of the library, I soon came upon Darwin and his theory of evolution. The fossil record unearthed skeletal remains of species placed side by side, that had existed millions of years apart, showing scaled gradations of limbs and posture in progressive evolutionary stages; illustrated charts, when your eyes scanned the ladder of ascent, became animated like the photo sequences of trotting horses and running men by Muybridge.

In gradual eon-long stages, the smallest primeval crustaceans grew to huge, armored reptiles and horned carnivores taller than the trees of the forests around them. They stood in place, not needing to move in order to gore or snag with claw, horn, and sabre-tooth, the plentiful game—often including their own kind—that abounded. The earth was a slaughterhouse of mammoth phantasmagoric species each on their way to adaptation or extinction.

Higher up on the branches of the evolutionary tree, like furry leaves, grew the crouching primates and hairy simians, humankind's earliest ancestors.

In the first frames, an amphibian had crawled ashore on its fins, and on the next level, its successor with modified stumps for locomotion, drew itself up on all fours into the frame above, where its modified heir strode, first hunched, then erect on two legs, and finally—original leathery fins transformed into elegant airy wings—aloft!

Was this fossil record—the eons-slow struggle for survival-of-the-fittest exhibiting the ingenious adaptations of natural selection—to be trusted? Could it have been faked or tampered with? But that was not how I understood science to operate. Not convenience or custom, but tangible, provable evidence was its litmus test. Evolution's fossil layers were a solid, if incomplete, record of what lay deep beyond human tampering—even beyond imagination—before being unearthed and codified by men like Darwin.

One evening after the other students left, I stayed and asked Hacham Shlomo, "Rabbi, how can it be according to the Talmud's interpretation of *Beresheet* (Book of Genesis), that the world was created 6,000 years ago, when scientists have found fossil bones of animals millions of years old?"

Turning his head in repugnance, he fingered the top button of his jacket, and replied: "God put those bones there to fool the scientists," and picked up his prayer book, dismissed me, and strode out of the room.

On my way home through the dark streets, night felt like an even vaster hallway than at home, open-ended in space. What sort of God had we been learning about? Could the Creator of galaxies more numerous than all the grains of sand on all the shores of the world; the Creator of a universe whose immensity by now had enlarged exponentially for me with my reading in astronomy; could such a Creator be so spiteful as to play a hoax on his creatures . . . to delude them? Could those gigantic bones of reptiles and T-Rexes be the handiwork of a cosmic prankster? So petty and perverted was this ploy, it sounded too much like what only a human was capable of thinking up, and made the Creator of the universe into—what?—a sadist? Wouldn't that be what local wise guys called working "ass-backwards"? Was creation, then, simply a joke on a captive audience? If that was the case, then appearance was even more of a hoax than I had imagined.

Wouldn't any Talmudist have seen the absurdity of attempting to justify such devilish contempt in divine behavior? Once understood as a developing process, the gradual nature of evolution over eons of time had the force of a self-evident truth rather than an heretical theory. Yet the rabbi had assured me . . .

Try as one might, when the heart is not in it, part of one's being is held back, so that, through applying reason, I couldn't help but imagine how much more wondrous it was for humans, along with all other life, to have originated from a single-celled ancestor and evolve through infinitesimal variations of natural selection to their present forms. This would make time an active, ongoing agent in the process of creation . . . and human development along with it.

In these nightly walks home I began to feel confused and troubled; whatever strength had held my earlier belief was now turning, by necessity and reason of incremental evidence, to questions I couldn't answer with inherited models. Could it be that customs were habits, and the repetitions of habit were seductions; that tradition and authority were mere holding actions against the unknown and unpredictable; that, in present fact, nothing from the past could help anymore, and as these moments went on, there was no appeal outside of the present, that each moment of the present was an ongoing beginning as well as an end? Religious belief was a practice in discipline and remembrance to ward off uncertainties of the immediate present. But each moment—like a flare going out, not some sacred past we owed allegiance to, nor a promised future without immediate substance to its claim—each present moment was the very heart of time.

THE NIGHT I WAS INTRODUCED TO SIGMUND FREUD

Walking home after Hebrew school was a ritual, unwinding a process of thought led on by more rapid, deeper breathing. Rhythm was the key: the rhythm of walking—alternating left, right—both lulls and alerts. Repetition's regular movements numb us into trance, dulling discomfort, even pain, and seems able to stall and reverse the erosion of time by setting back the psychic clock.

At night, darkness merged surfaces and erased volume, canceling the divide between objects, and canceling the objects themselves by abolishing the sense of space. In that darkness, with chinks of starlight, it didn't take much to imagine being in the belly of a beast, like Jonah, but vaster than any eye could measure; which made the eyes themselves an immeasurable dream.

Some nights I'd walk home from Hebrew school with a fellow classmate, Isaac Malek. It was a few blocks to his house and we'd head there first. The walk would have taken no more than fifteen or twenty minutes of slow going, but in my memory those night walks take up more weight and volume than the clock-time in which they occurred.

We walked at the leisurely pace of our conversation, which usually began with the subject of our lesson. Often, when we'd reach his house, still not having finished our discussion, we'd turn around and start toward mine, then, still absorbed, having concluded nothing, we'd turn back again toward his house. One night, after having read the story of the Exodus from Egypt, as we strolled, Isaac stopped, faced me, and said: "You know, Moses wasn't a Jew."

I was startled—as much by the audacity of a mind that could think in that way as the unsettling implications of the remark.

His face under the streetlight came into somber focus, then appeared bisected as he turned, and the separate angles of his features came forcefully together as I had the uncomfortable feeling I was being challenged while listening, absorbing his comments like blows to my hollow midsection. We were both around ten or eleven, with similar slight frames. Isaac's expression was usually intent and serious, but now he laughed in a loud cackle, with a hiccuping action at the end, like the pop of a cap pistol. I tried to argue, but unrelenting doses of his mockery blocked me at every traditional turn I took as he bared his lethal heresies. I felt a powerful tug of a hollowness in my gut and quicksand underfoot. Lit for an instant, choices flashed by like precipices that, looking down from, made me dizzy, propelling me headlong into who knew where, and calling for what scrupulous effort, what exacting search? Could a boy dispute the Bible, the foundation on which our religion was based? Did I want him to continue to be my friend? I was afraid of the answer to both: Yes.

Isaac was shameless, enjoying his waste-laying evisceration of the Biblical version of the six days of Creation, the Flood, the crumbling of Jericho's walls by Joshua's trumpets, when, as he put it, "Joshua didn't even know that the Earth—not the sun—moves," and gleefully concluded, "All that horn-blowing—for the wrong miracle!"

His scornful laughter is what I most remember, more than the words of his arguments; the self-assured, sweeping glee of one so convinced of the irrefutable truth of his case, so at ease with its confounding implications; he had a hand he didn't need to show.

When I asked him what he meant, he said that he had been reading Freud's "Moses and Monotheism." According to Freud, Moses had been an Egyptian of royal birth, a disciple of the Pharaoh

Akhanaton's radically new monotheistic religion: it banned the practice common among the Egyptians of sorcery and of worshipping many gods.

"Read it yourself," he said. "Make up your own mind. I don't want to be the *yah-sir ha-raah* (evil spirit)," he snickered.

A few days later, over inner qualms, I took the book out of the library. Reading Freud was like trying to make out hieroglyphics inside a cave; the slippery, subterranean text was like a language of night. Following where Isaac had left off, reading this felt like racing for my life, so dreadful did the images and ideas take shape. So plausible did Freud make his theory, I could follow the trail he traced from the primitive Egyptians' many gods—chief among them the hawk-headed sun god Amon-Ra—whom Akhanaton replaced with the one and only divinity, Aton (later transformed into the Hebrew "Adonai"), unique, universal, without form. But, Freud conjectured, the old habit of polytheism persisted so that the suppressed priests, after Akhanaton died, reinstated Amon-Ra to the people for whom Aton had held no appeal. One of a small circle of royal disciples of Akhanaton (here I quote from Freud's text), "Moses conceived the plan of founding a new empire, of finding a new people and leading them out of bondage and to whom he could give the new religion that Egypt disdained." This could also tell us as much about Freud's motives and ambitions as those of his Moses.

Freud hypothesized that our earliest ancestors lived in small groups, each ruled by an older male who governed by brute force, appropriated all the females, and enslaved or killed the younger males, including his own sons, out of fear of being displaced. Circumcision, in the later Mosaic law, became a symbolic substitute for the castration the primeval father dealt his sons who showed their submission to his will. This patriarchal system was ended through a rebellion of the sons against the father, killing him, and consuming his body. This repressed father-hate, Freud concludes, "bears the characteristic of being never concluded and never able to be concluded with which we are familiar in the reaction-formations of obsessional neurosis."

In support of his thesis, Freud notes that one of his sources, the German historian Ernst Sellin, refers to what he claims is evidence in the Prophetic Books that, after the exodus from Egypt, "Moses was killed in the desert by the tribes to whom he had introduced the new religion and which they then abandoned. This murdered figure, Moses, would later in their Babylonian exile become the basis for the future Messiah: the one they had killed would return from the realm of the dead and lead his contrite people into the Promised Land." It is with the early consciousness of this communal guilt that what Freud calls "this Father religion" began. Judaism, originating as a new religion of fugitive, wandering immigrants would be granted as its redemption the eternal Promised Land.

I remember being more disturbed not so much because what Isaac was saying might be true, but that it was *conceivable; it could* be true. Combined with what I had begun to sense about human nature—my own included—this prehistoric rebellion and cannibalism set off a suspicion that shaded into a recognition, like a dormant visceral genetic memory.

Freud also noted the similarity of names like the Egyptian gods Aton and Jahve with the Hebrew Adonai and Jahveh; that Moses was an Egyptian name *(mose* meaning child, a common abridgement of the fuller names of Egyptian kings, such as Ah-mose, Thut-mose, Ra-mose); that there was an unmistakable echo of the early hymn to Aton, "O Thou only God, there is no other God than Thou," with the later Judaic "Shema" ("Hear O Israel, Adonai, our God, Adonai is One"). Was all this mere chance, coincidence, or might there be omissions, deletions, distortions in traditional roles whose traces might be uncovered through links, hints, echoes, clues? Did words and their roots share a common source? Freud continues, "What interval elapsed between an event and its fixation by writing, we are naturally unable to know." But even with his several demurrings and misgivings about any certainty in what he proposed, Freud had opened the door to the possibility that history might have been tampered with and rewritten to accommodate a preconceived design.

It was as if the darkness in which Isaac and I stood was not simply a nightly presence, but was surrounded and smeared with successively dark layers from the past; nights blacker, older than the mortar of Egypt, enveloping us, a tunnel in time linking all preceding nights to original, primeval night.

Another evening, Isaac went on to explain Freud's theory of the unconscious; that, as the psychic development of humankind is repeated "in abbreviated form," in the development of each individual, the human race was still in its infantile stage and subject to the explosive "return of the repressed" (such a powerfully charged recoil in the phrase) for the guilt of killing the father.

As we stood, Isaac explaining (or, more exactly, asserting) and I listening, I tried to imagine being alive then: Egypt, a nightmare of unceasing labor, bloodshed; darkness and dunes canceling visual edges and boundaries, everywhere desert; visible darkness and vaster darkness within.

CHAPTER SIXTEEN

AT UNCLE ABOOD'S HOUSE

On my way to the library, when I'd pass my Uncle Abood's house near the corner of 21st Avenue, I'd try to make sure I wasn't seen by my Aunt Sarah.

Uncle Abood, his wife, and their five adult children were among the few people I knew, especially family, who owned a house; everyone else rented. Uncle Abood, tall, soft-spoken, well-to-do, owned a sewing factory in Manhattan that my mother had worked in as a seamstress when she'd arrived from Syria, and before she married my father. Uncle Abood, my mother's oldest brother and the oldest member of their Cohen family, was of a height (around six feet tall, rare among Arabic men) and a fleshy bulk that accentuated his aura of gentleness. Patient and tolerant, he was always kind to me; a look of pleased surprise on his face when he'd see me.

Aunt Sarah, however, was his opposite in temperament, manner, appearance, and aura. This contrast made it likely that theirs was also an arranged marriage. They seemed to have little in common. Short and stocky, dressed in dark sabbatical attire, she made herself a martyr to unattractiveness, demanding the same of others around her. Strict, Orthodox fault-finding was her calling, more-Orthodox-than-thou. She took her revered Biblical name as license to despise what she considered religious laxness. *"Ruh-chut il k'neese yo'meh* (Did you go to shul today)?" she'd ask you at any time, on any day, religious holiday or not. If you hesitated, or guiltily looked away, she'd reply, *"Eyb, ya boom* (Shame on you, bad one)!" Or she'd blame you for prolonging the tardiness of salvation by wiping her hands and sarcastically inquiring: *"Ya faheem, chalasnah? Il Mashiah mah bijee* (O wise one, are we finished? Is the Messiah not coming)?" And if you dared,

self-protectively, to sheepishly grin for lack of a reply, she'd reprimand, *"Ishu hadah, duhkeh* (What's this, a joke)?" Once when she
saw me with an Italian friend, she asked with a grimace, *"Minu
hadah, talyani* (Who's this, an Italian)?" Her Arabic was a com-
pendium of objection and displeasure; among her favorite words
were: *dib* (fool, male), *dibbeh* (fool, female), *zbaleh* (garbage), as those
times when she'd spot me carrying a book not a *siduhr* (a Hebrew
prayer book) and ask, *"Ish ahn'dak, zbaleh* (What have you got there,
garbage)?" and waving her hand, *"Kish min witchee* (Get out of my
sight)!" Everywhere she went she spread censure and resentment;
everything soured in her presence.

Pleasure, to her, was a vice: the only benefit she found in it was her
ability to condemn it—as strongly and self-righteously as possible—
a virtue she found endless opportunities to practice. When we'd visit,
seeing me without a yarmulke, she'd ask my mother: "He goes around
without a hat on?" With equal disdain, my mother wouldn't answer,
pretending she didn't hear, or that the jibe did not deserve a reply. She
was on a social visit to her older brother, not a defendant in a religious
trial. To her credit, my mother was suspicious and contemptuous of
such arrogant fanaticism. She was all-too-aware of her own short-
comings in observing the letter of religious law; to her, fanatics, by
nature, were hypocrites.

The one pleasurable memory I retain from visiting my uncle's
house with my mother was one Shabbat afternoon in summer, sitting
in the large comfortable glassed-in porch looking out onto the street,
I heard the inviting jingle of ice-cream bells approach, and there
appeared through the stained-glass window a colorful mini-fireworks
display. The window suddenly turned into a revolving wheel of
sparkles. I had seen the phenomenon before in a drop of water. What
a riotous, delicious palette was this spectrum, and full-screen!—
quickly glinting one colored pane of glass off another, till everything
in the air, moving or still, spun in prismatic accents from the back of
the truck filled with open tubs of fruit-flavored sherbet I was forbidden to taste that afternoon. But, in my mind, their variegated glitter
still sparkles with delectable sharpness on that long-ago summer
afternoon, as little else does from that time.

DRUNKEN BOAT

My bed was a raft, I imagined, beginning when I had my own room, after having shared one with my sister Renee until our brother Nat, the youngest, was born, and after which they both shared until the time for her to have her own room. I was about ten or eleven and my sister eight or nine. I suppose that, as a girl, she should have gotten the room into which I was moved, adjoining the kitchen. But I was glad to have it; small as it was, a few paces wide, gray-walled like the rest of the apartment, its very bareness allowed for a focus on reading, thinking, and what would soon be at hand: a microscope and chemistry set I was to acquire.

As a bed is a door opening the outer to inner worlds, so is a child's imagination often set free when lying down.

At night, reading a book was the best adventure. After moments of concentrated reading, the material bed would lose its solidity and I'd drift and levitate, much as later when working as a seaman on a freighter in the south Atlantic, standing on the top deck, closer to the sky than to land, I'd have the sensation of flying more than sailing.

With reading about the great navigators, the adventures of Tom Sawyer, a history of the American Revolution, how to grow microbes in a petri dish, came a rush of perceptions and tonalities of feeling. The act of reading released something like a hormone that activated an inner world—not *another*, but this one, more intensely. Going from word to word was an adventure of expectancy, creating an alternative reality to the tedium of plodding days and weeks and months past and to come. This promise served as an advance on time, and was no less real (if, by "real" we mean what affects us deeply) for being imagined.

The more exasperated I felt at being subject to time's passing helped make what I imagined even more real.

In those days I could go without speaking to anyone; sullen, angrily discontent, an uneasy sense growing that by becoming isolated I was trapping myself in my body, which was growing more rarified on thin air and thinning flesh. Going for a walk, or going about the activities of a normal day was sometimes a relief, a liberation.

When older, writing or walking would become a dissolving of landmarks and limits, a freshening of perception in the vividness of roused sensation.

Before embarking on the dream-voyages that made up much of my sleep, I'd lie on my side and read adventure stories like *Kidnapped, Robinson Crusoe, The Voyage of Sinbad,* tales that traveled farther than any present moment could in the time it took to read them. Stories were units of concentrated time, more dense with excitement than daily life's tedious duration. Having too much time is a condition children dread, just as adults dread not having enough.

I soon grew fascinated by the life and work of the French poet Arthur Rimbaud, whose precocious poetry envisioned a purity believed only in childhood. In his "Seven Year Old Poets" he wrote, "And the mother, closing the exercise book, went away satisfied and very proud, without seeing in the blue eyes under the pimpled forehead the soul of her child given over to loathing." The tempestuous seascapes and delirious dreams of his "The Drunken Boat," written in his mid-teens, were as much prophecy as poetry, an imaginative rehearsal and intimation of what, soon in his short life, would become actual: working in a lime pit on Cyprus, escape to Africa, gunrunning in Aden, slave trading in Harar, losing a leg to gangrene after having carried on his person the money belt filled with gold coins he had amassed in order to gain financial independence, at last emulating the miserly mother he had earlier loathed. Alas, his poems were more successfully crafted than his life, the latter half wasted in isolation and bitterness before his death at thirty-seven. But Rimbaud's rebellion and travels had great appeal, especially when I read he had learned to speak fluent Arabic and worked as a translator in Africa for European traders; I even imagined that, with my knowledge of the language, I might be able to do the same one day.

Compared with Rimbaud, Shakespeare was a paradigm of health and compassion, as in *The Merchant of Venice:* "The quality of mercy is not strained; it droppeth like the dew," with its sound-aura spun of the unsubstantial, paired "quality" and "mercy" merged with the substantial "droppeth" and "dew," creating a linguistically precise, palpable embodiment of what is being expressed, and possessing the cadence of conviction. Shakespeare possessed a great natural force in both the directness and awareness of human complexity in his language; the brute meat tenderized by mercy. What came to mind was the feeling I had at times when summer rain, falling softly all around, felt like family.

Another discovery was Christopher Marlowe and what our English teacher emphasized one day when we were about to begin reading *Faustus:* "Marlowe's mighty line." ("I'll leap up to my God; who pulls me down?") In short doses, I found Marlowe could be even more exciting (because more brutally violent) than Shakespeare, just as later the speed of thought, feeling, and imagery enacted in propulsive cadence drew me to Gerard Manley Hopkins, Francis Thompson's "Hound of Heaven," Hart Crane, and Dylan Thomas.

On my bed, together with my sister and brother on either side, I'd set off telling a story, taking my cue from whatever adventure I was reading at the time. Crusoe was a sure way to begin: shipwrecked seaman marooned on an island, having to improvise methods for survival. After all, what else was the world for us then, besides an adventure!

Shortly before her death, at age fifty-nine, during one of my weekly long-distance calls to her at the time she was undergoing radiation treatments, Renee reminded me of the tales I used to make up, of being shipwrecked and surviving on a desert island with makeshift tools. "The Black Hand. Jackie, don't you remember The Black Hand?" I didn't. Besides the eerie connotations that came to mind at the name, I didn't recall imagining such a thing, much less the details of those yarns. Renee was about to tell me, but along with news of breakthrough cancer drugs and radical interventions, we somehow lost the urgency for answering that minor question. I put it aside; other more pressing matters came up. And it didn't have a chance to come up again before she succumbed, making her fate the answer to the question.

How much more I have forgotten of those early years, and how much she took with her, I have no idea.

The writing I did then—imitating Shelley, Keats, and Tennyson (with a jaunty bit of John Masefield's maritime music thrown in: "I must down to the seas again, to the lonely sea and the sky, / And all I ask is a tall ship and a star to steer her by")—I kept private, secret from both my family and friends. More than embarrassment, I would have felt exposed if anyone in my family read a line of what I'd written, since it would have revealed how opposed to their concerns were my own. I was, as I could see in puzzled and worrisome looks from my parents, already considered "strange"; I didn't want it confirmed by something I'd written. Though my mother couldn't read English—she didn't need to, knowing her son as only a mother can—my father and siblings could, and I didn't want to fuel their suspicion. I never understood how people could show their writing to their parents, like showing your hand to those it was raised against.

With my friends (not that they were curious or even cared), I didn't want to have to explain language and imagery often archaic and out of their realm of interest. Better that they saw me as "a regular guy," the popular password assuring you were not "irregular," or in the retail lingo we were all familiar with, "seconds," damaged goods.

If one of them dropped in, I'd put away my writing and take up whatever activity they had in mind: cruise the runway that was Bay Parkway to meet girls, or check out the park, or the several local soda shops (the biggest and loudest, and appealing to the most socially mobile crowd, was The Chocolate Cove), play ball or cards, or goof in someone's basement. Whatever was happening, I would adapt; it may not have been my preference, but coming after I'd been concentrating on writing, it was, if at first an interruption, in the end, a welcome relief.

CABINET OF WONDERS

A drop of water was the first magnifying lens; in effect, the beginning of modern science. That intriguing detail drew me to a popular biography of Anton van Leeuwenhoek, Dutch tradesman in Amsterdam, who in 1683, with hardly an academic education and in fact never having written a research paper in his life, became the great "layman" father of microbiology by discovering a hidden dimension of which people up till then had no inkling: the world of invisible bacteria.

The biography related how one day Leeuwenhoek noticed that when he spilled a drop of water on a tabletop in his lab he could see the grain of the wood enlarged clearly beneath the convex swell of the drop's transparent center. He wondered how he could reproduce that effect in a more permanent way so he could examine materials and objects more closely. This practice made actual the scientific principle of taking the next step: an observed natural fact built on for further experiment and observation. One could claim as scientific proof only what could be observed and measured.

The magnifying effect of a drop of water I had already noticed when, out walking, a drop of rain on my sleeve would enlarge a stitch in the woven fabric; the same phenomenon as when I'd spill a drop of water onto a linen napkin where the nubs, bulkier to begin with, appeared larger than those of more tightly woven fabrics, like cotton. This enlarging of what was ordinarily small and insignificant was a revelation: being pure in its elements and simple in expression gave it the authority of a truth, which once realized and expressed seemed self-evident: truths out of which further propositions could be conceived, experiments tested, effects measured. The biography went on to relate how Leeuwenhoek used his discovery to construct a magnifying glass using the more solid, stable prototype of a waterdrop: a glass lens whose magnifying powers he could modify and adjust by polishing to a fuller roundness at the center and set into a wooden spatula could be carried around and held above objects to observe more closely, thus the first handheld magnifying lens. The next step was to align two lenses—one set slightly above the other to produce further magnification: the first microscope.

These claims, while dramatic to a boy, I'd later learn were inaccurate. Leeuwenhoek did not invent the first magnifying lens nor the compound microscope (a microscope using more than one lens). However, where his predecessor, the Englishman Robert Hooke, made lenses that could magnify objects twenty to thirty times their natural size, Leeuwenhoek's skill at grinding lenses enabled him to build microscopes that magnified over 200 times what his colleagues achieved.

"In the white matter between my teeth," under his homemade microscope he saw "millions of microscopic animals, more than there were human beings in the united Netherlands, and all moving in the most delightful manner."

Some historians conjecture that he was a friend of the painter Jan Ver Meer, of Delft, since he acted as Ver Meer's executor, and he may have known Rembrandt, who also lived in Amsterdam. Around the same time Benedict Spinoza, a fellow Amsterdam citizen (did they also know each other?), having been excommunicated by the Sephardic rabbis for his heretical philosophy, also took up lens grinding as a way to earn a living from failing Dutch patrons' eyes.

Leeuwenhoek's innovation—so simple a child could appreciate—was the deep seeing behind my growing interest in obtaining a microscope set, which I did, but don't recall how. I'm sure I didn't buy it; it must have been given to me, but by whom? Not my parents, nor can I imagine any relative so observant as to be aware of my interest at the time. How then did it appear one day on the table in my room? A wooden cabinet, when opened, revealed rows of slender glass test tubes held at their necks in grooves, and the Gilbert microscope with its elongated black binocular tubes, one fit inside the other, a silver wheel at the side to adjust for sharper focus, the round mirror beneath and the horseshoe stand spread below, holding it up. With an eye dropper, I'd tint with blue stain a feather, then place it on a slide and as I turned the small mirror underneath, light caught there reflected the delicate distinct arrowed fibers, illuminating what earlier appeared as solid surface, showing multipockets of varied textures and a deeper hatched design than visible to the naked eye. For evidence of living organisms, I'd leave a small piece of raw meat in a dish of water for a few days and when I'd then inject a drop onto a slide and stain it, at high magnification I could see the tiny amoeba and rod-like paramecia moving, twisting, splitting. A few times when I had left the meat out for too long, the foul smell of decomposition would be noticeable in my room and my mother would throw it out.

In a pod, a leaf, a fly's wing: in whatever object I'd examine under the lens, life flourished—ran rampant—below the visible surface of everyday life. The microscopic world was, for me, the true original magical world. Everywhere you turned, strange alien organisms were born and reproduced while attempting to overtake their basic survival needs, food supply, and territory; organisms, often with nervous systems that responded more quickly than human nerves did, were numberless, as were their slower victims.

In the gradual process of evolution, ugly and beautiful became so intermixed, it made no sense to differentiate between them: creatures grew multiple eyes for panavision; others without eyes grew feathery cilia to feel their way toward food and shelter, while still others developed poisoned barbs to deflect enemies; species that survived perfected ways to navigate through surrounding predators and hostile environments. Nature was guerrilla war, every perilous step of the way, and along with each step, sights such as the close-up of a Japanese kimono pattern on a luna moth; a miniscule pulsing pool sequentially enlarging into an amoeba, and the infinitely fine lace intricacies of a pesky housefly's wing I examined after swatting it against the window.

CHAPTER SEVENTEEN

WHAT'S IN A NAME

There must have been something of my father's temperament that my mother saw in my face whenever she'd notice me reading a book, poring over a test tube from my chemistry set, or peering into my microscope. It prompted her to order me to go outside into the bright afternoon sunshine and *shim 'il hehwah* (breath the air). When I'd look up, she'd throw up both her hands in a vehement gesture of splashing her face with sunshine and shout, *"M' bussaet! M' bussaet* (Be happy! Be happy!)."* What I couldn't say was that I *was* happy, but not in any way she would recognize or approve.

I didn't at the time, but now suspect my father's self-effacing social manner disguised a high opinion of his own worth. My mother would often mock-imitate his pronounced Manchester English accent rounded in Middle Eastern tones, its formality and fussy correctness; she'd scoff at his timid, conciliatory nature and within earshot, sneer in Arabic, *"T'eel i-dem* (Slow, heavy blood)."* There was an inborn, elegiac quality to his forbearing, guarded look, and my hunch is that in the lulling ease it engendered in others he had time to more carefully appraise his surroundings: a veteran survivor's fixed attention kept on a low flame.

Like many European Jewish immigrants who felt the need to reconfigure their family names, deconstructing, flattening, or cropping their native "inskie," "heimer," or "witz" to proper Anglo-American size, in order to "blend in," my father tailored his Arabic family name to the social norms of his adopted country.

From as far back as I can remember, I had assumed that, in order to assimilate for business purposes, my father had Anglicized his family name to "Marshall" from the Arabic *Ma' shah' lah,* meaning "Praise

Allah." Only recently did I learn from my brother that the original family name was in fact *Mash' aal,* meaning "torch." I wonder if my father, in deciding on the closely corresponding English surname, had first calculated the social risks of inciting disfavor in his adopted land by keeping the family's Arabic name and using it in the family business. If interpreted into its English meaning, might "torch" be taken for insolence? However arrived at, the Anglicized "Marshall" was used as a badge of safe conduct through the new world of the European mercantile class; much like raising your country's flag in treacherous times to avert suspicion, or daubing a cross on your door at news of an approaching pogrom.

I remember in grade school when learning to write the English alphabet in large, full-rounded cursive script from left to right on the wide-staved pages of my copy book, my father, one evening after returning home from work, patiently and precisely writing out in ink the flowing, hook-tailed wavelets of the Arabic alphabet from right to left. Then, with firm precision, he wrote out in graceful Arabic letters our family name, the glossy black ink flowing smoothly with no pause or break. At other times, his handwriting in English had the same liquid fluency with a different script. Years later, he would write with equal exactness the English-lettered signs and price tags for the merchandise in the window of his own dry goods store.

The name "Marshall," called out by a teacher in school or an official in a public place, embarrassed me; it felt oddly unfamiliar, even alien. When spoken, rather than denoting a family's trade or profession (as in Goldsmith, Baker, Silverberg, etc.), I had the feeling that the thin film of identity had been pulled aside, exposing a wide hollow underneath.

In grade school kids would call me "Texas Marshal," granting me a sort of mock authority of which only one's young peers can appreciate the irony. But when I was alone and I'd repeat my name, it would begin to fade like smoke, dissolving in the distance; then after several more evaporating repetitions, vanish. At first made uneasy by this verbally induced disappearance, I soon came to feel that in not attaching to me a socially defining identity, this freed me from automatically being assumed a member of any particular ethnic group. If a name could be a cipher, "Marshall" was as close to being a vacancy as I could imagine.

I have at times wondered how a family name might affect its inheritors? Might it perhaps, in subtle ways, influence how others viewed and reacted to the family's descendants? Could we be influenced, even somehow determined, by the properties of the names we bear?

Recently, my brother Nat told me of having been introduced on his visit to Israel to a distinguished Sephardic rabbi in Jerusalem who informed him that in an earlier time the *Mash' aal* family was royalty—"princes" was the word the rabbi had used. It's common knowledge that flattery, another patent art of disguise, is not unique to certain peoples, but as perfected in Arabic, hyperbole is creatively polished to the point some would consider poetic license and others outlandish fantasy, caricature edged with sarcasm.

I asked Nat if he'd thought the rabbi's remark might have been flattery. He e-mailed back:

Jackie,

I don't think it was flattery. This was a sincere and of course wise rabbi in Israel, from England; I think even from Manchester, where Pop and his family moved from Baghdad. He knew something about our family's history but he didn't go into it. He just said "Princes." Who knows, maybe a relative we know nothing about is a prince in the Royal House of Saud. Yeah, right.

BEDOUIN-KIN

I.
There was (or is?) a colonel on my father's side
he once showed me a photo of
in the *New York Times,* must have been

late 1940s. Picture with me if you will
a Bedouin-kin, baked stoic
look in a lean face, earnest gaze,

much like a younger version of my father
with the added dash of a military-bar mustache
above the tailored uniform of the Iraqi elite corps—

uncle? cousin? nephew?—who
knew? In the time it takes to
glance and register a node

of hardly any interest to a boy,
I noted the family face, like an echo
visible down the ages, and looked away,

taking in as little as I could then.

2.
It comes
as no surprise: the older you get
the further back it takes

to reach some bare,
buried note
no matter how random or remote

a recognition or fleeting
trace.
                    Except for an obscure

oddball uncle or two, we hardly knew
his side. . . . He didn't offer,
we didn't pursue—not unusual

for a boy whose total consuming mental effort
was: not to be there.
Families are to flee from.

3.
In the cyanide light of recent events,
I wonder what became of him: did the high command
know he was a Jew?

Might he have survived the cabals, purges, coups
that periodically irrigate
those bloodthirsty Biblical sands?

If he converted to other
than the double masquerade of the Marranos,
did he pass, or what loopholes slip through?

All that is moot.
As with the rest of his clan, I never asked
or gave him a thought.

In the annulling anonymity of time that makes us
all the same age at once, little more than
a pang says he has most likely been erased

from human eyes. When mine last saw his,
he could have been anyone—anonymous
as an atom—as my father is and I will be,

so that if only for the moment it takes
to tell of hardly
any difference between a possible life, partly

mine, and certain extinction, which is everyone's,
let this memory pass as virtual
elegy and its fleeting

(as his life most likely long-since did)
take place in the real.

THE GRAVES OF ANIMALS

When Pop arrived home from his salesman's job in the city, the first
question he'd ask was if I had moved my bowels that day. No doubt he
was checking with me for signs of what must have been troubling him,
though he never admitted it. His question was an embarrassing intru-
sion, which I guess would confirm us as members in the same dis-
comfited gene pool. Repeated over time, his question communicated:
"If you listen to me, you will become this"; like a fate one secretly
intends for oneself. Other times it seemed as if his voluntary surrender
to the circumstances of his life verged on a kind of hard-won serenity.

Nearly every day he'd repeat to me his cautionary, mercantile mantra: "Mind you, make money in due time, but don't *do* time for making money." Though he was as religious as he could afford to be, the nature of his job in a 5th Avenue linen shop required that he work on Shabbat; he may even have allowed himself to believe that God would excuse that violation, for he had to support his family. In regard to most other Jewish holy days, he was observant, if not meticulous.

Coming home late, he'd wearily go about washing up for dinner after the rest of us had eaten, if my mother had left enough of the *mih'shee,* or *ser'chee-chaah,* or *kibbeh.* But if he was tired of the breast of lamb stuffed with ground beef and rice, or the chicken roasted in potatoes she'd basted on a slow heat in the oven all day, she'd throw up her hands and walk away while he'd look downcast around the kitchen, then go about making himself a simple plate of *baed 'oo 'benadorah* (scrambled eggs with tomatoes) and eat his dinner at the table by himself. On those occasions, usually religious holidays, when we did eat together, I'd notice my father's finger-grooves worn smooth and sheened with a silvery film from handling coins all day. In all the daily and holiday meals we shared, none of us noted that we were the graves of the animals we ate.

CHAPTER EIGHTEEN

THE ANSWER MAN

In our pre-TV days, the news broadcasts on the radio had relatively little power to cause psychic damage on us, thanks, no doubt largely, to the absence of grim "reality" video footage. Our old stand-up Philco was the visible temple of invisible voices that kept me enthralled: leaning close to the cloth-lattice under its arched dome, I listened intently to the weekly quarter-hour adventure series whose musical themes, I would later learn, were derived from classical compositions. *The F.B.I. in Peace and War* was Prokofiev's *Lieutenant Kijie Suite, The Green Hornet* was Rimsky-Korsakov's *Flight of the Bumble Bee,* and *The Lone Ranger* (whose rousing, galloping intro was, unbeknownst to me, my first exposure to classical music) was Rossini's *William Tell Overture.* The last, which, even after we'd learned its identity in music appreciation class, when asked by our music teacher (the scowling, rumored bewigged Mrs. Cutler), a classmate would answer "The Lone Ranger" and get easy laughs. On the day that she told us we were about to listen to a piece called *Scheherazade* by a Russian composer named Rimsky-Korsakov, we pounced on the golden opportunity and soon renamed him, together chanting, "Rimsky-Take- Your-Corset-Off!" to Mrs. Cutler's frantic, wig-shaking dismay.

My last discovery of music-matching was the most surprising: having recited that rousing national anthem for years, it was not until I one day heard on the radio the gradual up-swelling bars that open Smetana's *Moldau* that I realized I was listening to the melody of "Hatikvah," the Jewish national anthem. Could no Jewish composers write an anthem? What about Felix Mendelsohn? (I'd read that, for business and social purposes, his father, like many assimilated Jews, had converted to Christianity.) Surely something from his *Midsummer's Night Dream*, or better yet, my favorite, the *Fingal's Cave Overture*, in which I recognized the lyric tidal surges of another musical source (less well-known than Rossini's *William Tell Overture*) used as background for radio episodes of *The Lone Ranger*. I wondered if whoever put the fervent, patriotic lyrics of the "Hatikvah" to the music of a Bohemian composer—a goy, no less!—had been aware of any irony in the borrowing. I later learned that the *Moldau*, composed in 1879, had been derived from a Moldavian-Rumanian folksong; it and "Hatikvah," written by Samuel Cohen in 1895, had been drawn from the same source. Nevertheless, this music, exuding such stirring ardor and longing, was particularly well-chosen as expressing the ancient Jewish yearning for homecoming. Memory doesn't care whose wings may launch it, nor longing care what may send it forth.

Another favorite program was the spine-chilling *Shadow*, with its eerie voice-over that snarled, "Who knows what evil lurks in the hearts of men?" and the spooky snickering reply, "The Shadow knows . . ." signing off with a blood-curdling, cackling "heh heh heh heh heh heh!" which I heard as the signature glee of all-knowing derision. Another favorite was *The Answer Man;* I was impressed by how listeners could send in questions about any subject and hear the answers on the air the following week. How so many various, rare topics could be so thoroughly researched and answers found to questions dealing with everything, literally, from Art and Automobiles to the Zodiac and Zoology, attested to a great mysterious power that could be tapped for everlasting use.

Of the songs that most characterized the patriotic times during and right after the war, there was something reassuring in the comforting tones with which Frank Sinatra crooned the popular "The House I Live In," suffusing its hymnal melody and public-spirited lyrics with the ambling grace of an idealized American street that claimed to welcome the immigrant butcher and baker and stranger that you meet every day, sung by an immigrant's son in a paean to the country's democratic principles, and summed up in the refrain, "That's America to me." Years later I'd read in an interview with Sinatra a candid quote about his craft: "My instrument is not my voice, it's the microphone."

FROM BAGHDAD TO BROOKLYN

BOIINNGG!!!

Neither my brother Nat nor I will ever forget one particular day in
Seth Low Park. I was about thirteen, and Nat seven. It was an early
summer day; our mother shooed us out of the house, saying she
was going to do some housecleaning, and we headed for the park.
Since it was a weekday, nobody was using the parallel bars, and the
basketball courts were empty; the regular players, who on weekends gathered to choose up sides, were at their jobs; the wading
pool that day, hot though it was, had not been filled. Mothers with
their baby carriages and strollers had apparently found cooler
paths to stroll in. Except for the slap and squeak of a couple of
handball players' sneakers in the far courts, and the crisp smack of
the ball, a sound distinct even from far away, almost otherworldly,
against the concrete wall beyond the outfield gate, the park was
nearly deserted.

Having left Nat to his own devices, I sat on the steps of the park
attendant's shed and was concentrated on playing checkers against
myself (I liked the fast moves, jumps and double jumps, without a
partner and without pausing), when I suddenly heard a loud, echo-
ing BOIINNGG!!! Looking up, I saw Nat in mid-recoil from a basketball pole, thrown to the ground. Head down, he'd run into the
steel upright unawares; the force of his speed equaled the counterforce of his falling back. I ran to him; he was moaning and writhing,
grabbing his forehead. The echo of that sickening sound reverberated in the air as the park attendant ran up behind me, took one
look and ran back to his shed. The right side of Nat's forehead had
become a raw, red knob he clutched. The attendant returned with
a cold compress he put on the already swollen lump. Only a
moment later, it seemed, an ambulance arrived, driving right into
the park and up to us. A medic leapt out of the front seat, and after
a quick look, we helped him place Nat on a stretcher and into the
ambulance; I got in, thinking we were going to the hospital. The
attendant asked me where we lived; I told him and, siren wailing,
we headed home. Arriving, we helped Nat walk unsteadily up the
three flights to our flat. When my mother answered the door, she
took one look at Nat and uttered her one-word all-purpose Arabic
wail of woe: "Oolleeee!" To this day, I can still hear that hollow

tubular clunk resound, like those radio and TV sound waves that keep traveling in space long after we Earthlings have heard them; this one returns and smacks me each time I recall it, literally, in the head; Nat too.

Fortunately, he recovered, and has since grown adept at butting his head against banks, mortgages, creditors, wholesalers, insurance companies—all manifestations of seemingly immovable entities.

I should own up here that, growing up, six years older than my brother, I used to take an older sibling's satisfaction in first cajoling, then bullying him into a wrestling match when our parents were out of the apartment. I'd urge him, he'd demure. When I'd promise not to hurt him, he'd beg to differ and point out that, last time, I had grabbed him in a stranglehold and nearly choked the breath out of him after I had made the same promise. I reassured him that at the time I had meant it; I, too, was convinced that I had meant no harm, all the while closing the distance between us, my hands reaching for his head, and he ducking away.

Nat, at age seven or eight, was small—certainly smaller than me— and I could easily wrestle him without fear of being beaten; and that certainty added impetus to my further urging what I surely wouldn't have fallen for from anyone my own size. Of such certainty that guarantees no possible harm to themselves are bullies made.

The way I saw it, Nat had already been suckered in by the mere fact that we were discussing it. You get someone to "discuss" a situation they've presumably decided on, and you've already won: talk dilutes action. Thus is a negotiator's prime tactic: "Keep them talking."

We both knew the outcome: I'd grab him in a bear hug, he'd gasp, falling on the bed in a heap, and I'd put a stranglehold on him and, once in motion, a rarely felt exhilaration grew in me to a mindless frenzy I couldn't or didn't want to control; not intending to injure Nat, I wanted to feel this exuberance grow, to overflow. I could barely restrain myself from tightening my grip, like a vise whose spinning rod doesn't stop until its sides clamp their teeth shut. Under his struggling, only when I'd hear his moans and muffled shrieks that he couldn't breathe would I cease. A few days later, with no one else in the apartment, the whole inevitable ritual would start over.

GLADIATORS

The children's wading pool in the park holds another place in my memory. One day an argument over a play at home plate that would have decided a game being played for high stakes broke out between the Panthers and a rival team from another neighborhood, sponsored by a different bar. Just before the quarrel reached the bat-swinging stage, the two parties decided that, rather than a messy all-out brawl ending bloodily, each team would match their strongest man against the other and battle it out, bare-knuckled, inside the gated wading pool, which that day happened to be empty.

The concrete enclosure within the four gates would be the arena where the two men would fight it out, no holds barred. As the other players, their wives and families and the rest of us spectators moved en masse to get a close view from behind the six-foot bars, I watched to see which man each team would choose. After a huddle, the largest man from each team gravely emerged from their midst, stepping forward as if having taken shape for just such a calling. I hadn't noticed either of them in the game before. Each man stepped forward, looking grim, apprehensive, as if having just awakened to the full danger, and needing to take a moment to gather into himself the collective will of his teammates, giving him the chance to size up his opponent from a distance.

They looked as if they had done this before, had been stand-ins for their teams in just such a contest. As both men, followed by their teammates, walked toward the pool, you could see in their faces, in the moment before it could be bluffed away, that look of resolved determination that comes over someone who finds himself facing imminent danger.

As they entered the makeshift arena, neither man seemed angry or vengeful or even upset: they looked "deadly," as in the age-old accurate description: "deadly serious."

Because the day was hot and dry, and the wading pool's water jets had not been turned on, the dry concrete floor glinted with mica. People crowded against the bars; it was eerily quiet for a crowded day at the park. Even the park attendants in their leaf-green uniforms knew better than to try to stop this. They had witnessed the Panthers' displeasure before, and wanted no part of it; they watched discreetly from the top step of their cement-block office, which, overlooking the pool, gave them the best view.

The combatants didn't bother with the customary tapping of fists. Bare-chested, bare-knuckled, resembling gladiators more than boxers, they edged toward each other, circling, but with no pretense of evasive moves or distractions. Rather, slowed by the day's heat radiating from the empty pool's stone floor, they began taking turns pummeling each other as if with the other's tacit permission; first one would swing with full force, his bare fist slamming into his opponent with the thick, chunking sound of a cleaver cutting meat on the block; then, after taking the blow, absorbing it, the other would take his turn and heave a punch, until their faces began to show swollen welts and bloody bruises, swinging less vehemently but no less grimly, until panting and exhausted, having no one and nothing to turn to, they leaned on each other for support.

After a moment holding one another up, breathing hard, they'd separate and start swinging in grunting slow motion, like wounded brothers lapping each other's sweat and blood from face and neck. In midswing, not seeing who fell or who was left standing, I decided not to stay until the end, and walked away.

The pool, in Seth Low Park, was a baseball-throw away from my Aunt Becky's house, a block away, toward which, usually for relief, I found myself headed.

THE PLEASURES OF FEASTING:

Pesach at Aunt Becky's was my favorite holiday of the year. I'd look forward to going to her house for the long evening service and the relaxed dinner afterwards. During the week before the holiday arrived, the entire house had to be thoroughly cleaned of any trace of bread (including crumbs), cake, pastry; anything leavened was *ha'-maes* (not kosher for Passover).

Walking from our apartment seven blocks away, we'd carry a large pot of rice and the traditional sweet *haroseth* (pureed dates mixed with honey and nuts) my mother had prepared for the ritual service and to have at dinner. When we arrived, the long dark-wood table in her dining room would be crowded with the traditional dishes for the evening's *seder*: squares of unleavened matzo, the hard-boiled eggs, lamb shank, bitter herbs—the Israelites' diet of deprivation (which seemed not at all deprived to me!) as they wandered in the desert after escaping from bondage in Egypt. Afterwards, the *real* evening's meal, the fragrances wafting in from the kitchen, would be carried in by the girls and women, one steaming dish after the other.

After dinner, when my parents were getting ready to walk back home, Aunt Becky would ask if I'd like to stay over, and I'd jump at the chance, sleeping on a mat on the floor between Nat and Gilly's beds. For breakfast the next morning, she'd make me a bowl of matzo soaked in milk that I'd sprinkle with sugar and wait for it to soften before spooning. The trick was to chew while the matzo was soft on the outside, but not soggy, and still crisp in the middle.

GILLY

When it came time in the Haggadah service for reciting the list of thanks to the Lord for the miracles of the ten plagues against the Egyptians, Gilly initiated the chanting of the response of *"Dah-yaenuu* (it would have been sufficient)" after the recitation of each plague. Across the table, impishly grinning, he would improvise his own syncopated version, breaking the word down into its component parts and toy with them individually, tantalizingly, *"Dah-dah* (It would have been)," followed by *"yaenuu* (sufficient for us)," the phrase reiterated four times with growing emphasis on the final note of gratitude, *"yaenuu."* He would repeat this after mention of each successive scourge the Lord sent down to free the enslaved Israelites from their Egyptian masters; each affliction meant to persuade the stubborn Pharaoh—"If You had smitten them with pestilence, *da-yaenuu;* if You had filled their wells with frogs, *dah-yaenuu;* if You had cast them into darkness, *dah-yaenuu;* if You had killed their first-born, *dah-yaenuu . . .*" even had the Lord not afterwards inflicted an even more devastating calamity, "It would have been sufficient," yet even so, with each successive misfortune the Lord showed even greater munificence.

This playful rendition caught on with us so much it became a tradition for several years afterwards, cheerfully, raucously led by Gilly's tapping, rousing slow down of time. Had this *"dah-dah-yaenuu,"* been allowed to continue even a little longer, it would have been sufficient; however, a few years later, after Gilly married and he and his wife were expecting their first-born, after complaining of various aches and a rapid softening of his muscles, he was diagnosed with leukemia and died soon after, before his son was born. To think that while he lived and kidded with us, and played ball with his friends, and sat with us improvising his catchy melodies about liberation, the leukocytes were proliferating in his blood, is to catch a glimpse of the ways of the Lord of Darkness that are more than sufficient.

After years of observance, I began to think of the Passover story as a metaphor for the enslavement of the ego; its stubborn, often suicidal resistance, like Pharaoh's, urged to set free his enslaved self—with conditions set by a demanding taskmaster; a myth about arrogance and its punishing plagues. "Stiff-necked" is the term often used by God when referring to his unrepentant people, and exemplified in the tale of Exodus by the Pharaoh-ego, holding out against necessity. The story could be a cautionary lesson in the tactics of the entrenched ego resisting change.

Some years ago, during one of my visits back East, my brother Nat showed me a video of Gilly and his wife on their honeymoon at a bird sanctuary in Florida. Startling to see him again, this time covered with tropical birds standing, plumage outspread, large wings flapping, on his head and shoulders, along his outstretched arms, and his wife, in similar array, standing beside him. They both appeared more natural-looking than ever, honeymooners, in their true element. Pink, orange, green, blue, the big wings fluttered all around and atop them. With their arms spread, they stood in colored leafage, wincing and ducking and laughing, profusely aflutter with happiness.

THE PLEASURES OF FASTING

Besides feast days like Passover, there were the pleasures of fasting: of those fast days prescribed by the rabbis, Yom Kippur (Day of Atonement) was the ultimate antifeast day. Fast days, like feast days, gave significance to a day's beginning as well as ending: daily quotidian was transformed into the sacramental, and dulling time became ceremonial.

Fasting made you realize how—unlike days when the habit of eating was automatic as you went, sated, about your business—the body's processes slow down without its daily replenishment of nutrients, making demands you ordinarily would not think about. Deprived of nourishment, the senses sharpen, the bodily mechanism is put on alert for stimuli: smell, sight, touch, hearing—all plentiful, except taste. Like a squeezed sponge, your stomach groans for refueling, the tongue thickens, avid to absorb like a blotter, taste buds grow parched and porous, and movements slow while the mind feels lighter and thoughts wander.

During those fast days, when I'd take a walk, my slow pace made me breathe more deeply than usual, and in the effort to inhale a full breath, though far from any ocean, I'd become aware of the least trace of salt in the air, and could taste the briny alkaline molecules dissolving on the back of my tongue, which sharpened my breathing even more.

Later, I'd notice that after fasting for twenty-four hours on Yom Kippur, at home, my father's features looked smooth, tranquil, revived through the self-discipline of deprivation, as if having endured a sustained ordeal.

At day's end, people looked more peaceful, solemn, as if sobered by the effort of having made a long journey.

Water again tasted like a pure elemental liquid, unadulterated, and for the first time in twenty-four hours, bread had the texture and warmth of flesh. Sitting down to the dinner, which ended the day's fast, renewed the pleasures of flavor and smell as my mother served my favorite dishes, stuffed squash and roasted chicken with tomato spaghetti, over which my taste buds salivated like the gaping mouths of baby chicks.

CHAPTER NINETEEN

THE JESUS SHOW—"THE GUIDING (GOYISH) LIGHT"

From an early age I was enamored of the word "eternal." I don't know why.

One Sunday evening, switching stations, by chance I happened on a voice whose eerie, otherworldly reverberation, obviously audio-enhanced, sounded infused with a serenity so all-embracing and compassionate, it made credible that, if Divinity had a voice and could be heard, this sound, infinitely tender and pitying, surely would be that voice:

> *Verily I say you are the salt of the earth. You are the light of the world. Let your light shine before men.*
>
> *Consider the lilies of the field, how they are garbed in glory greater than Solomon's. They do not spin, neither do they toil.*
>
> *Verily I say unto you, when that which is perfect is come, then that which is in part shall be done away.*

A voice from the past drew each word back to what felt like its origin, where it was refreshed, then returned to the silence that preceded speech, and the next word sounded spoken from that silence. I realized I was hearing the sermons of Jesus from the Christian Gospels. Not *reading* them—I had earlier torn out from my copy of the English Bible the entire New Testament when I had bought it, since its text was forbidden to read. Now, hearing them spoken, the words sounded autonomous, as though they were speaking themselves out of a world-wideness, and I wondered if, in hearing them for the first time, I was held as fixed as were those who first heard them.

That repeated word, "verily," intrigued me; I had not heard nor seen it before, and though I didn't immediately look it up, the impression the sound made was akin to truly, fully, justly. Checking the dictionary confirmed my hunch.

Words so spare felt transparent; needing no intercession or interpretation, nor any doctrine to validate them. Once heard, they seemed self-evident, then evaporated into a universal anonymity. What remained was the clarity of a truth touching everywhere and everything, for all time. And what was universal had to be true; because that's what truth meant. So that anybody could know truth, wherever and in whatever time or place they lived: all they had to do was pause, wait, and perceive: there were no false notes or break in the words, no falling away:

> When I was a child, I spake as a child, I understood as a child, I thought as a child; but when I became a man, I put away childish things.
> For now we see through a glass, darkly; but then face to face; now I know in part; but then shall I know even as also I am known.

And oddly, there was no melancholy in the words, no room left for sadness or grief. Instead, a radiance emanated, as though they were present everywhere, in all directions.

I listened as the voice seemed to expand; as though the infinite, summoned into sound, spoke; or, not so much spoke as stirred, breathed, made manifest through the means of the ordinary. The Word made flesh. Verily.

Against my Orthodox upbringing, a part of me suspected that what I was hearing was not apostasy. That an actor's voice, reproducing the words through the medium of radio, could elicit such a feeling of union made the words spoken centuries ago by a "heretical" rabbi all the more potent. Hearing them was like eavesdropping on a past to which the present caught up and apprehended a moment only now becoming manifest. Even mechanically enhanced and re-enacted, the words were no less true no matter who spoke them, and once encountered, could not be forgotten or dismissed: language bare as an elemental force; a poetry of the most clearheaded, far-reaching dimension. This, I realized, was what "self-evident" meant.

I listened despite knowing I was breaking a rabbinical prohibition, caught up by this enlarged and forbidden (because enlarged?)

moment, beginning to suspect that, by way of shielding, religious taboos kept one bound. I returned to the program for several Sundays until I wanted to be rid of religious questions, and I stopped listening.

I began reading as much as I could in science, about the mineral makeup of the earth and planets, down to the molecule, then on to the chemical properties of the body that I had a premonition I would have to slog through on foot.

BRITANNICA

One winter night an *Encyclopedia Britannica* salesman appeared at the front door, trying to interest us in purchasing a complete set for "the youngster's education." What was this man doing out this late at night in the freezing cold? The narrow velvet collar of his overcoat and the thinness of his graying hair parted in the middle of his bare head didn't look like they gave much protection in this weather.

At my urging, and more, at first, out of politeness than any real interest in what the fellow was selling, my father, already on his way to bed in his bathrobe over his pajamas, reluctantly let him in.

Hunched forward, intent as a proselytizer of a midnight religion, the man entered, looking like he must have been out in the cold for some time. Despite the late hour, the icy weather, and his obvious discomfort, as the man began reciting in a steady, at times even enthusiastic voice the benefits to the young to be gained from knowledge, my father must have recognized a fellow worker in need of some rest and was extending, at least for a while, the courtesy of one salesman to another. Inside the flat, especially at this hour, whatever minimal token heat had been sent up during the day had long since dissipated and the flat was cold enough to make you feel your bones stiffen and set, unless you were fortunate enough to already be asleep.

Without wasting time to remove his overcoat, the man sat in the kitchen across from us and took out a large volume from his briefcase and began to extol the intellectual advantages and financial profit in acquiring knowledge about a variety of subjects condensed in these one-of-a-kind volumes, "All at your fingertips in the index," he said. To me, whatever contained such a large store of knowledge of the world and how it worked, all bound in a set of volumes whose control center was an alphabetical index, seemed an ingenious solution to something like an intricate mathematical problem, and was indispensable. Slowly turning the pages of a volume open on his lap and noting my growing interest, the rhythm of lifted and back-flipped pages became mesmerizing as they fell away, showing in alphabetical order photographs of Charles Darwin, Charles Dickens, a dirigible, a dragonfly.

"A fixed point of view . . . is a disadvantage, even . . . a dangerous thing," the man said. "Here at your fingertips you have an invaluable collection of human knowledge from ancient times . . ." he continued, looking first at my father, "till now," he said turning to me, "to help you become aware of new discoveries and modern inventions. We all need help to get out of our own way. Don't we?" I wasn't sure what he was saying; the words were reassuring, but their meaning was unclear. I could see vapor puffs from his breath as he spoke.

For my father, sitting still in the cold must have been an extra burden on his fatigued shoulders. They hunched lower as he held the robe closer in the minutes proving more of an ordeal than he'd counted on, while my interest was held by the impressive array of information and pictures before me. After noticing my father's eyes closing, I let myself lose sight of his discomfort and began to question the salesman. Finally, he too must have grown tired—of the cold, of no offer of warm refreshment, of my questions and, from the looks of my father nodding off, of the likely prospect of no sale—when he suddenly offered a thirty-day trial period at a reduced rate. My father, nodding awake, politely not saying no, thanked the man for taking the trouble to show his "wares" (the word he used for merchandise), kindly explaining that he needed to go to bed to get up early to go to *his* job.

Giving us a look of disappointment, with practiced movements of his hands, reluctantly, as if unwilling to give up on potential converts, he closed the volume and, appealing with his eyes, offered an even more reduced rate as he leaned over, reaching for the briefcase at his feet and with a skilled movement, opened the black flap—I could smell its polished leather—and slid the volume back in its alphabetical slot. My father got up and, summarily wrapping his bathrobe around him, shuffled off to bed.

As he was taking his leave at the door, turning up his coat collar, the stranger remarked almost to himself but aware of my presence nearby, "The more we come to know, the less need be said."

That was the last chance I had of acquiring such a vast library of knowledge at my fingertips, at home.

KOSHER BACON

When word got around that a new product called "kosher bacon" (a thin-sliced beef cured to a smoked, salty, baconlike flavor) was on the market from Hebrew National Company with the stamp of rabbinical approval in large Hebrew letters printed right on the package, still our rabbis prohibited it, already tainted by the label's absurd oxymoron. Having conceived and marketed the idea into an edible item was brilliant and blasphemous at once; on a par, it could be argued, in its convoluted casuistic reasoning and justification, with Talmudic legalese: one could argue the case for or against—either way. True, it was just beef, "kosher" to the letter of the law, but this rabbinic prohibition was consistent with the spirit of the ancient ban on pork: to approve a product whose name crossed the line of permissible association—even if only suggested in words—(already an insult!)—would then gradually, faced with temptation, lead inevitably to further erosion of the Biblical "kosher" laws, *kash-root.* And who knew where this crack in the edifice of the mandate—with no exceptions—would lead, when little Jewish kids would soon be devouring—like pigs!—the unclean flesh forbidden in the commandment.

Traditionally rigorous, observance had to be consistent with both the letter and spirit of the law: the new product was ruled *assurr* (forbidden), because, although certified by rabbis as beef that *was* kosher, the fact that it even *looked* like bacon (they wouldn't have known that, when cooked, it also *smelled* like bacon), was enough to brand it as *tref* (unclean). The mere appearance of transgression made it so. You couldn't argue with that rabbinical logic.

And they were right—at least as my case proved. For, soon after I had tasted the sizzling pungency of this new ersatz "bacon" down to its crispy curled edges, I graduated to the next level of sin. On many a Sunday after dark I wouldn't return home for one of my mother's usual Arabic dinners of roast lamb shish-kebab or veal breast stuffed with rice or baked spaghetti in tomatoes. Instead, I'd go to the truckers' diner on the corner of 66th Street and treat myself to what was a truly exotic meal: *real* bacon and eggs. My first taste of that fatty, burnt flavor swallowed me into the belly of the unkosher beast.

All the *ka'aak, kibbeh,* and *lah'hahm ajeen* waiting at home—what many Americans consider exotic—were to me, in those days, commonplace. Palates, like people, grown bored with regularity, reach out to wider worlds of flavor. But on the other hand, the Koran teaches, "Paradise is under the feet of your mother," and Italians advise a man to live with his mother, in the same house, as long as she lives.

MUEZZIN IN THE HOUSE

Every language has its supreme interpreter of love songs: at that time in America, it was Frank Sinatra; for many, in Arabic, it was Uul-Kulsuum, the dark-eyed, voluptuous Egyptian mistress, it was rumored, of Egypt's then-president Gamel-Abdel Nasser. Both she and Nasser were seen by their people as equally devoted to their nation. My father used to listen to her regularly on the radio. Her rich, piercing voice could cast a note into the deepest well of lament and longing, while her concentrated ardor could arouse a passionate urgency: the more hopeless the longing the more powerfully ardent.

I heard in Uul-Kulsuum the pure sounding of this directive, reaching ever more extreme frequencies in the spectrum of yearning, knowing hopelessness while helplessly driven to make her appeal, transcending the personal for the elemental, and drawing others together in a summons to the primitive, desolate actuality of existence, experienced by all.

Years later, after reading Kierkegaard's *Either/Or,* I was reminded of Uul-Kulsuum, how her voice seemed an embodiment of the great philosopher's "counsel to despair," by which I understood that if one were to take on the consciousness of what it is to be human and to suffer time, thereby recognizing their affinity with all of humankind, they would of necessity come to despair; for, whereas depression is private, despair is universal. This radical enlargement of the personal to the universal, Kierkegaard explains, is essential in taking on the full weight of living awareness: the counsel to despair.

Whereas the call to prayer of the muezzin arises from their needle towers, Uul-Kulsuum's appeal was made from street level, expressing dramas and longings enacted on the level of daily human affairs, as if the yearning for the absent lover, originating from different levels, was one and the same impulse.

When I'd enter our front room overlooking Bay Parkway, and my father, listening to Uul-Kulsuum on the radio, would be standing with his back toward me, facing the window, I'd hear him accompanying the song in a subdued falsetto I can only describe as lovesick, longing its way back to its source, coiling so far away and long ago, it felt ageless. What surprised me was that he'd show such intense feeling openly, since it was not his habit, even though he was unaware of my presence; usually he'd be more discreet. I noticed an unembarrassed flush on his face when he did notice me. A kind of youthful radiance softened and relaxed his features, and I was taken aback by this display of intense fervor.

The few times he'd come home from work and complain of a backache or muscle pain and have to stay in bed, he'd first ask my mother—who'd refuse—then ask me to apply the mentholated Vicks, greasy and reeking of eucalyptus, or the even more repellent sludgy black salve that, when I'd rub him with it, would smear like tar. Those moments return now when I experience my own aches and pains caused by no particular injury; they feel more like impacted time: time's revenge on itself. When I think of him sick in his bed, a vestigal vapor floats down the years, a drift of belated sympathy for one no longer able to receive it.

In the generational spinning down of paternity, there must be a law, unwritten except perhaps in crumbled tablets or in retrieved memories, that the father, the one who was first, is approached late, and recognized last.

CHAPTER TWENTY

LOCATION, LOCATION, LOCATION

In summer, workers returning home from their jobs in Manhattan would step out of the subway station and, trailing heated swirls of fetid electrical dust and gaseous whiffs of ozone sweeping out around them, their bodies clammy and sweating, their mouths dry from the long, crowded train ride, exiting the swinging doors, they'd practically step right through the side door of Herb's Fountain for a soda, a snack, or a pack of cigarettes before heading home.

Since it was just across the street from where I lived and I'd often drop in to buy ice cream sodas and candy, when I one day asked the owner, Herb, for a job after school, he promptly hired me to help him in the evenings, during the rush hours. Cigarettes and sodas were especially popular with the commuters. Girlie magazines kept in display racks off to the side had their own regular visitors who'd ease over and flip through the glossy pages of nudes posed lounging and available, no doubt more so than the wives to whom they were returning, if they had wives at all. So seductive were their expressions it didn't take me long or farther than the sensuous blond and brunette outstretched on the cover of *Night and Day* to become aroused and have to slip the magazine in its rack and get behind the counter. Herb, a balding, mildly harried man, but not an especially demanding boss, didn't mind my occasional look as long as there was a lull in the flow of customers; but, given that trains arrived almost one after the other during rush hours, lulls did not come often. He told me that he didn't care if men bought the magazines or not: in fact, they were bait, to draw customers into the store and hold their attention while the sweet aroma of candy, chocolate, and ice cream would work on them until they'd grow thirsty, or hungry after a long ride home on the train, and nature would take its course and business would pick up.

Which it did. So much so that I'd return home reeking of lactose, like a dairy, and even showering and scrubbing with a bar of black Lava soap (how ironic a name!) could not get rid of the smell in my pores.

It was a "dream job," having all those Snickers and Hersheys and Baby Ruths, all that ice cream and soda at your fingertips! It was one of those lucky jobs kids hoped for, like working behind the counter in a deli with all the hot dogs, knishes, salads, and cold cuts you'd always craved, right in front of you. But, as I found out after the first few days of gorging, you soon grew sated, then indifferent, then came a loathing verging on nausea for the very sweetness you once craved.

MOM WORKED FOR UNCLE ABOOD

One day, when I was about fifteen, accompanying my mother on the train to Manhattan to "use her connections" and find me a job after school, as we came out of the underground tunnel into bright daylight, approaching a run-down redbrick building visible through the crisscrossing bridge beams, my mother pointed to one of its windows, and told me she had worked there.

Until each married, she and her sister Becky worked as seamstresses in Uncle Abood's factory, operating sewing machines, hemstitching tablecloths, handkerchiefs, curtains, and pillowcases for sale to fellow Aleppoans, who, in turn, would peddle their wares from store to store to fellow Syrian Jews on the Lower East Side and upper Manhattan. Many of these immigrants, starting out as peddlers, had opened small retail stores of their own that eventually prospered and grew into retail chains from 14th Street to upper 5th Avenue.

In the instant we passed, I saw a row of smeared windows, and in them, rows of seated Asian and Latino women bent over their machines; one absently staring out the window.

In later years, each time I'd cross that bridge under the geometric shadow-patterns cast by the network of beams and cables, passing her building, I took to imagining my mother as a young woman, sitting at her machine, tired, glancing up, unaware of her future son's glimpse of her, passing in the present. Time somehow felt rounded. I'd wink inwardly, waving as I passed; the powdery spore-riddled building itself—looking ancient—would outlast her and, most likely, myself.

CHAPTER TWENTY-ONE

CREATOR BOOKKEEPING

Speaking often felt like a curse: the effort that went into conceiving, then formulating and forming with the tongue those hollow vowels and grating syllables for the sake of social manners struck me as habits of meaningless mumbling.

This feeling was followed by another: that often, when people talked to you, your silence would allow you entry into their way of thinking, if not their true thoughts, and provided an impression, however incomplete, of the kind of world they inhabited, what they wanted, and, sometimes, even what it felt like to be them. This was before you allowed them access to your thoughts by speaking. This was the so-called "give and take" of maneuvering for social advantage, called "conversation."

Far from automatic, the mental effort of finding a meaning and form for the words that fit, the choices needed in order to reveal (not often) or conceal (more often) motives, the alternatives rejected in favor of what was socially acceptable, all seemed a maze of equivocations and cross-purposes woven on a loom of fabrication. Spoken words were thrown outward, most often as camouflage and ambiguous vagaries; rarely, if ever, as lifelines. One had to store up a lot of silence in order to speak truthfully. The rest was entertainment—good for the moment, but forgettable; or else, with anything related to the acquisition of power, downright lies and obfuscation. The tactics were to be expected, given their intended ends.

These predilictions must have been why, from early on, I was drawn to the *Zohar.* Beginning with the title's lightning-flash first letter, *Zohar,* The Book of Splendor, was my favorite Cabalistic text.

The fact that its reading was forbidden by rabbinical edict, not only for its mystical interpretation of Biblical phrases and events, but also for its recognition of the magical powers inherent in blasphemy and in the transgression of Holy Writ, loomed for me even larger since its ban even extended to rabbis under age thirty-five (reputed to be the age of wisdom). At the time, still in my early teens, I was far from anywhere near the age of wisdom.

It was in a translation of fragments of this volume of mysteries that I first encountered a primary example (perhaps the ultimate one) of Judaism's emphasis on words and numbers; words possessing numerical value: according to this arcana, the Creator of the universe allots to each person before they are born a certain number of words to speak in their lifetime; when we exceed our allotment, we must pay a tax on the extra words in the world to come. I've always been drawn to that bit of Creator bookkeeping. It is for the purpose of avoiding overextending their account that devout Jewish men refrain from speaking anything but prayers during Yom Kippur, hopefully lowering their debt.

GUIDE TO THE PERPLEXED

My cousin Nat, who I didn't think of as much of a reader, was the cause, by chance, of my first interest in philosophy. In his room, on a low shelf, books stood in a row alongside his bed; a dark brown covered series, each volume contained the works of a single philosopher. Strangely, Nat never referred to those books, or mentioned that he was reading any of them. And if not, what were they doing there? Were they remnants of a college class he had taken? But as far as I knew, no Syrian, male or female, had been to college. Unlike Ashkenazic Jews, whose sacrifices for their children's college educations were legendary, for Syrian parents, mostly without formal education themselves, and recently emigrated from an ancient mercantile tradition, academic education was not a priority. In fact, it was actively discouraged as an obstacle to getting on with the business of living, which was *earning* a living: leaving school (as legally early as possible), and getting a job (the sooner the better), in order to help support your family, your *main* business.

Nat, like most sons, worked for his father in his dry goods store. College was out of the question. So where and why had he collected this small philosophy library? I'd pick a volume up at random, read a few lines of airy, abstract musing, and my thoughts would sail out into space. If Nat ever noticed my interest, he never let on. I never heard him utter a single thought that might be considered "philosophical," or even mention names like Augustine, Schopenhauer, Aquinas, Descartes. I don't recall asking Nat about them either. When he wasn't in the room, I would pick up a volume and browse through what seemed like endless tracts of monotonous metaphysics, noting key words—eternity, infinity, absolute, mind—until I came upon the writings of Spinoza. In reading the brief biographical introduction, I was fascinated by this Sephardic Jew, who, in seventeenth-century Amsterdam, wrote what the rabbis charged were heretical views on the nature of God (that God *was* Nature!) and excommunicated Baruch ("Blessed") de Espinoza from the Jewish community. To finalize the social break, he changed his birth name to the Latin "Benedictus." No one was allowed to acknowledge his existence; he was banned from family ties and social attachments. A rabbinical edict of excommunication was passed on him: "If he were to be seen approaching you on the street, you are to quickly cross to the other side; if he might come close, you must keep a distance of at least 50 feet between you. He is banned forever from the sight of Israel." Here was a marked man, if there ever was one.

A close friend of Spinoza's, Isaac de Silva, earlier excommunicated and later shamed and isolated, had begged to recant, and was required to crawl on hands and knees before the congregation in the synagogue as penance. After this further humiliation, he returned to his room and shot himself in the head. Fortunately, it turned out, Spinoza was not so easily intimidated by social pressure; he left the community and lived alone, developing his philosophical ideas.

In a single rented room, grinding lenses for a living and weaving a stoic metaphysics based on a framework of rigorous axioms dividing infinity into a harmonious sequence of rational proofs, he posed questions concerning the existence of God in eternity, and through a series of logical steps attempted to formulate in mathematical propositions the structure of the Absolute and its universal laws. Called by his Christian townfolk "this Jew, the only man among us who talks like Christ," too solitary and shy to be a hero (no man, in his heart, believes himself a hero), this feverish, tubercular silkworm, lungs eaten from inhaling countless hours of finely ground glass, could become absorbed watching a spider spinning a web in the corner of his attic room while creating the precise language of a divine proof through Euclidean geometry. But heretical? I read the massed words that, without understanding, I could feel growing in a sustained wave of purpose toward a rational system describing absolute qualities. On the page, as I remember, his brief axioms, followed by intricately phrased proofs, had the look of solidity. Given as fixed, stable (some would say stern) geometric axioms about the nature of God and the Absolute, the proof was drawn in a speculative language of which the fulsome paragraphs unfolded like sails swollen with rare metaphysical air I hadn't breathed before. I coudn't see why people called this kind of thought "heavy," when it seemed the opposite: weightless.

I'd never encountered thought so stripped of self-interest; the words, though their meanings were obscure, felt oddly chaste, incorporeal, certainly much too impenetrable to bring a charge of heresy and damnation.

Beneath a dark dome of hair cut at the shoulder, Spinoza's portrait shows a high, smooth forehead and an expression of benevolence in warm Semitic eyes. For some twenty years, the ostracized freethinker ground the glass and breathed the dust of lenses he made for the failing eyes of Dutch patrons before breathing himself an early grave on February 25, 1677—anniversary, two hundred fifty-nine years later, of my birth.

CHAPTER TWENTY-TWO

ALVEOLI

Nat drove us in his car through a snowstorm. We were returning from the hospital where Pop, finally retired at eighty-eight and fading fast, had said to me all he would say to me about dying, "This is my job." I thought it was an odd but strangely apt description, which called to mind his favorite quote from the gospel of the clock-watching god: "Time is money and money is time. Make money in due time, but don't *do* time for making money." He'd repeated it almost daily over the years when I lived at home; reciting it like a limerick, obviously taken with the balanced rhythm of the four-beat first two lines, followed in the last by the punchy stress on the extra syllable, *do,* (subtly suggesting, in fact—and I wonder if he was aware of it—the opposite of what it warned against). A life's credo summed up in doggerel.

Last there five years before, I flew from San Francisco to Nat's side after his vw was crushed by a speeding car at an intersection in Brownsville. The stop sign—knocked down in the days of Mayor O'Dwyer—had been left there, facing skyward, to warn off what? Fallout? ufos? Highflying suicides whose vision, suddenly sharpened midway in their dive, would save them? While I flew the friendly skies—the only creature able to eat chicken soup 30,000 feet in the air—Nat had lain eleven hours under the knife, being pieced together; a scar the size of a quarter at the base of his throat is all you can see with his clothes on. Since then he's had six cars—all Chevys—stolen from him. To no longer draw attention, he explained, he bought the Lincoln Continental—two-tone, with wire wheels, c.b. radio, and armor shaped like grillwork—we rode in. We hadn't—neither of us—brought up Pop yet. His slow sly grin told me we weren't about to. He lifted the c.b. "Me and my friends got them," he said, an anticipatory pleasure, as with a new toy, lit up his eyes. I knew he was going to clown for me: "Breaker, breaker, this is Crazy Kibbeh calling the Jewelry King. Hey good buddy, what's my traffic like on the ole Skyline to Starret City? Can you read me? This is One Crazy Kibbeh just outta the bin, lost in the frost, calling the Jewelry King for some info. Can you give me a copy, good buddy?"

"It's poetry," I said, and meant it. Then I heard a squawk of voices cooked from transcontinental fits and static crisscross the channel, but no Jewelry King. We were headed for south Jersey, where Nat and Viv, once more trying for a girl, just had their fourth boy in a row. It runs in the family: at last count, Nat and I have six sons between us, and our sister Renee had three girls.

As we rode, I thought of Pop in the hospital: my first sight of his sleeping face looking hollow and melted; a yellow wrist tag on his hand holding the bedsheet, and his loose white tuft of hair gave him the look of a shrewd, rakish lifer. Opening his eyes, I was surprised, thinking he recognized me . . . then he looked startled. I took his hand and, tipping forward, felt myself pour into a long last-minute kiss of hopeless retrieval and leaned over him as over an edge of a roaring high wind I had seen in times of stress before, but no person had been in it; and now there was a person.

We had brought some things—money, stamps, an electric shaver—all positing a future. "Don't," he said, almost fiercely; the pupils of his eyes I didn't remember ever being so black and worn out with ardor and fear, staring at the open doorway. "Don't leave anything. They come when I sleep and steal everything. They don't come when I call them to help me take three steps to the toilet."

I wondered about the cancer in his prostate and the pain he must have been feeling, not allowing the doctors to remove his testicles. The cancer cell acts like a spermatozoan, taking shape like fetal tissue, but a fetus never finished, that keeps on growing, never reaching a limit. The tumor spreads—spreading is all it *can* do. It would spread to infinity in the cells if infinity could spread in the body, and the body with it. He looked up. "I want to go home," he said. "Take me, sneak me out," he pled with the craftiness of the doomed, "tell them you're taking me for a walk. I have money, I'll give you money so you won't be miserable like me." He turned to Nat and nodded toward me: "He'll go soon, like always. You take me out of here. If not, you're leaving me a dead man. I'll throw myself from the window."

For a blank moment, I forgot we were on the ground floor, my confusion recalling the man on a panel of survivors I once saw on TV who told of capsizing with his three children in a storm at sea, and having an instant to choose, chose to hold on to the two youngest; a choice, luckily it turned out, he did not have to carry through, though the guilt was still with him long after they all were rescued.

This was where time, speeding toward an end, slowed as if in one final effort at compensation, and there followed a moment that felt like centuries breathing down our necks as Pop awaited a reply he wouldn't receive, in a silence without end, and I felt us enclosed in a lowering glass cone, tight as a phone booth, where nothing moves while something is sifted; nothing stirs as something is shaken; nothing distracted from his gaunt face lifting toward me on a shifty hot wind that can't be trusted; that has roared through time in an overcharge of current; and sweeping up all the light behind him, opens a chasm through which air rushes out, and the infinite distance closer. This was no dream, unless the eyes, too, were a dream. If he fell back, it would take years for his head to hit the pillow.

Something swift, final, not nearly understood, passed between us. Too late, I thought, but how could I be sure since that day on Van Ness Avenue when what I had thought were charbroil fumes from the nearby Hamburger Heaven were coming from Delmore's Mortuary behind me. I carefully brought his legs around and down to the floor, encircled him with my arms under his arms, and lifted him, deadweight, to standing position. Nat came over and helped, but it was no good; the three of us together couldn't make it halfway to the door.

Just then, a pretty black nurse appeared through the door, teasingly, as if it were a burlesque curtain, and she, cinnamon candy. Smiling, she came in, checked us over, her flashing black eyes blacker, brighter, for being set in all the surrounding white, and motioned that time was up.

We eased him back into bed, made a date to return, and walked out to where the leafless fossil-tips of trees swayed delicately, icily stiff in a driving wind and headed back to the living of winter.

Years after my father's death, I would notice a man sitting in front of me on the bus holding his hat bottom up, like my father's felt hats, the brown and the light gray, the wide silk band, and at the bottom of the well, the trademark word: ADAM. Trying to make the sound of one generation with the mouth of another. Hopeless. I only hope he was taken by a source with the power to ease the defeated in their final moments.

CHAPTER TWENTY-THREE

HURRICANE RIDGE

Those once close to us who have died gradually begin to take up more and more space in our past, like nail heads that memory's repeated tap-tap-tap over time flattens and spreads out.

My sister's breast cancer, originally diagnosed twenty years before, in her early twenties, was excised at that time in a double mastectomy that gave her a thirty-year remission. In her mid-fifties it reappeared and began to metastasize, despite repeated doses of chemotherapy and the latest drugs. With her three daughters married and bearing her grandchildren, after the tumor was detected, she left her job as receptionist for a Japanese firm in New York, and began gathering her remaining energy after the enervating chemo treatments to spend as much time as she could with her daughters, her grandchildren, and husband, while putting in order what she wanted to leave behind.

In her thorough, systematic manner, she made piles of photos, letters, journal pages, phone numbers of various doctors and treatment centers, her medical history and pharmacy prescriptions. With the precision that a travel agency would be proud to advertise, she methodically arranged a trip for Nat, me, and her, to a forested mountain area in northern Washington state called Hurricane Ridge, reserving rooms in advance in cabins and hotels nearby (it was the closest we ever came to camping out), and listing contact numbers for them in her pocket calendar. Nothing, especially now, would be left to chance, since it was once again chance that had put her in this condition.

Thanks to her exacting arrangements, at the agreed-on time at the San Francisco airport she and Nat, having taken the same flight, met me at the arrival gate an hour before our scheduled flight together to Seattle.

I hadn't been back East for some years, since our mother died of a stroke. At the time, I had been working as an office temp at the University of California, San Francisco hospital and one morning at my desk I received a call from Renee in New Jersey. Her voice was hurried and alarmed: Mom had had a stroke; she was unconscious and the doctors didn't know how long she might have, or if she'd regain consciousness; and if she did . . . would she be . . . ? Renee didn't finish, but we both knew what she meant. "I know," I said, answering her silence. The specter of mom regaining consciousness but unable to speak or communicate was too awful to contemplate.

Renee was weeping. "Come right away!" I assured her I would. I called the airline, reserved a seat on a red-eye flight that night, and called Renee back to have Nat pick me up at the Newark airport the next morning.

The rest of that day and evening and during the midnight flight, I was haunted by the possibility that Mom might not regain consciousness but lapse into what was all-too-graphically referred to as "being a vegetable," and the dreadful choices we'd have to decide among.

Fortunately, we didn't have to make a choice: by the time I arrived and met Nat who was waiting for me at the gate, he told me that Mom had gone.

In San Francisco, before the trip to Seattle, waiting to one side at the gate, with people milling around waiting to greet family and friends, I spotted Nat: his curly, white-haired head and thick dark eyebrows stood out in any crowd. In the early seventies, when he'd sported a full, stylish, macho mustache and his dark curly hair began to be peppered gray, he was often taken by people for the actor Elliot Gould. Both men—with Semitic eyebrows and lean leathery faces—had the inward, measuring gaze and vigilance of those who've been screwed over. In those days, someone would approach Nat on the street or on a beach with his wife and kids and, with that celebrity-spotting gleam in their eye, not so much inquire as positively claim him as the actor and ask for his autograph. He'd try to explain that he was not Elliot Gould, but the likeness was so striking, the fan would shove pen and paper in his famous face and persist, assuming the noted movie star was trying to ward them off, and finally got his signature. "It was easier just signing," Nat said, smiling the very same winning smile that had invited the mistaken identity in the first place.

When I spotted him coming through the exit gate, he had no mustache, no longer any likeness to the actor who himself had passed his prime. Nobody edged up toward him as he looked around for me. I waved, he waved back, and then I saw Renee. She had been squeezed behind him by the crowd. When she emerged, I saw that what remained of her hair was cropped close to her head (she'd soon be wearing wigs), and with her slight, flat-chested figure (after the breast surgery she refused any cosmetic enhancement except two thin foam pads) she could have easily passed for "one of the boys."

There is a photo of her that Nat had included along with Pop's letters: a girl of about nine or ten years old; skinny arms and stick legs standing beside our older cousin (who, in the traditional recycling of parental names was also named Renee), Aunt Becky's daughter, who my sister laughingly told me used to call her "the little Ethiopian."

In the photo, the plain summer dress she wears is caught billowing in a breeze, so loose it yanks and fills like a sail around her; if our cousin weren't holding her by the shoulder, she looks as if a puff of air might have sent her aloft. But she grew to marry, raise three girls of her own (who were all married and beginning to have their own children), hold a job, and run a household. After my father died and the house in Brooklyn was sold, Nat found Mom a small apartment near him in Deal, New Jersey, so he could keep an eye on her; he'd drop in most every day on his way home from the train station nearby. He'd check on her, see if she was taking her medicine for her diabetes and glaucoma, and if she needed any groceries.

When I'd fly back to see Mom about once a year and make a detour to the other side of New Jersey to spend a few days with my sister and her family, I'd always be struck by Renee's loving, fiercely entwined, no-nonsense interactions with her daughters: like a house buzzing with four sibling sisters. They'd bicker, bond, argue, and consult. She'd encourage and egg them on in their sports and social life. She'd drive them everywhere: to their friends' houses, to parties, to basketball and running practice; she'd help them decide which boys to go out with and what clothes to wear for a date. Having grown up with two brothers, she could finally revel in sharing—even squandering—girlish ways.

Since hearing about her relapse, I had flown back several times to be with her at her home. On my return to San Francisco, I'd check out the new science periodicals that came through the office I worked in at the UCSF Medical Center and, finding an article about some new cancer drug "breakthrough" or "intervention," I'd cut it out and send it to her. She was always ahead of the curve. Whatever new innovation I might send, she had long known about, had investigated its effectiveness and side effects, and had the information stored in a card file on her kitchen table at home. Determined not to let any new possible treatment fall through the cracks, she was, as far as I could tell, ahead of the doctors, inquiring about drugs they knew nothing about yet. But on the phone, she'd pretend that it was new, and thank me for sending it, and say she'd follow up. I tried to imagine what it must have been like to follow so closely the inescapable trail of what would eventually turn on you and take you out.

Now, among the airport crowd, she spotted me and her eyes lit up in surprised delight.

"Hiya, Natie—I mean Jackie!" she corrected herself. I had forgotten how she would often confusedly call me—especially when we were all three together—by my brother's name; perhaps her way of reminding me that though absence may make the heart grow fonder, it makes the brain forget. But the sound of that fond childhood diminutive "ee" at the end of my name was still there, still retrievable, and I loved how it reconfirmed our early intimacy.

We hugged and kissed and traded news about her daughters and my sons. Was it by chance, I had wondered, that both Nat and I fathered only boys: four by him, and two by me; and that Renee and her husband had three girls? Or is there some mysterious genetic imperative doing its alternating balancing act somewhere in all our coiling comedic DNA?

Then perky and positive as ever, she began running through our itinerary like the tour guide she would have excelled at being. Nat and I were glad she did. Even sick and depleted by bouts of chemo, she took the initiative.

We flew to Seattle, rented a car, and drove four hours to our first overnight cabin where, at a small restaurant nearby, we had a delicious dinner of broiled salmon and a walk around the nearby lake, and then stayed up late trading stories of when we were kids, which all began with "remember the time . . . ?" We laughed so hard and long, the people in the adjoining cabin had to bang on the wall several times before we heard them—"Hey! You know what time it is?" they yelled—before our gargantuan laughter subsided to giggles, and then exhausted sleep.

On this trip together we ate well, drank good wine, and in the restaurant lounge with its dark redwood beams overhead, we sat near a fireplace that cast flickering shadows. Renee's complexion was pale, the sparseness of her hair emphasizing her features at which I couldn't help staring when we were silent. To break the spell, she plunged right in and asked me why I had left her and Nat when I was eighteen years old, and she sixteen and Nat twelve.

"*Left* you?" I was taken aback. I had never thought of it that way. "I left because I had to. It was either that or suffocate."

"We thought you'd left us," Nat said.

"No. I couldn't breathe. It was . . . stifling."

"You left so suddenly . . . You never told us . . ." Renee's entreating voice trailed away.

"We couldn't figure why," Nat added.

"It wasn't you," I said, realizing for the first time that they might not have experienced it that way all these years.

"You left us alone," Nat said. "I didn't know what to tell my friends. I didn't know myself."

"We missed you," Renee said, "just when we needed you."

I tried to explain. "When I was living at home, I literally couldn't catch my breath. When I'd try to take a deep breath" (here I inhaled and held my breath) "I couldn't" (then exhaled). "Like sheep, you know, that can't jump the fence, I couldn't get a full breath over the top. It was only when I left and began traveling, on the road, that I could breathe. Something about walking and hitchhiking in all that open space. At home I felt smothered. Everything was *bi'zohr* (forced)."

In the pause, I noted that whenever we were together, we'd start speaking in English and then I'd hear myself revert to the pidgin Arabic we'd switch to while growing up: English words becoming more abbreviated, atomized, Arabized. And the pig Latin or pidgin English we'd use with our friends became mixed with Arabic shorthand, an improvised pig Arabic.

"Pop wanting me to take over his store . . . It was going nowhere . . . I hated wholesale, and I wasn't any good at retail. . . . And all that useless praying . . ." I blurted it out before realizing how it would upset Nat.

"Aww," he groaned, eyeing me, a pleading censure in his look, and then he glanced at Renee whose eyes began to redden.

On my last visit East, when I stayed at Nat's house for a few days and we had gotten into an argument about religion, Nat's wife Vivian, watching television, said, "You know, Nat, usually Jackie is pretty mellow, but when he gets on religion, he gets *crazed!*" I was taken aback. I didn't think she'd been listening. But not only had she been listening this time, apparently she had at other times too—and I realized she was right. And I was doing it here, again.

What right did I have to argue them out of any bit of faith that might help make what was inevitable more bearable? Though I thought this, I didn't say it. But, at the time, it seemed, faced with the evidence of just a *single* human case (Renee's, for instance), to even entertain the idea of a merciful God was nonsense. Yet all religions espoused it, while slaughtering each other for the supremacy of their version.

And yet (I thought without saying), despite all the evidence, we still feel this need to address our utmost appeals, as well as our enraged blasphemies, to a source of the universe. This appeal, however hopeless, needs to posit a harbor, a hearer. The word, uttered *in extremis,* throws out a line to an unknown, hoped-for-listener. Every such appeal, then, was, perhaps instinctual. Belief or unbelief had nothing to do with it. Even atheists have moments in which they cry out, "God help me!"—and mean it.

But again, I couldn't help myself. My backed-up anger at Renee's condition spilled over in a crude summary: "All that crap about a merciful God." With the red wine we were drinking and the warmth of the fireplace, I was beginning to heat up, bitter, careless, heedless of the last vestige of possible hope my ill-timed words were undermining. I persisted. "Where do you see God caring? Why must we ask His forgiveness? Why must we be more perfect than He is?" Then remembering that Yom Kippur was coming, I said, "He should ask for *our* forgiveness!" By now, I was carried away, losing sight of what was in front of me, and addressing what I had earlier disavowed existed, and growing angrier because what I did not believe existed would not be present.

"Jackie, please . . ." Nat said, alarmed.

"And if there *is* a God," I concluded, with a triumphant clincher, "I'm against him."

Nat gasped and glanced at Renee. Her eyes had filmed over with a deep red, her head tilting languorously to the side; I wished I could have placed a pillow under it. Softly weeping, as if to wash away all this bickering and blaming, she seemed to take on an expression of serene acceptance of the inevitable; with her appeal denied, she had made her peace with surrender. It said: what matters is our being here together, probably for the last time.

(Some time after these events, on recounting my remarks to a friend who had been a Jungian therapist for many years, she smiled knowingly, and replied "Yes, and how much longing there is in that denial!")

That night, in our cabin, before we turned in, Renee said she wanted to apologize for something that took place when I was about to marry my first wife who was both a Christian *and* a minister's daughter—a double abomination to Jewish parents.

It happened after I had moved out of my parents' house in Brooklyn and rented a room in Manhattan not far from where I worked as a shipping clerk in a wholesale handkerchief company on 34th Street during the day. I had enrolled in a poetry writing workshop given at the YMHA (Young Men's Hebrew Association) in the evenings. Attending the first night's class, I was taken with a striking redhead sitting across the wide table from me. Her name was Kathleen. We went out a few times and, at her suggestion, attended several recitals, one by the magnificent gospel and folk singer Odetta and another performance by the great cellist Janos Starker of Kodaly's intricate and powerful sonata for cello that he played all the way through, sitting center stage, eyes shut.

Soon, in no time it seemed, I gave up my small room and moved in with Kathleen in her larger apartment. Three months later we decided to marry; we'd fly to southern California where her father, a Presbyterian minister, would marry us in his church. Certainly not expecting my parents or any members of my family to attend, nor even to approve, but as a point of information, I phoned and told my family of the coming event.

The rest of this story comes from Kathleen herself, since I wasn't present. As she told me right afterwards, about a week after I had notified my parents, she received a call from Renee asking to have coffee with her. When Kathleen arrived, Renee, biting her inner cheek, met her and turned to a male companion seated beside her and introduced Nat Shamis, my Aunt Becky's son. Getting to the point, Renee said she and Nat were there on behalf of my parents to ask if she would reconsider her decision to marry me in view of the difference in our religions. Kathleen said she didn't think I practiced any religion. Then Renee asked her didn't she think "there was something wrong with Jackie? Maybe . . . his sanity?" Kathleen replied that I was the sanest person she knew. (Though since then and during our protracted divorce, I'm sure she had reasons to question her early diagnosis made in the first flush of new romance, but that's another story.) Then my cousin Nat brought out an envelope. Apologizing first, Renee said the family would offer her ten thousand dollars if she did not go through with the marriage.

I remember my amazement when Kathleen returned to our apartment and told me what happened. Were they serious? Ten thousand? Where would they get that kind of money? They certainly didn't have anything like that in savings. Did they borrow, or appeal for (from whom?), or were they given it outright? My instant response was to feel flattered and flabbergasted at once. My parents and I had long since cut down on our contact. I'd phone now and then, but I rarely visited. I suppose they had given up on me and hoped they could dissuade my prospective bride from encouraging my lunacy.

We couldn't help but laugh at the notion that our illicit union could elicit that much cash. We certainly could have used it. With no car, no college tuition, no house payments, no big appliances, my family had never spent that kind of money on anything. I had become their biggest expense.

I told Kathleen she should have taken the money as a dowry (hijacked though it would have been) and we could have eloped to Paris, Hawaii, Acapulco. Instead, we flew to southern California and were married by her father in his church, with only Kathleen's family and friends in attendance.

For this long-ago episode (to me comedic, to Renee crass) she now wanted to apologize: what must have been for her a dutiful daughter's quandary more than thirty years before, and for me, forgotten soon after, my sister, with terminal cancer, was now asking my forgiveness. Unbeknownst to me, she had been carrying her guilt all these years!

Glibly trying to make light of it, I said the marriage eventually broke up anyway, and ten thousand bucks had been saved! We laughed, I more nervously than either she or Nat.

On that trip—hiking to the top of Hurricane Ridge, where her amazing stamina showed itself, thanks to her daily regimen of running (she, who Mom used to tease, calling her *"Renoonae mej'nunae* [crazy Renee])"—Renee most often took the lead up the steep trails, around sharp bends and across streams, while Nat and I gaped, amazed, as we slogged on behind, trying to keep up. Then, abruptly, her energy would give out and she'd stop, leaning against a rock, long enough for us to catch up. We'd gaze out over the valley below, inhale the spicy forest smells, take some pictures of each other, and start off again.

The great surprise for both was my driving: they'd never seen me drive a car before, nor heard me express interest in driving, and there I leaned, elbow out the open window of a rented car, steering them down the narrow, twisting mountain road from Hurricane Ridge with the screen of trees a ferny blur in the distance, as I brought us down safely to sea level and on through traffic to the car rental at the airport for our separate flights back home.

While driving that precipitous route, I knew they both watched me closely and had to suppress their anxiety. Afterwards I felt being together on this trip we had come to share a sense that an earlier bewildering time had been relieved and we had been restored in a new place.

Before leaving, Renee told me of a dream she'd been having lately: Mom and Aunt Becky (both dead) were each standing on either side of her. I asked what they were doing. Warning her, she said.

"What did they say?" I asked.

"Deer ba-laek (be careful)," she answered in Arabic, then repeated what they had told her in English. "The stairway you're on has no handrail." I didn't ask any further.

CHAPTER TWENTY-FOUR

I. F. STONE

Soon after the Korean War began, my cousin Nat, having joined the Army, this time legally, was stationed at Fort Benning, Georgia. The family worried that he might be sent overseas for combat. I was fourteen at the time. One day I picked up a newsstand copy of a daily paper new to me, the socialist *Daily Compass.* In its muckraking pages I first discovered the columns of I. F. Stone, who unnerved me with his exposés of the American military's doublespeak and congressional cover-ups. Rather than promoting his opinions in editorials, Stone simply quoted directly from congressional reports and comments by military leaders that were incriminatingly at odds with official government press releases and news reports.

The discrepancies juxtaposed the alleged reasons the u.s. government gave for its "police action" in Korea with what was actually reported taking place on the battleground. In more recent times such disparity between reality and propaganda "spin" has been legitimized as "misinformation." Back then, I read Stone's columns each day with a growing sense at first of apprehension, then alarm, at being lied to by our own government, which I could no longer ignore or justify to myself. In my zeal, I cut out and sent Nat clippings of those incriminating quotes and reports. My sense of betrayal was much like that of my disenchantment with religion. First God, then government . . . what next? Was there no end to the pervasive deceptions spreading all the more widely the further and deeper one looked?

At the time, it didn't occur to me that mail to and from military personnel might be censored, so I'm not sure Nat ever received the letters I sent him. After he was discharged, I didn't ask him, but thinking back, I shudder to imagine what might have happened, especially to him. We were learning that one did not have to be a card-carrying Communist to fall afoul of the likes of Senator Joe McCarthy.

During this time, my last year in junior high school, I had a young civics teacher whose tolerant manner in class, unlike many older, despotic teachers, made me want to show off the wide range of my knowledge of world history and current events. I, no doubt, had a crush on her, sensing something enigmatic that she warily held back. Petite, with a thick mass of shiny black hair framing her dark Germanic features, making them stand out even more, Miss Klingor possessed an intensity she kept under wraps, looking tentative, circumspect even, in her handling of the class discussion of current news, especially the McCarthy hearings.

She never gave an opinion, passed a judgment, or posed questions that might be interpreted as critical of such a controversial matter. She had taken political neutrality a step further, adopting (as well as she could) the look of a blank screen. She left it to us to interpret, give our opinion of the ongoing proceedings, and she supported our views with quotes she read from newspaper accounts of the verbal sparring between the senator from Wisconsin and witnesses who pleaded the Fifth Amendment. On TV, a mean, nasal whine characterized his hectoring allegations and threats bellowed in an inquisitor's bluster that, though alarming, proved as hollow as his head was bald.

Mr. Jacobs, our popular boys' gym teacher, fell victim to McCarthy's reign of terror. He was fired, along with several other teachers, for his (earlier? current? suspected? fellow traveler?) membership in the Communist Party during World War II. Not too long after he left, and I switched from public junior high school to *yeshiva,* I was surprised and glad to see him again on the basketball court across the street from Talmudic Academy. Now our *yeshiva's* gym teacher, he looked less agile on the basketball court, slower on his feet, more cautious.

On the day it was my turn to give a presentation in front of the class, I delivered what I considered a factual appraisal of the unconstitutional methods of the senator and his shrill assistant prosecutor, Roy Cohen. Reading from I. F. Stone's columns, I quoted that the charges they were making were without evidence, and pointed out that the tactics used were without legitimacy, were mere gossip, broken rules of law, and character assassination.

I expected to see Miss Klingor upset, even if no one else in the class would be. I glanced at her standing to the side of the first row. She neither stopped nor tried to interrupt me. In my talk, I made an effort not to show any bias, but to let the facts speak for themselves, as Stone did. When I finished, there was a long silence: it may have been above their heads or below their adolescent interest, but no one raised their hand. Finally Miss Klingor spoke up: "Surely someone has a question," but no one did. A moment later the end-of-class bell rang, and students, visibly relieved, made for the door and the room was soon empty.

As I collected my papers, getting ready to leave, Miss Klingor approached with an uncharacteristic, though guarded, grin and animated eyes. Close up, she appeared vivacious, and then, as if recognizing the effect of her attraction on me, grew flirtatious, excited by an idea, and whispered, "Would you like to join the Socialist Youth Party?" Taken aback by such an unexpected question, I instinctively resisted committing myself to a possibly dangerous call. I don't remember answering her. All right, her expression seemed to say, if not now, later. Before I reached the door, she approached and whispered in my ear more fervently, *"Fur Freundschaft und Frieheit!"*— which I later learned was the socialist workers rallying cry, "For Friendship and Freedom."

Some years later, by chance, I was in the New York Main Public Library on 42nd Street, waiting for the elevator, when the doors opened and among the passengers exiting, I noticed a short, intense-looking man with a large nubby hearing aid in his ear, wearing thick Coke-bottle eyeglasses that enlarged his lemur-looking eyes. He held an oversized, brimming portfolio of papers in one hand and magazines in the other. I recognized his face from a newspaper photo, but didn't know he was hard of hearing, which, at first, made me doubt my initial hunch. But I knew, even before having it later confirmed while reading of his several physical disabilities, that he was I. F. Stone.

CHAPTER TWENTY-FIVE

TALMUDIC ACADEMY

Despite my growing doubts and attempts at reconciling the conflicting claims of religion and science, at age fifteen, on graduating from public junior high school, when Hacham Shlomo (perhaps to set me back on the path he must have sensed me straying from) suggested that I apply, with his recommendation and a scholarship, for entry to Talmudic Academy, Yeshiva University's preparatory high school, toward obtaining a rabbinical degree, I did just that. Why? One practical inducement was the ninety-dollar monthly scholarship check I received from Magen David and handed over to my mother to help with household expenses. But even with that added bit of income, my mother, with her often uncanny prescience, must have seen something willful, and forced, in me—like my recent (failed) attempts at independence—and predicted that I would not last at the *yeshiva*. And for me, perhaps, *yeshiva* was a last attempt to convince myself of the primacy of inherited faith over a disillusion fast burgeoning into ever more irrefutable reality, and a last effort at fending it off.

One was born into an all-encompassing ancestral tradition and obeyed its age-old precepts as givens, just as one inherited his family and obeyed his parents and their customs . . . or must he? Might faith and family be what one had to flee? At times I felt such apprehension and anger at my parents' constant quarreling and petty feuds, I'd imagine they were not—*could* not possibly be—my real parents; that they lived somewhere else, anywhere but here.

And that guilt, I suppose, prompted me to try a last-minute, rapprochement, however tenuous or tentative, with family and faith.

After I accepted Hacham Shlomo's offer to apply to Talmudic Academy, I received a letter asking me to show up for an interview with the academy's chief rabbi. On the day of the appointment I took the train to the Franklin Avenue station, and as I walked the few blocks to its address, I noticed in the distance a large steel facade with flying pennants: Ebbets Field, home of the Brooklyn Dodgers. This might not be without benefit, I thought.

Talmudic Academy, an old, two-story building whose brown-stone front blended with the private houses nearby, had its administrative office on the ground floor and classrooms above. As soon as I set foot into the lobby, I was hit by an odor of disinfectant filling the air, all the way into the office. There I was met by an aggressively attractive young woman at the desk whose full, dark hair formed a mane around her head, which may have been (I couldn't tell then) the customary Orthodox Yiddish woman's wig, but whose fulsome plump breasts, about to spill over her blouse top, were surely real. She seemed either unaffected or desensitized to the fumes. Without smiling, with hardly a look, she directed me to a room on the second floor where Chief Rabbi Karlin was waiting to interview me.

Milling about in small groups, or on their way to classes, the young male students, wearing yarmulkes or black broad-brimmed hats, didn't seem to mind or be aware of the chemical vapors either. Perhaps they had over time grown so acclimatized to the smell, they associated it with their study of the ancient texts.

Climbing the wooden stairs didn't leave the stench behind, and it abated after I entered the room where the old rabbi was seated, and closed the door. Small, compact, with a full beard, wearing a high black hat and a long robe, he motioned me to sit. Inside the close room whose walls were lined with full bookshelves hung a smell familiar to me from the Magen David basement and prayer hall: the ancient, oaken emanation of mildew, like a vapor released from the pages in those large tomes, whose origin had been wood.

For a moment he eyed me with a look of steady appraisal and then, speaking in a deep, almost subterranean voice, said something I didn't understand. I must have looked puzzled. From behind the broad bulk of his beard I saw his cheeks and eyes raised in quizzical surprise: *"Du bis ein yid?"*

My look must have shown my puzzlement. After a pause, he translated into English, "Are you a Jew?"

Surprised, it took a moment to catch a note of ironical whimsy. *"Kehn* (yes)," I answered in Hebrew. I was taken aback; did he intend to begin the interview by making me convince him I was a Jew? By speaking Yiddish?

"Attah loh m'dehber ivreet (You don't speak Hebrew)?" he asked.

"Kehn," I replied in Hebrew, *"aval loh Yiddish* (but not Yiddish). "

"La-mah loh (Why not)?"

"A-nee Sephardi (I am Sephardic)," I said.

"Ahh, Sephardi," he exclaimed, sagely nodding. I couldn't tell if there was irony in his tone. *"Tohv* (Good)."

I was relieved he had no trouble understanding my Hebrew. I had passed my first test.

"Ach'shav la'avodah (Now to work)," he said.

He motioned me to sit beside him at a desk where I could see by the look of the text—the stoic-looking script, bare-boned, angular, stripped of punctuation—it was Rashi's commentary on a Biblical passage. He pointed and I read from it, my years of instant decoding from Aramaic to Hebrew while reciting Rashi put to good use, and I felt a confident fluency in my reading that kept up with my understanding, both of which, through lack of usage, have long since eroded.

In Hebrew, he asked me, "Tell me, what do the letters R-A-S-H-I stand for?"

"Rabbe Shlomo Itzchaki," I said.

"Ha-eem atta yo'dai'yah l'odot shel nefesh Rashi (Do you know about the life of Rashi)?"

"Kehn," I replied.

Then I told him what I thought he wanted to hear about the legendary rabbi, which he already knew: How Rashi, the outstanding commentator on the *Tanach* (Five Books of Moses) and the Talmud, born in France in 1040 A.D. (4800 by the Hebrew calendar), survived the massacres and forced conversions of the Crusades; how, while the cross was turned into a sword, Rashi miraculously escaped the horror all around him; none of it reflected in his work. Over many years, his commentaries and explanations of the *Tanach's* ambiguous phrases, paradoxical meanings, and complex grammar were written down and collected by his students. The commentaries passed down to us were not written by Rashi himself, but were his answers to questions from his students, or his answers to rhetorical questions he put to them that they would write in the margin of the parchment text. While the early rabbis wove a multilayered palimpsest of story and legend, comment and elaboration, argument and counterargument upon Biblical passages, Rashi abridged, simplified, and explained the principles behind the text, both of the Five Books of Moses and the vast swathes of midrashic legalese that comprise the Babylonian Talmud. Practical as well as scholarly, this great sage supported his family and the academy he founded from the income of his wine manufacturing business in Troyes.

To impress him even more, I introduced the irony that it was a Christian, despite his Jewish-sounding name of Danile Bomberg, a Venetian printer, who first published Rashi's commentaries in a Hebrew Bible in 1517, by inventing the distinctive characters called "Rashi script," which he set alongside the original text, inside the margin.

Familiar as I was with the rabbinical fondness for legends and parables (even if they superseded accuracy or even credibility), I concluded with the tale of the crusader Godfrey, who, gaining an audience with Rashi, asked whether his forthcoming military campaign would succeed. Rashi replied that he would initially be victorious but his forces would eventually be routed and he would return with only three horses. Enraged at what he took to be a curse, Godfrey swore that if he returned with even four horses he would destroy the Jewish community of Troyes. But Rashi's prediction came true. Godfrey's forces were defeated, and when he returned with his remaining four horses, which he guarded with his life, determined to carry out his threat, as he passed through the city wall of Troyes, a stone loosened and fell from the wall and struck one of the horses dead.

We then went on to a Talmudic text he had me read aloud, give my interpretation, which he then asked me—with thumb and forefinger extended, and speaking in that distinctly see-sawing up-and-down, now-on-the-one-hand, now-on-the-other flip-flop of options known as Talmudic *pil-pul*—to elaborate on, and followed with questions equally giving rise to alternate meanings and conflicting conundrums.

In the Talmud's convoluted permutations explaining the multi-meanings attached to sentences, isolated phrases, even fragments of words, the original Bible itself had become a pretext on which generations of venerable rabbis—who were also diplomats, physicians, mapmakers, merchants, and financial advisors to their royal Muslim hosts—had overlayed a web as richly drenched in speculation and folklore and fraught with queried hesitations as living itself. Responding to these legalistic queries and ever-unfolding explications put to me by my patriarchal examiner, I felt confident in responding in the authentic Hebrew of precise, dental-dotting Sephardic enunciation, closer to Arabic, than what I thought of as the coarse, unwieldy Eastern European inflections in the Hebrew I'd heard spoken by Ashkenazic Jews like himself. After a shorter time than I had imagined the interview would take, Rabbi Karlin raised his hand and said "Enough." It seemed too easy, too quick. This was one of the rare times I felt my confidence had been convincing.

It was only after I left the building and was on my way home on the subway that I wondered if I was fluent enough in Hebrew, if my Talmudic interpretations were intricate and hair-splitting enough. A week later I received a brief letter (a note on official letterhead) from Talmudic Academy: I had been accepted. I learned later that I was the first Sephardee to ever have been admitted, whether by dint of knowledge and ability or through lack of other Sephardic applicants, I never found out. Had Rabbi Karlin's decision, in large part, gone in my favor because of my Sephardic accent, so unlike that of his Ashkenazic students, not to mention his own? I also wondered how much my scholarship tuition, paid for by the Magen David synagogue's committee, may have contributed to my being accepted. I was the only Sephardic student in the school.

The following term, when I began attending Talmudic Academy and had to commute by train, I grew increasingly self-conscious about having to wear a yarmulke in public, since the constant wearing of a yarmulke among Sephardeem was not traditional. At first, I felt a defiant pride in wearing the black silken cap, while feeling marked and vulnerable. I believe my taking up this practice had less to do with prescribed orthodoxy than pride in visibly standing in opposition to bare-headed goyim on the streets and trains, who would often glance or stare as they passed.

Among the required subjects of study in the *yeshiva* was a music appreciation class. In this oddly chosen subject for religious training, one day the teacher put a record on the turntable and said we would hear Beethoven's Seventh Symphony, which I had not heard. After the brief stately opening, which builds to a propulsion, then rest, then gradually skips into a driven dance, a lilting rhythm leapt in the air, exuberantly infectious, and was repeated in slightly varied chord gradations of the original run of notes. Beethoven had somehow stirred all of nature to this ecstatic dance, skipping, then darting, creating a tension that stretched, then stopped, and finally released, and was repeated from the beginning. This dance movement was followed in the next section by a funeral march, which made the contrast of speeds and moods more enlivening than if either were prolonged without its opposite.

One day, after class, on my way to the toilet, the young woman from the front desk was just coming out of the men's room, carrying a pail in one hand and a mop in the other. I'd often noticed other students, before entering the bathroom, reach their hand into their jacket pocket and, using the inner lining as an inside-out glove for added sanitary protection, grasp the doorknob to open. I made way for her; avoiding my eyes, she sidled past, as the reek of disinfectant hit me as I shouldered open the door.

GRAND ARMY PLAZA

Early in my time at Talmudic Academy, I discovered the Grand Army Plaza Library in nearby Prospect Park; it had a vast literature section as well as a large record collection of classical music. I began to visit there regularly before taking the train home.

The library, with that imposing name, was an equally imposing structure with large white Roman columns flanking the entrance. When you entered, sunlight was diffused through a glass dome, giving a religious aura to the spacious lobby. This library, so much larger in size and contents than my local library, was a veritable palace of books. Vast and uncrowded inside, its full shelves held books on all of the same subjects as my local library, yet on a much more expansive scale. Whereas in the local library you might find a few dozen books on subjects such as biology, history, or poetry, here were hundreds on each subject. Wandering from shelf to shelf in any subject, I'd accidentally spot a title that would catch my interest. Reaching for it, I'd notice another title alongside, above, or below it on another shelf, an even more surprising discovery, until my arms were piled with more books than I could hold. After setting them down on a nearby table, the process of chance discoveries would begin again, until, in the excited confusion, I'd forget where I had left my first choices only moments before.

One afternoon, wandering around in the English Literature section, I spotted *The Collected Poems of Dylan Thomas*, with the young poet posed aureoled in curls, the cherub in the painting by Augustus John. I had heard Thomas's oracular, orotund reading voice in English class. I had never heard anything like it, and found the incantatory intonation mesmerizing. At first, it was the unusual passion in the voice of our English teacher who originally read out loud to us Thomas's "Fern Hill" that made the poem fascinating: I'd never seen or heard a teacher so excited about any subject, so happily taking delight. His appearance, bland and noncommital when reading other texts aloud, grew animated, eagerly enjoying the syntactic pleasure in enunciating the cadenced vowels and alliteration.

He played the poet reading on the first Caedmon recording. Airily voweled and rhythmically gripping, there boomed forth a deep bass-toned voice, from an altogether other world; a magic instantly memorable. It began:

> Now as I was young and easy under the apple boughs
> About the lilting house, and happy as the grass was green . . .

And ended:

> Time held me green and dying,
> Though I sang in my chains like the sea . . .

Nature, not only made active, was set to a deliriously paced dance in a liberated English, language that oxygenated the lungs.

Next to Thomas's book stood *The Poems of Edward Thomas* and *The Poems of R. S. Thomas* (a contemporary of Dylan Thomas, and also a Welshman). Having picked Dylan Thomas, I felt that was enough for the time being, and thus missed the chance of discovering the work of two of the finest other Thomases in modern English poetry until years later, long after my enthusiasm for Dylan Thomas's sumptuous imagery and tangled metaphors waned in favor of the more stoic, plainer-spoken poetry by both other Thomases.

There, too, I haphazardly wandered my way into discovering the works of Whitman and Dickinson, then on to modern American poets such as Edwin Arlington Robinson, Hart Crane, Robinson Jeffers, Robert Lowell, and John Berryman; each of whom in turn led to other poets unknown to me, like Randall Jarrell, Theodore Roethke, W. S. Merwin, and Frank O'Hara; who led me to European poets they had translated: Rilke, Garcia Lorca, Mayakovsky. I would later find the work of Eugenio Montale and Giuseppi Ungaretti in a Penguin paperback of modern Italian poetry, where, at the bottom of a page of the original Italian, ran a "literal" English prose translation in italicized type so tiny and packed, the letters looked like a swarm of scurrying ants. I kept it over the years as its pages of cheap paper turned brown and crumbled, much like the leaves mentioned in the poems themselves.

There again, I listened to Beethoven's Seventh Symphony in the library's large classical music record section. I'd play it each time I visited, over and over, sitting with earphones at a long mahogany table. Soon, I was listening to Schubert, the lovely whistleable melodies of his symphonies and the aching, heartwrenching melancholy of his last quartets and piano sonatas; Brahms's broad, majestic, autumnal passages; Grieg's "Dawn" in *Peer Gynt,* the shimmering strings calling forth the fresh morning spaces between one mountaintop and another; while the ravishing opening of Mendelsohn's violin concerto drew a power that could thaw and tenderize feelings.

Listening to pieces such as these began to make me feel that, rather than the daily rote repetitions droned from ancient texts, it was the playful freedom and surprising depth of emotions stirred up by such music that had the power to move me. And I craved more.

OUR FIRST TV SET

Not until I was about sixteen years old, after what must have been steady pestering by us kids, did we convince our father to buy our own TV set, after practically all our friends had one. Television was introduced to our neighborhood by the owner of an electrical appliance store across the street. Physically huge, the man loomed above the Philco and Magnavox sets on display.

In his window stood a (for those days) large fourteen-inch black-and-white set he'd regularly turn on to draw an audience to this new gadget. On Tuesday nights, he got more than he bargained for when, at eight, he'd switch on the *Milton Berle Texaco Comedy Hour.* It seemed the entire neighborhood, anticipating this night of new free entertainment, turned out in force, thick as the moths drawn in tiny cyclones to the streetlights overhead.

We would be there early, right up against the window, waiting for him to turn on the set, while the adult men, returning home from their jobs, had barely enough time for dinner before arriving, so that when the "Texaco men" came onstage and began crooning their punchy trademark intro, "We are the men of Texaco, we work from Maine to Mexico," the crowd, pressing behind, would push us so hard we could feel the glass shudder, which we knew would bring out the owner. Soon, with his broad bulk in the doorway filling up the frame, he'd threaten to turn off the set. Almost as one body, the crowd took a step back. In order to watch Berle, in his outlandishly puffed and plumed drag costumes, or smacked by a stagehand with a wallop of powder puff makeup, literally run through his campy, manic comedy skits with all their live scene-smashing mayhem and mishaps, we'd obey any order, like good soldiers. My father never came to any of these mass public viewings, but must have caught sight of a TV program somewhere, and finally gave in.

Soon after, our family would gather—kids on the floor, Mom on a chair, and Pop, his lap covered with a blanket on the couch in the living room—to watch *Mama,* a popular sentimental show about an immigrant Norwegian family living in San Francisco. The lulling pastoral theme (from Grieg's *Holberg Suite,* I'd learn later) came up as the idyllic family members sat and talked together around the dinner table in their cozy kitchen while we sat enviously watching them in our cold, drafty flat.

It wasn't long before Pop began to enjoy watching the Bob Hope specials and the zany, sweaty antics of Jerry Lewis and Dean Martin. These were among the few times I ever remember him uncharacteristically laughing out loud. I feel (though belatedly) glad that he could enjoy these moments, so rarely did he allow himself the luxury of laughter. When he did laugh at a punch line and my mother didn't, she'd nod toward him and without turning to face him, sarcastically ask in

Arabic, "*Ha'lah btifham* (So now you understand)?" deriding what she implied was his pretending to understand what she didn't, and therefore was surely beyond him, just as she'd often mock his British accent as an affectation. Her ignorance of English was due to her refusal to make any effort to learn it; refusal of anything new was her way of being—and staying—in her world, just as derision was her way of leveling the field between her and my father.

ON FIRST SEEING A LIVE TV CONCERT

Arturo Toscanini, with slicked-back hair, wielding a baton as thin as his mustache, had the look and mechanical manner of a mini-Tuscan tyrant. He conducted the New York Philharmonic with a signature scowl on his face; the severe stare, black eyes beaming for absolute obedience (carrying to the farthest row of drum and cymbal), looked permanently displeased with every bar his cowed musicians played, or might be about to play. His stiff L-bent arms pumped like pistons. As if avenging the deafness of his musical God, Beethoven, he led his symphonies like heroic hurdles, conducting the Fifth so four-squarely it filled my head as if a sonic boom had cleared my sinuses to a more keen-eared, enlarged world of dramatic sound, lyrical landscapes.

Yet so primitive was the technology of the time, the figures of the orchestra members on the screen were a grainy blur, ghostly shadows, though their movements produced such shimmering sounds. All this breaking up, bridging, and broadening out of lyrical time only to break up again was driven by the thin baton in the maestro's hand, and beneath the watchful eyes, the mustache bobbed up and down, also keeping time.

I was coming to realize that my everyday hearing was a passive act, performed unconsciously, whereas listening required focused attention. It was refreshing to hear such a harmonic language without words; like going out the door and not knowing, though eager with anticipation, to what catchy melody or strikingly new harmonies you might be treated. The music resonated in an interior space while enlarging, reaching new layers of feeling.

It was still too early in my musical experience to have grown bored by the constant repetition of nostalgic workhorses—overtures, concertos, symphonies—played on WQXR, the New York classical radio station, until their original excitement grew as dulled as the predictability of sentimental pop tunes, and would, in later years, turn me away from the orchestral repertoire to more intimate chamber music, such as Schubert's quartets and piano sonatas with their spare means and stark, shimmering overtones; their summons to attend the poignancy of the moment passing, and the enormity of the silence, sad or serene, when the last sound died away.

"BLESSED BE HE WHO PERMITS WHAT IS FORBIDDEN"

While I was discovering classical music, I continued reading in evolutionary science and astronomy while I attended *yeshiva*. After a few months, I realized I had made the wrong choice: the conflict between the science I was reading, opening a wider world to me, and the ancient laws and traditions that closed it down, came to a crisis. I started to take my yarmulke off soon after I'd leave the *yeshiva* and ride the train back home without it. I felt relieved, unburdened, and people in the street no longer gave me a second glance.

I suppose I did this also as a dare to the other *yeshiva* students waiting on the platform, who came over to admonish me. With them, I'd exploit the opportunity and soon have them embroiled in Talmudic *pil-pul* right there on the noisy Franklin Avenue train platform, in an argument I'd pursue with relish, convinced that scientific facts refuted the Creation in the Book of Genesis with fossil evidence that was indisputable; that was, literally, imbedded in solid rock.

In the same heated breath of argument, they'd veer from rabid protest to tongue-tied perplexity. I knew their irrational arguments because I had invoked them myself in attempts to buttress my own waning faith, and failed. In my vehemence, I was intent on having them experience the full measure of their failure.

With a growing recklessness, I could feel myself careening down a slope, not knowing where it was headed, or if it would end. There was a gleeful sense of gratification in the arguments I made. I felt what my old friend Isaac Malek must have felt when he gave his demonic laugh at what he was provoking. I took pleasure in seeing the confusion, distress, and resistance on their faces when I made a point they couldn't rebuff, after which they'd switch to another tack, the more desperate for being so absurd.

Fending off their weak parries and weaker reasoning, I felt a growing sense of relief, of bidding good riddance to what could no longer hold me, and with a liberated quickness and lightness saw that only those who have faith can have doubt; but for one without faith there is no doubt.

After invoking the evidence from Darwin, I'd paraphrase from Thomas Paine's broadside, *The Age of Reason:*

> Whenever we read the obscene stories, the voluptuous debaucheries, the cruel and tortuous executions, the unrelenting vindictiveness, with which more than half the Bible is filled, it would be more consistent that we called it the word of a demon, than the word of God. It is a history of wickedness, that has served to corrupt and brutalize mankind . . .

The implication was not lost on these hair-splitting rabbinical students that in my estimation they too were ignorant, superstitious fanatics. On sensing that, many earnest faces turned beet-red with rage, unaware that their train had entered the station, and was leaving without them.

My parting shot was that, in practical terms, each person had to be his own Messiah.

My family also noticed the change in me; to them it appeared sudden, inexplicable. One Shabbat, like all the others before it, I was in shul, and the next I was not; the mornings I'd get up early for morning service abruptly ended, though it took months for the doubts to become convictions and to undermine my habits, and finally to hatch from their cocoon into open dissension.

When, soon after, I quit the *yeshiva*, thereby forfeiting the monthly scholarship allowance, my mother, gloating scornfully reminded me: *"Ish il-tilak* (What did I tell you)?"

CHAPTER TWENTY-SIX

SANDY KOUFAX AND MOOSE

Lafayette High School had been built early in the years of the New Deal on a landfill on the way to Coney Island; students liked to joke that it was sinking about an inch a year. At that rate, kids on the top fifth floor would be neck-high in garbage by the year 3000, so we didn't have to worry. That was the word going around school, which, however much mathematical accuracy it might contain, seemed more an expression of a collective wish.

You reached the school by taking the bus to 86th Street and Stillwell Avenue, the last stop at the far end of Bay Parkway. There, for several blocks, was a thriving open market of stalls loud with vendors and crowds milling underneath the rattling rails of the El trains above. If you rode one, you'd see the huge domed storage tanks that leaked a thick oily gunk in black pools so rank with a foul sulfur smell you had to hold your breath going by.

Because earlier in Brooklyn's past land was cheap, immigrant Sicilian and Italian farmers had settled a small shantytown and tilled vegetable plots to sustain their families. At the edge of this town, a communal dump was filled in and overlaid with cement, and on it, to commemorate the Frenchman who had aided the American forces in the Revolutionary War, was constructed a squat institutional slab, Lafayette High School, whose classroom windows overlooked a noxious industrial waste zone.

No wonder going to school each day felt like we had walked into a penitentiary. The usual apparatus of judgment: tests, grades, homework, the whole system of "getting an education" felt more like being indoctrinated into servitude than practicing independent thought.

When I left the *yeshiva* and entered Lafayette, there were two students I remember most from my homeroom class; one a star, the other a disaster.

The star—even then—was Sandy Koufax. Tall, lean, and handsome, Sandy was a popular student, who, at that time, was a basketball celebrity on the school's team. Sandy, encouraged by his stepfather in his interest in sports, used to regularly play basketball at the local Jewish Community Center on Bay Parkway. Often, when you went there for a social youth event, there was Sandy in the gym, shooting hoops. Occasionally, he also pitched for the baseball team, drawing the interest of the Brooklyn Dodger scouts. After graduating, he went to the University of Cincinnati on a basketball scholarship. There, too, on occasions when he pitched, baseball scouts urged his parents to have him sign. He did, with his hometown team, the Brooklyn Dodgers, in 1955, for what in those days was a munificent bonus of $30,000.

After his relatively brief (ten-year) strikeout-record-breaking career, Sandy would become a first ballot shoe-in to baseball's Hall of Fame, his pitching arm gone lame and nearly paralyzed from throwing so hard and often, with usually only two or three days rest between starts. After each game he'd have to plunge his arm into a bucket of ice. Besides his pitching prowess, what would endear him to Jewish fans was his refusal to pitch the opening day of the 1965 World Series against the Minnesota Twins because it was Yom Kippur. Instead, his teammate Don Drysdale was given the start. Taken out early in the third inning after giving up six runs, Drysdale returned to the dugout, head hung low, and told his manager Walt Alston, "I bet right now you wish I was Jewish, too."

For all his enviable gifts as both an athlete and student, I recall Sandy as a good-natured, intelligent fellow. Far from being "stuck up," Sandy would enter homeroom in his quiet, graceful stride and immediately be surrounded by eyes, and most often females, who tried to engage, or at least be noticed by him. Having been an exemplary student, it came as no surprise when in 1966 he announced his retirement in front of a battery of cameras and reporters in poised, articulate language not usually uttered by major league ballplayers. His teammates told about when they were on the road and they'd be out partying at night while Sandy was back at the hotel "reading a book."

The disaster was "Moose": that's what the kids in school called him—to his face. In the hierarchy of victims, Moose was a natural-born top candidate, a prime case history, all by himself.

I think his name was Alan, but am not sure, having myself all these years thought of him by that rude appellation. His head was large and long, and from his oversized shovel-shaped ears floppy lobes hung nearly to his shoulders. It would not be physiologically inaccurate to say his features resembled more those of a bull elephant than a moose, especially with that large fleshy nose preceding him when he'd shamble into class, head down, huffing, already exasperated from the merciless teasing he'd endured in the hallway, out of breath from chasing and cursing his tormentors, first thing in the morning.

Though he towered above us all, kids would taunt him with comparisons of his prodigious "shnozz" to his "schlong," examples of juvenile alliteration in the service of humiliation. In truth, it was hard to choose which physical characteristic, from such an array, to watch for his reaction when he'd curse and groan, spittle flecking the corners of his thick, twisted lips, his head slouched between caved-in shoulders, as he'd bluff preparing to rush a tormentor. When he did, the teacher would reprimand him, being a single target, rather than have to confront a mass of hecklers. The victim was victimized further for bringing trouble. From one side of the room to the other (but from which corner exactly? and from whom?), a low mooing would be heard, then gather, and as the helpless teacher tried to bring the class to order, the sound would grow, an ominous cattle call, until the room sounded like a bellowing stockyard: "Moooo-ooosse" He'd turn toward the sound he had become so attuned to, and, standing still, try to pin his glaring eye on the culprit. "Moooo-ooosse," as his face grew redder with fury, and his lanky jaw hung open like an overstuffed boxing glove, he'd feint a move to chase the suspected mooo-er, and yell "I'll break your fuckin' head, ya cocksuckers!" But he'd just stand there, on the spot, rivetted, in outraged confusion, his long arms hanging stiff as logs at his sides, fists knotted into helpless stumps. And even as he yelled "I'll kill ya!" the spit that flew from his mouth backfired on him. In the schoolyard, at recess, when he'd run to the nearest teacher and point an accusing finger at one of the kids taunting him, the teacher would turn away, not wanting any further trouble from this potentially dangerous giant.

One day the entire student body assembled in the auditorium to watch a nature film, girls seated on one side of the hall, boys on the other. After the noise of chases and catcalls, of paperclips shot from rubberbands pinging off walls and chair backs, and the banging of seats subsided, the lights dimmed and on the screen came a *National Geographic* documentary about the American Northwest. After the camera finished panning across the obligatory mountains and wide rushing river on whose banks stood now a bear, now a deer, now a bear chasing a deer, out from behind a thicket of trees, just as the tips of the rack appeared before its full array of antlers, the familiar call began to converge and swell like winds from all sides of the auditorium, "Mooo . . ." and gathered like a rumbling gale, "Mooooossse!" "I'll kill ya, motherfuckers!" went up the cry from where he sat only two rows in front of me. Teachers scurried around, trying to restore order, and, as usual, especially in the dark, to no avail. The mooing came in waves, followed by an animal moaning; a forsaken, inconsolable bellow of protest. Kids were howling, stamping their feet, whistling, jeering. Suddenly a seat was slammed back, books were thrown. His looming, threatening figure stood, rocking, in the aisle, his enlarged shadow cast on the screen, while he shouted and cursed and was jeeringly "Moooo"-ed down; he then stalked up the aisle to the doors, his fist raised, pumping the air. "Die, ya bastards!" he cried, spasmic sobs catching in his throat as he nearly pulled the door off its hinges. "You're all gonna die!" And deep down you knew he meant *you!*

BERNIE

I doubt, though, that he meant to include Bernie H. in his mass curse. Bernie, a friendly, intelligent boy, was well-liked, especially by the girls; in particular, the prodigiously developed ones, savvy with the knowledge of their budding allure. Sweet-smelling girls with deliciously defined features, red mouths, and wing-tipped eyebrows; girls in white blouses whose full breasts sloped in frilled, snowy cones; girls with satiny pink skin in full bloom, who, far from betokening promise, were already beauties as they stood, laughing, chewing gum, gossiping with friends. For these girls, out of our reach, Bernie's appeal, besides his natural good looks, was that he was at ease with them, attentively present, assured and anchored in that knowledge.

He stood, relaxed and amiable, enjoying himself in the hallways between classes with them, joking, laughing, affectionate, with no trace of guile or motive, only pleased and giving pleasure, which, from the looks on their faces, included them. One couldn't begrudge him that. It seemed his natural circle, rightfully so, with none of the usual awkward, inane, hemming-and-hawing of teenage boys daunted and thwarted in the presence of a group of girls.

So gentle and unaffected was Bernie's manner, so endearing, I doubt any of us begrudged him his popularity. No one spoke enviously or even unfavorably of him. I, too, felt an admiration in his presence, even if he was unaware of me, as I'd watch him captivate a girl's attention, her books clasped against her breast, face raised to take in Bernie's laughter; herself not so much courted as made to feel included in the stirring light of Bernie's attention.

Even with Moose, I noticed Bernie was kind. When he approached, Bernie would pause and listen to what Alan had to say, rather than turning away. There was something sturdy and admirable in him; he could have easily acted stuck up, but never did. Poised and dignified, he didn't need to exploit his popularity like others, less self-assured, and less generous.

Only a couple of years later, in 1953, a short while after we'd graduated, I was sitting at the back of a Bay Parkway bus and noticed a fellow getting on having trouble mounting the front steps. I saw the top of a cane hook onto the post beside the door as he lifted himself up and into the bus; it was Bernie, his legs encased in metal braces, slowly, stiffly taking one hesitant step at a time. The last time I had seen him he was healthy, and now he looked much older, ingrown, tottering—a victim of the dreaded polio. And yet only a little later in that same year did Dr. Jonas Salk discover his vaccine, but it was too late for Bernie.

AN INVITATION

Much like the other subjects I was interested in, such as science, history, and geography, my attention to poetry grew in proportion to my curiosity and sense of affinity for it, which I actively sought in the school and public libraries.

The other required subjects in which I had little interest—in fact, disliked, chief among them algebra and trigonometry—I studied only enough to pass. Those required subjects I considered energy drains from my real interests. I'd cut my losses and do just enough, but no more. Since my grades were not reviewed at home, there was no need to excel. Since "education" seemed to consist of passing tests, I would cram before taking one (though sometimes not enough), and barely pass. The subjects I found interesting, I'd study on my own.

By this time, along with my disinterest, as well as my determination to choose how I'd use my time after graduating high school, college was not real to me, and I wasn't preparing to apply. While kids around me were intimidated by their parents into getting high grades for college entrance, I could pick and choose my subjects, barely passing the difficult ones with c's and d's. Through a family connection, I had gotten a part-time job after school in a retail linen store in Manhattan, and could get other jobs as I might need them. In the business world that I knew, calculus and trigonometry were not required. If you were a relative, could work a cash register, and could understand the basic Arabic used as a code among salesmen in the presence of customers, you had a job.

At the library, in one of those multicentury poetry anthologies, I was enthralled by Walter de la Mare's "The Listener"; its opening question and haunting rhymes:

"Is there anybody there?" said the Traveler,
    Knocking on the moonlit door,
And his horse in the silence champed the grasses
    Of the forest's ferny floor:
"Is there anybody there?" he said.
But no one descended to the traveler;
    No head from the leaf-fringed sill
Leaned over and looked into his grey eyes,
    Where he stood perplexed and still.

I could hear the speaker as if he were on the other side of the door, and we, on this side, being addressed. Hearing no reply, with only "the stillness answering his cry," the Traveler

    . . . smote on the door, even
Louder and lifted his head: —

"Tell them I came, and no one answered,
   That I kept my word," he said.
   ....

   Ay, they heard his foot upon the stirrup,
And the sound of iron on stone,
   And how the silence surged softly backward,
When the plunging hoofs were gone.

Elsewhere, in his elegiac tribute to Thomas Hardy, de la Mare manages, in Edwardian tones, to condense the paradoxical nature of poetry itself:

   . . . lorn thy tidings, grievous thy song;
   Yet thine, too, this solacing music,
   As we earthfolk stumble along.

It was the dense sensuousness of Keats's imagery, the high-octane passion for liberty that oxygenated Shelley's verse, and Tennyson's "innumerable murmur of immemorial bees" that held me. And in Thomas Hardy's poems about his old age, I found a more private tragic sense in his confessions of having been uncaring of her love when his first wife was alive.

And then (not likely to have been a class assignment), I happened on a poem whose title, "The Hound of Heaven," intrigued me, as well as its centered layout on the page, the lines step-like, jagged, propelled:

I fled Him down the nights and down the days,
   I fled Him down the arches of the years;
I fled Him down the labyrinthine ways
   of my own mind and in a mist of tears
Hid from Him.

Such a visually graphic sound-enactment in pouncing, plunging lines; a headlong rush of torqued circuitry sustained through three image-packed, grammar-gnarled, propulsive pages! In contrast to his contemporary, the celebrated poet laureate Tennyson, Francis Thompson, a London street derelict addicted to laudanum, had articulated a force equally of flight from, and fervor toward, the Divine. In that paradox lies its coiled energy.

Once, being asked by our teacher to recite a poem that we'd been assigned to memorize, I began to recite "The Hound of Heaven" quickly—to the teacher's utter surprise—so as to be able to slip into the already running stream of the lines in my head, and then riding them more assuredly as I moved along, their urgencies cuing me, their sounds were their sense, and neither could be pared from the other. Of that recitation, I managed about two-thirds of the first page before my memory gave out.

I would feel that propulsive force again later, reading Lorca's *Poet in New York;* Thomas Wolfe, D. H. Lawrence, and Faulkner's novels: each led to other writers. With Henry Miller, I was moved more by his passionate enthusiasm for writers such as Céline, Giono, Hamsun, and Rimbaud than the infamous sex scenes that (after eagerly reading, of course) I sensed lacked true feeling, and were, finally, forced and mechanical.

A special favorite was Joseph Conrad's *Heart of Darkness,* in which I read, like an invitation to a voyage:

> I watched the coast. Watching a coast as it slips by the ship is like thinking about an enigma. There it is before you—smiling, frowning, inviting, grand, mean, insipid, or savage, and always mute with an air of whispering, "Come and find out."

Several years later, I would be drawn by that and other descriptions by Conrad of his journey up the Congo River:

> Going up that river was like traveling back to the earliest beginnings of the world, when vegetation rioted on the earth and the big trees were kings. An empty stream, a great silence, an impenetrable forest.

But it wasn't in the library or in school that I first came upon the work that spoke most to me at the time with great urgency. It happened by chance: one afternoon, while sitting in a doctor's waiting room, I noticed on a nearby table a small leather-bound volume, its brown cover nearly as dark as the wood paneling in the room. It was *The Essays of Ralph Waldo Emerson.* Opening it at random, I came upon "Self-Reliance" and wherever in it I read was so peppered with rousing positivism, I felt I was hearing the hidden side of my own inner voice:

A man should learn to detect and watch that gleam of light which flashes across his mind from within, more than the lustre of the firmament of bards and sages. Yet he dismisses without notice his thought, because it is his. In every work of genius we recognize our own rejected thoughts: they come back to us with a certain alienated majesty . . .

Wherever in it you looked, each and every phrase contained the spirit of the whole:

Trust thyself. . . . Society is a joint-stock company, in which the members agree, for the better securing of his bread to each shareholder, to surrender the liberty and culture of the eater. The virtue in most request is conformity. Self-reliance is its aversion. . . . Whoso would be a man must be a nonconformist . . .

This was curative. For whatever reason I had come to that doctor's office, I left feeling healthier, fortified, and far more buoyant than I had before. Whatever license I may have lacked, I would take from Emerson, a true soul-healer.

One high school English teacher, Miss McDermott, was encouraging when I'd show her poems I'd written, usually on the train to my job in the city. Hackneyed, fuzzy poems of love and longing, I doubt she knew I'd written them with her in mind. Well-groomed and dressed in a conservative, fashionable manner, Miss McDermott had her gray-streaked hair regularly cut straight across her brow and at her shoulders. In private, her look of concern and interest made her attractive face, in class usually undemonstrative, even more animated and engaging. I'd bring her a poem I'd written in longhand; she'd read it, offer praise, and say that she'd show it to a male friend, a critic for a professional journal. A few days later she'd report that he, too, liked the poem and that I should continue writing. Which I did, and which, for the time being, added to the store of poems she herself had inspired.

CHAPTER TWENTY-SEVEN

CHA-CHA-CHA: DANCE LESSONS

Off the corner of Bay Parkway and 72nd Street, around the corner from my Aunt Becky's house, lived one of my friends, Louie Shrem. Directly across the street was Seth Low Park. On Saturday nights, we'd drop into a popular ice cream parlor, the Chocolate Cove, with its cushioned booths no clubhouse could compare to, and its festive, frantic make-out atmosphere, to meet our friends and check out the girls. Like us, the girls clustered in groups and, from their intimately shared giggles and gossip, you sensed they intended to stay together, if necessary, for social protection, the rest of the evening. Obligatory greetings and ambiguous exchanges were traded, and if not enough erotic charge was generated just then, further mingling would be left for another time.

Afterwards, we'd usually end up at Louie's apartment and spend the rest of the evening playing cards. Blackjack and poker were the house games. Louie and Al Safdie were the leaders in first coaxing, then coaching the rest of us how to play. What I learned from them, though, was how good they were at bluffing. They were experts, seeming to possess an innate talent for dropping false leads and showing sham alarm; throughout the game their faces would have such a look of confidence I couldn't tell the difference between their pretense and their assured, "Hit me!"

A poor bluffer and face-reader, I'd often dismiss my first impression as too improbable or suspicious, or ascribe motives to a look where there later proved to be none; trusting when I should have been wary; doubting my judgment when I should have trusted my instinct. But, as I soon learned, instinct wasn't to be trusted either, nor was judgment (at least not mine) an accurate reader of the hand showing or of the facedown card waiting to be played. I hated being rushed while trying to consider the possible combinations of the cards I held, as the others would rush me to make a call, which confused me even more (obviously its purpose), and would unnerve me into a too-quick call. Maybe that was the problem: that I was trying to figure it out, rather than to play the way someone like Al or Louie did, out of a well of confidence that the single-minded seem to possess, as if ordained, for well or ill.

Sometimes the thirst for profit would turn into blood lust, especially on long muggy nights, and we'd play "knucks," where the loser of a game would have to make a fist and hold it palm down as the winner, grasping the full deck, would slam it down *hard*—edge first!—against the loser's exposed knuckles. Worse, at times the penalty would be the tight deck slowly, surgically, card-edge-by-edge, scraped like saw blades down the white, raw knuckles before the final down-chopping hammer-blow drew blood.

Otherwise, so intent were we to align our kings, queens, jacks, and aces, so engrossed in the magic of divining the next card in the deck, or wishing it forth out of a shuffle, that we at first didn't notice Louie's older sisters moving quietly in and out of the room.

They'd appear from their bedrooms, as if from an inner seraglio; they were getting ready for their dates to arrive. We'd be playing a hand, and in they'd saunter (it was their house!), wearing a robe or a slip, their shampooed hair wrapped in a towel, and start to tease us with disparaging remarks about our manhood. As girls with younger brothers in the house, there wasn't much they didn't know about our ways. In the competition for husbands, having brothers was an advantage in acquiring foreknowledge of male inclinations.

Each *bee-jenen* (Arabic, "gorgeous") one of them was the cream of Syrian genes: olive skin in the prime of voluptuous bloom, dark-eyed brunettes, all three, each younger one more beautiful than her predecessor, making the youngest, Louisa, the prettiest and most playful, my favorite.

If sexual allure is the carrot held out on the stick of marriage, Louie's sisters were straight caroteen, unadulterated Vitamin A, pure sunshine.

How often they were met with the cry (incredulous, dazzled—struck!—by the sight of such beauty) *"Yah-aaeneey* (O my eyes)!"

The dating scene was such that, for status and marriage availability, young teenage girls went out most often with older men. Since Louie's sisters were in their late teens and early twenties, the men they dated were in their late twenties and early thirties. But in the boasting of inexperienced boys, the slogan bandied about girls was summed up in the credo of the 4-F Club: "Find 'em, feel 'em, fuck 'em, forget 'em," and our success with the first was as scant as our chance to practice the rest.

Trying not to stare at a friend's sister while she's dressing for a date is not easy, calling for concentration the equal of playing a game of cards: neither can be done casually. Coming into the room as they did, in mid-makeup, wrapped in a towel or half-undressed, unconcerned about our presence, soon created an atmosphere of easygoing intimacy between us, much like brothers and sisters. One of them would lean over, teasingly swelling out of her bra, and suggest we stop wasting time playing cards and learn to dance as a way of meeting girls. When we showed no interest, they'd flippantly suggest we play this or that card. Then, standing back, they'd watch us a moment, mutter something trenchantly caustic about our gutlessness, and leave. They were a veritable live-in charm school wasted on the likes of us.

When I'd try to refocus on the cards, I'd find that I had no talent for playing hunches, or bluffs, or reading faces. Playing poker took me longer to see a possible sequence of cards I could arrange and hold ready in my hand than it took the others to figure out a strategy they were, by their looks and gestures, already putting into motion. The key to successful bluffing seemed to be in the conviction that whatever hand you held was, or could be turned into, a winning hand, no matter what the odds. A show of confidence—even obvious overconfidence—worked, finally, to undermine an opponent's will, like a general uncaring about casualties as long as a plan was boldly executed. Clearly, I was no general.

Meanwhile Louie, assisted by the continual distraction his sisters provided, cashed in. If I were a conspiracy hound, I might assume they were diversions in Louie's strategy; but, if so, they were worth it, and his ploy had earned him his winnings.

Al, the suave, make-out man of our group, also had the knack for quick calculation, and constantly won big. Al was living proof that timidity held no appeal for girls our age: they were interested in boys and young men who were self-assured.

Al's soft auburn hair, fair skin with a bit of residual baby fat plumping his smooth cheeks showing no sign they'd ever need shaving, his slightly pouting lips—features that in his twin sister were positively pretty—were a magnet for girls.

Repeatedly, he'd draw a comb out of his back pocket and study his reflection in a store window or a parked car's mirror and run it casually through his hair, smoothing the "duck's ass" tuft at the base of his neck. He dressed in slacks and fitted sport shirts—beige, tan, ochre, ecru—all with his monogram imprinted in fancy letters on the front pocket. Cashmere was his favorite fabric: his sweaters, jackets, even coats were made of the soft material. For comfort, on his splayed, flat feet he wore loafers with tassels, a shiny copper penny in the slot of the shoe-top.

Al's pick up method was to approach a single or a group of girls on the street or in the park and, smiling as he passed, whisper something in one of their ears, and as if by magic he'd get a phone number. His manner, friendly yet persistent, must have flattered the girls to be chosen by so single-minded a suitor. He plied his skill like a trade. Whatever needed saying, he'd say. The rest of us hung back. The turmoil of our own overeagerness to "score" derailed us, while experts like Al, who "made it," didn't seem to press their urgency on a girl because their experience allowed the girl's attraction, perhaps not yet evident to herself, to be stirred.

Still, there was one social grace that even Al lacked, knowing how to dance.

One Saturday night, in however much time we took to notice, Louie's sisters entered the room with big-hooped curlers in their hair and still half-dressed, muttering how cowardly we were, hiding behind cards. Even with only modest daubs of lipstick, blush, and mascara they were vivacious and vibrant. They were trying to be more helpful than we deserved. Their intention that we teenage dolts learn to dance for our own benefit had taken on the zeal of a mission, and that they would convert us should have been obvious.

Why couldn't girls our own age be as caring and helpful? Girls in their teens—however unintentionally, unknowingly (if that were possible)—were emanating waves of sexual allure. For what other purpose were the eye-liner, rouge, lipstick, perfume, not to mention the tight-fitting sweaters and sack dresses? They could give off the scent while acting as though they weren't doing anything of the kind.

Preoccupied with our cards, killing time, we'd look up and see Louie's sisters "dressed to kill" and "good enough to eat." We had mistaken their presence at this late hour for their not having dates. Not so; as it turned out, they were on what was referred to as "S.Y. (Syrian) time": the time it took for a Syrian girl to "get in the mood" and ready to show up at a party.

This ritual took long-considered preparation: applying layers of makeup, scanning her wardrobe, selecting, then slipping into an outfit no one had seen her in, and, in no hurry, finally heading out, and as if in just passing by, come upon the party by chance on her way to some other social event in her evening's full schedule, and drop in for a minute.

If a party was announced for 8:00 p.m., "Syrian time" in effect meant more like 11:00 p.m. at the earliest. To make oneself scarce, "hard to get," not to appear eager, was the norm. Since arriving early betrayed being "hard up," to maintain their status of exclusivity, girls did their utmost to show up last. And boys did the same.

One Saturday night, hunched over our cards, we noticed all of Louie's sisters had finished dressing early. Their dates hadn't arrived yet. At that time in the early fifties, Syrian girls wore large rings, jangling bracelets, hoop earrings, heavy eye shadow and lipstick: the full treatment.

The sisters came in, in full regalia, hovered over us, then announced that it was time we learned to dance, especially the mambo, the craze of the time. They would teach us.

Dismissing our usual grumbling and moaning, Louisa put a new Tito Puente record on the turntable; its opening brass blare silenced our protest with a visceral thumping of trumpet calls that shook our solar plexi, spreading up from the floor, into our legs and thighs, "carrying" us off, with conga drums pulsating like tree trunks in syncopated rhythms. The girls pulled us up toward their swaying hips, bobbing breasts, and undulating shoulders, and onto our feet. In the presence of such lively girls, you knew instinctively that the intensity of desiring them could determine your happiness—or unhappiness—from then on.

Our first impression of the mambo's dance steps was confusion and impossible intricacy. We protested; it was too difficult, we'd never get it, we weren't interested. They wouldn't give up.

Taking the male partner's lead, they showed us a basic three-step for both the mambo and rhumba: legs apart, left foot lifts, swings one step back, then right foot lifts, steps back, then left foot back again, all along keeping knees bent, a flexible hinge; then, as variations or "breaks," the same steps taken forward, sideways, or in a circular motion.

"Wherever the rhythm leads, you go," said Louisa. That was it. Simple. Anyone could pick up in minutes what we, from arrogance, had put off for so long. Dance was a response to rhythm's visceral summons. It became clear why music—especially dance music—and even more so, Latin music—was considered by the Orthodox "profane": limbs eased and stirred to further arousal, more sensuous movement.

The doorbell rang. Their dates had arrived. We were on our own.

And, on our own, practice with the basic step gave us a sense of confidence, and we were hooked. We began seeking parties to which, invited or not, we'd show up—I, in a gray-spotted jacket of soft cloth, with a bar of black velvet on each shoulder and a tie-belt at the waist that I got into the habit of nervously tightening before a dance, to feel compact, focused. I had bought the jacket on 42nd Street after seeing one like it on a tall guy with light-brown skin, the leader of a bunch of older guys, who walked into a party we had crashed one evening. This fellow wore large dark glasses and sported a miniature Vandyke tuft on his chin.

As soon as they walked through the door, as if welcomed, they dominated the floor with the expertness of their moves to which the girls gave themselves, gladly, without hesitation.

It didn't feel like they were trying to cut anybody out—least of all us—they were concentrated on having a good time dancing with these new friendly girls they had chanced upon. You could tell from their expressions and smooth movements that they, too, were carried away by the music. You couldn't begrudge them their luck. Vandyke was the happiest of the bunch, as he alternately grinned and grimaced in the throes of swaying, dipping, breaking, spinning, all the while leading with his tufted chin suggestively stuck out under the red hue of Chinese lanterns glinting off his dark shades. His quick-changing elated expression returns to me now, looking as if he were mugging for posterity, his beard like that of a Sphinx, while the rest of him is a whirling dervish in memory's perpetual motion.

There was no shortage of girls standing around, eager to dance, in bright, clinging dresses, skin flushed and glowing with erotic antici-pation. We hit the dance floor accompanied by whichever girl grasped our outstretched hand and followed our lead, matching our moves, copying the breaks we initiated and on which they improvised at a signal tap-and-step away, then rejoined us in a hand-clasp and summary twirl at the end.

Exhausted afterwards, standing between records, our sweat was a slick balm cooling us with a film of earned languor.

In the early fifties we knew nothing of drugs; beer and liquor were the sole intoxicants available, at least to our group. Once tasted, though, dancing became a "high." We couldn't get enough of how moving to music enhanced our pleasure and confidence. We grew accomplished at the rhumba and mambo. There was another dance, the merengue, whose jerky, side-to-side moves were said to have been created to accommodate a Latin American dictator's peg leg. We'd go tottering through its staccato movements like spastic clowns.

When rumor of a party reached us via the grapevine of sisters, cousins, friends, or schoolmates, we'd interrogate them further for names and addresses, and, on the given night, after a decent amount of time passed to prove we weren't overly eager, we'd show up at the door behind which a din of laughter and chatter roared, music blared, and couples danced.

Our enthusiasm once had us make a bad call: after hearing about a sweet sixteen party in the neighborhood one Saturday night, we showed up at the door. Since I happened to be in front, I rang the bell, which was answered by members of the school football team standing in a scrimmage line. It looked like they were expecting us. When the squat lineman in front refused to let us in, as we stood, hesitating, considering our options, they swept into action. The point man, directly facing me, reached for my right arm, grabbed it in both hands and swung me rolling across his hip and over his bent-forward head in a somersault, landing me flat on my back, and shut the door.

After that, we asked more specific questions about who might be attending any parties we heard about.

CHAPTER TWENTY-EIGHT

ESSENCE OF AUTOMAT, EAU DE HORN & HARDART

From early on, I regarded retail stores as theaters, their display windows as stages, and their personnel as ushers and actors in the competitive drama called "making a sale." This sense extended from local clothing and appliance stores on the street I lived on to the high-line fashion emporiums of New York City, like Macy's, Gimbels, Saks, and Bergdorf Goodman.

Among Syrians, it was an in-group joke that an S.Y. store had only two notable days: a "Grand Opening Sale" (announced by a large, ornate-lettered sign left in the window for years), replaced one day by an even splashier sign, "Going Out of Business" (often displayed for decades).

My first job was as a part-time stock boy for Massur Bros., a fine linens shop on the corner of 5th Avenue and 48th Street. After my classes at Lafayette High School were over, I'd take the train to Manhattan, get off at 8th Avenue and Forty-Second Street and amble down to the nearby Horn & Hardart Automat. As soon as you opened the door, the thick smell of burnt gravy and overcooked meat enveloped you. I'd stand in front of the glassed cubicles and check out the display dishes, each one set on its shelf behind glass—the savory, stick-to-your-ribs baked beans; the cup of rice pudding sprinkled with cinnamon; the deep-dish macaroni and cheese, its edge baked crispy brown; the gravy-smothered Swiss steak (among my favorites)—and drop into the slots the exact number of nickels to open their doors.

There'd be several elderly men and women at a table, chatting, their cups of coffee or tea covered by a dish, and a thin, balding man alone at another table who'd glance up from his Yiddish newspaper, eye me a moment, then return to his reading. For all I knew, one of the men could have been Isaac Bashevis Singer in his favorite haunt, cooking up a bit of devilry for his next juicy tale.

Sometimes, postponing my snack until nearer my destination, I'd stop off at the Chock-Full-O-Nuts on the corner of 45th Street and 6th Avenue and, for thirty-five cents, have a tuna sandwich or cream cheese on raisin-nut bread, but I most looked forward to the coffee, more full-bodied than any I'd tasted.

At the time, I gave no thought to the workers' long hours, the minimum wages of the mostly black women serving at the counters, but from their expressionless faces I could have guessed what it felt like to be on their feet for hours, catering to the whims of testy customers rushing to work, or prolonging a break, or of shoppers resting between bargain hunting, lazing on their stools while customers standing behind them waited.

FRUITS OF THE TREE OF KNOWLEDGE

Often having time before I needed to show up for work, I'd head down toward 5th Avenue to the public library with its imperially wide white marble steps flanked by oversized stone lions, one paw raised as if a signal for your attention.

My destination was the main reading room, where almost any book or publication in existence could be requested for reference, but not checked out. Inside the spacious, high-ceilinged room, patrons sat in carved chairs, delving into books piled before them under the shaded glow of lamps on the long polished wooden tables. The overhead side walls were embedded with books that a ladder on rollers made accessible to attendants.

The entire room felt like a sanctuary dedicated to the idea that the uninterrupted labor of reading all the writing ever written would eventually put mankind's unanswered questions to rest.

I read there, thirsty as a castaway at a free tap, tracking down in obscure literary journals arcane interpretations of "difficult" poets like Hart Crane, (lovely, nimble name), which were more cryptic than the poetry they presumed to interpret. And even after much scholarly explication, I was not convinced that Crane's ambitious "The Bridge" (his strained bid for an American epic poem to rival T. S. Eliot's "The Waste Land") contained his most moving poetry, but rather his shorter lyrics struck me with their condensed poignancy: "Where the cedar leaf divides the sky . . . / I was promised an improved infancy," and, "There is a world dimensional for those untwisted by the love of things irreconcilable." What fascinated me was the precision of perception and emotion fused into images like these.

On my way from the library to my job, I'd stop at the newspaper kiosk around the corner and look over the new magazines and journals clipped to the side panels for display, with a handwritten "No Reading" sign to discourage loiterers.

I'd pick a *Partisan, Kenyon,* or *Sewanee* review and scan its contents for new work by Robert Lowell, whose majestic *Lord Weary's Castle* (with such jaw-breaking poems as "The Quaker Graveyard in Nantucket") had earlier dazzled me, and whose new, scaled-down, radically vernacular poems were beginning to appear and would later be included in *Life Studies.* I also wanted to follow what John Berryman was up to after his syntactically knotted *Mistress Bradstreet*, then the whacky, wrenching poems of *His Thoughts Made Pockets and the Plane Buckt*, which intrigued me with the increasingly bizarre breakdown into manic slang and heckling jive most recently spewing from Huffy Henry and his black-faced badger, Mr. Bones, in *The Dream Songs.*

Invariably, I'd get so caught up reading, I was unaware of Arnie, the owner, a bear-like man in his three-sided den, his eyes telescoped to gaping distortion by thick lenses, growing annoyed behind the counter, having to keep a lookout for "hangers."

In winter, with earmuffs pulled over a seaman's cap, and wrapped in layers of bulky sweaters and elbow-patched coats, he'd stamp his feet while making change with woolen gloves cut off at the fingertips. Perhaps out of some grudging empathy for my adolescent curiosity, or maybe just relieved that I wasn't pestering him for a closer look at the tabloids and porno magazines, he'd let me read for a few minutes, then, feeling his hovering stare, I'd return the journal to its clip.

One time, losing patience, he came from his stall and, straightening out the journal tree, asked sarcastically, "Studying? This is not Newsstand University. If you were a serious student you'd buy something." He was right; I was a dabbler, not serious enough for a sale.

RABBIT, I PRESUME?

On 5th Avenue, one day I noticed in among the passing crowd a man standing still, undistracted by the people milling around, his attention concentrated on one of the upper floors of a skyscraper, then lowering his head to jot in a pad in his hand. As he bobbed his head up and down, taking notes, I noticed a prominent feature of his angular face: his rather large, upstanding ears: they seemed familiar, resembling . . . what? who? What was I trying to recall? Then I realized, and before I could check myself, approaching him as he lifted his head up again, scanning some high cornice or facade against the sky, I blurted out, "Aren't you John Updike?" Surprised, with pencil poised, he looked at me. I was aware that what I had just said sounded more like a reminder of who he was than a question. "How did you know?" he asked, and though I could see he was genuinely puzzled, his question seemed oddly, but touchingly, naïve, for it was apparent to me that the first writer I had ever met, now standing before me, had described his own features in his first novel, *Rabbit, Run,* which I had just read, a physical self-portrait so accurate, in such detail (not all that flattering, and with the visual aid of a back cover photo) that even in a crowd on New York's bustling 5th Avenue he would stand out, unmistakable.

ZIFT (FILTH) AVENUE

Making my way through crowds and traffic, the closer I got to my job, the more men's attire grew stylish, continental, subdued. With their fingernails manicured and with shaven plump jowls, the pampered faces of executives glowed, tanned out of season by sunlamps in barber shops and private clubs; and women, drawn from the fashion capitals of the world, looked exclusively dressed, as if having sworn their couturiers to secrecy.

Flitting through the crowd went ponytailed, muscle-calved showgirls and dancers with leather bags slung over their shoulders, bouncing on their toes; pale, thin models swinging oversized black portfolios almost reaching the ground were tall enough not to meet most men's stares, scoping above their heads the distance they had to cover to their next shoot, their next contract, their next career, striding with that handy portfolio's side-sweeping snowplow motion, steady of eye and undeterred as teamsters.

One day I saw a vision on 5th Avenue: a young Indian woman wearing an embroidered scarlet vest and nearly sheer white pantaloons that hugged her swift ankles, fluttering through the mass of people across the street, darting like a butterfly through a herd. Her flowing movement, juxtaposed against men and women's business suits, seemed intercut from another time, another tempo. I was reminded of a travel poster on the window of the Air India office a few blocks away that showed a close-up of an exotic woman with a red dot on her brow; below it read: "Once you have been to India, India will always be with you." Later on I would come upon a lovely capsule description in a poem by Randall Jarrell: "The saris go by me from the embassies . . ."

Money promotes confidence, and confidence promotes more money. And where there is more money (as much as you can afford) there is more of God's blessing. On my way to work, on the corner of 49th and 5th Avenue, stood St. Patricks Cathedral. Passing it, I'd be struck by the vaulting, arched stonework and pink facade, and feel weighted down by the sheer sovereign tonnage. In that material volume in space, time was held, fast-frozen: authority cast in awesome weight. God looked *down*; judgment *fell*. Only the pillars of the church stood between.

The edifice also served to enhance the value of the avenue it presided over, not the least of which happened to include the real estate it occupied, tax-free; the ultimate bonus all other commercial enterprises could only wish for, with coffers that kept silent, eyes closed.

For the shops and businesses nearby, having such a distinguished architectural landmark as a neighbor must have lent legitimacy and bestowed privileged dispensation on the commercial enterprises under its wings, giving added blessed meaning to "location, location, location."

At the time, the archdiocese was officiated over by the renowned dumpling-shaped Cardinal Spellman, about whom we were hearing rumors: late-night escapades of the cardinal and J. Edgar Hoover changing into drag and makeup in the vestry and slipping through a back door for an evening of cruising gay and s & m bars on the upper West Side. From church to the clip joint I worked in was only a few steps.

The store was ideally situated to attract high-end clientele. It stood across the street from Rockefeller Center with its towering Atlas bearing the weight of the globe on his alloyed shoulders. Distinguished corporate names were listed in expensive lettering alongside the banks of elevators manned by operators whose gold-braided uniforms lent them the appearance of admirals.

My bosses, brothers Fred and Ralph Massur, hired me as a favor to my Uncle Al, who, as their wholesaler, was using his influence on my mother's behalf. I was to work from three to seven on weekday afternoons; Saturday was excluded since I claimed that I was a *sho'mer Shabbat* (Sabbath observer), which, at that point, was no longer true. I had been observant before they hired me, but had since abandoned religious practice. My new bosses did not know that, nor would they have cared except that I was, in fact, available to work on Saturdays, but I preferred the day off rather than working at a job I had not chosen and found dull. I had acquiesced solely for the pay (a pittance), of which the larger portion I handed over to my mother to help with household expenses, and what was left I kept for my own use. The work was numbingly monotonous. While working at this job, I began to sense that unless I could own my time, I'd be subject to the demands of others.

My duties consisted mainly of sorting and rearranging merchandise, refolding linens after a salesman displayed them to a customer, dusting shelves, "delousing" (code word for removing the telltale labels that, in the early fifties, were tiny flags betraying their cheap manufacture) the "Made in Japan" or "Made in China" items, and wiping down the glass showcases in which delicate linens from Madeira and scalloped Philippine pillowcases were on display.

When out-of-towners bought items they didn't want to carry in their luggage, I'd take them upstairs to the packing room and wrap, box, and ship them to their home address. I felt less as if I were killing time than time was killing me, slowly.

The monotony, along with Fred's surliness, made the hours more enforced. Although both brothers were well-groomed, nails buffed, fitted in classic Italian shirts with large cuffs, and suit jackets with the trapdoor flap in back, Fred, the older by a few years, was usually sullen and easily made irritable. He wouldn't suffer anyone, including customers, disagreeing with or even questioning the high value he placed on his merchandise: this, close up, was theater.

Several times during the day, he'd splash on cologne even though he hadn't shaved, and light up a cigar, so that your sense of smell was drawn or repelled in opposite directions. He'd sprinkle rose water on his thinning hair and comb it severely back in twin flat shiny wings. Leaning back in his Tudor chair near the cash register, a pasha puffing on a Panama rica, he would eye a customer who'd just entered, give them a grin of mock solicitude, and continue grooming, an actor getting ready to go on stage.

In his case, getting ready meant being "on." He'd let them wander around a while, to be impressed by the expensive, exotic merchandise on display. He'd act as if he were doing them a favor even allowing them to browse in his private domain so that they could gradually realize they had wandered into a haven of fulfillment even more precious than what they had dreamed of shopping for—and with no admission charge.

Only after one of the salesmen had sold them some small item, or failed to, sensing some lurking opportunity still unfulfilled, Fred would speak up from behind his cloud of smoke. Barely able to restrain his innate condescension, he'd first flatter the customer for their obvious knowledge of the merchandise in hand, then begin filling in the gaps in their knowledge: the finest tight weave of Irish linen handkerchiefs, the exquisite detail in the lace-embroidered tablecloths handcrafted in the Canary Islands over which nuns so painstakingly labored, devoting as much time to their work as to their prayers, so that they "finally went blind from stitching."

If that didn't work, he'd grow progressively more disdainful, bordering on belligerence, and then beyond, as the customer angling toward the door would suddenly get an invective earful of Fred's aesthetic:

"So, *dibbo* (idiot) you think you know everything about fine art because you've been to the Metropolitan and some hot galleries on Madison Avenue? You think you know? *Yin'aal-aboook!* (Arabic slur), *mab'tif'hahm shee* (you don't know anything). Museums are automats of art! Listen, learn something, *dib hamor* (idiot donkey). True art gets its hands dirty, and I'm not talking about the crap they hang on walls and label with self-important titles nobody understands. And the more they don't understand, the more they line up because they think they should understand what they're charged admission to stare at. What a racket! No, real art is made to be used and passed on, not hung like a carcass on a wall. Beauty has no price. Not for sale. I didn't buy these things," waving his cigar to include the finery on the walls and behind the glass cases. Confidence, like wealth, billowed from the rank smoke he wove in the air. "I was given them by my ancestors. See those Bakhara carpets back there?" aiming the ashen tip at a pile of rugs I had just the other day uncrated and deloused from a Japanese supplier, and trailing an acrid cloud, he'd continue, "The finest natural dyes pressed in and woven by children's hands and maidens. These Madeiras? Made on Cape Verde?" Pause. "You know where is Cape Verde?"

I noticed the way he often liked switching English words around like that, seemingly clumsy, like an immigrant, but actually just in play, or to tease the customer into thinking he might have an advantage with this "yokel." *"Eh-naak-phee-teezahkk* (Your eyes are in your ass)," he'd mumble under his breath, slipping under the customer's radar with Arabic slurs he'd throw in as bonbons to amuse the salesmen standing around, eyes averted, straight-faced, hands to their mouths.

He was far from caring about making a sale; selling wasn't the point anymore; humiliation was . . . which had to be oiled first by utter disdain. "Do you know who are my ancestors?" Pause. Silence. "Pashas." Pause. "From Aleppo. You know Aleppo? You know where is Damascus? You know why Queen Sheba crossed a desert to meet King Solomon? You know history?" Seated, aiming the glowing ash at the man—men got this treatment, which he enjoyed prolonging; with a woman he wouldn't bother, he'd just call them *sharmootah* (whore), and wave them out the door—with a man he'd take his time. "Believe me I'm not trying to sell anything. I wouldn't part with it for your money . . . but for love . . ." He trailed off. "But if you loved it, I mean really loved it, I'd give you . . . free. But first a little humility, please. Let's not confuse the viewer with the view: we can be gone tomorrow," his hand cut across his throat, "have a stroke in the *tesh'-maeh* (toilet), but beauty remains. Beauty doesn't care who possesses it; only that it be possessed . . . and by one who knows how to appreciate it. What's a beautiful woman without an admirer? A statue. A view without a viewer, right, *dib?* The finest art is not made to hang on museum walls, it's to be used each ordinary day. That's what makes it extraordinary. It takes time to plant and grow what will be spun into fiber and the fiber into threads and the threads into fabric embroidered with such exquisite delicacy no spiderweb can compare, no snowflake equal. The silkworm spits out . . ." pause, "what my ancestors, would weave . . ." pause, "fit for a king's table," as he pointed out a large ornate dinner table across the aisle. "You can make a reproduction of a painting and enjoy it almost as much as the original, but each of my things is one of a kind." Folding his arms imperiously across his chest, he'd mug the pout-lipped, monkey-faced grimace of Mussolini on the balcony in Rome, cheered by the throng below.

Entertained, intrigued, and insulted all at once, most male customers shrugged or stared ahead, their irritation stalled, wondering what might come next. "I don't need your money. I'm trying to open your eyes to a beauty too exquisite to need you to own it. You don't deserve it," he'd shout, feigned annoyance by now turned real, and order the man out.

In summer, during school vacation, I worked full-time and got to know Fred in a more revealing mode. I'd be waiting when he'd arrive at 9:00 a.m., driven to the curb in a black Cadillac by his zaftic, dark-eyed Syrian wife. And though the store was air-conditioned, after he opened, he'd lock up again and peel off the expensive shirt already soaked in perspiration. I would take it to his favorite men's store on Madison Avenue and buy another one exactly like it for which I'd pay with cash he took out of the register. Bare-chested, he'd wait till I returned to open again, or, sometimes while I was gone his brother arrived (also in a Cadillac with an even younger, more beautiful wife) and Fred waited for me upstairs in the cramped stockroom, not his favorite place to spend time.

A couple of doors away was a tiny, cramped eatery that could barely fit a counter much less standees, where I'd stop and get him his favorite sandwich for lunch: cream cheese and black olives on rye bread. The lone man working the counter, a lanky Texan, with tattooed arms briskly working on several orders at once, was the fastest, most efficient short-order cook I ever saw.

A virtuoso of quick moves in such a tight space, his precise pirouettes and chest contractions to avoid collisions, like a matador side-stepping the bull, were a phenomena to behold. Even as he was busy frying eggs, stirring pancake batter, flipping hamburgers on the grill, retrieving French fries out of their wire basket from boiling oil, slicing vegetables, topping a plate of tuna salad with garnish, he'd be responding to his boss's yelled orders to "Burn the British!" (toasted English muffins) or "Fudge the French!" (top vanilla ice cream with chocolate syrup). This was theater I found worth attending, and would linger there as long as I thought I could before provoking Fred's suspicions.

Fred's younger brother, more slender, and as elegantly dressed, Ralph, was soft-spoken, even diffident in his dealings with customers and sales help. More fastidious than his brother, Ralph was cautious, anxious about small details, minor worries to which Fred never seemed to give a second thought, such as treating civilly the customers, the salespeople, and me.

One of the freelance salespeople, Iris, offered relief from Fred's vulgarity. Thin, unmarried, middle-aged, Iris bobbed her gray-streaked hair so she would appear younger; her pale, tired face showed the strain of having been through similar experiences in other stores she'd worked in on the avenue. She treated customers with patience and respect, and to pass the time more aesthetically perhaps, she'd put on a small performance. Bringing out from the showcase a delicate handkerchief in which a customer had shown a passing interest, she'd carefully unfold and stand its four lace corners like a tent on the glass countertop where it would resemble a flower, a snowflake, a butterfly's wings, for a moment. She'd look over at me with her wry, weary smile, as if to say "Gotta put on a show," and allow the customer to take it in.

She stayed on for a couple of months, then apparently not earning enough (she, like the other salespeople, was hired on commission), was let go. Given her age, there was not much chance she went on to greener pastures. Within the year, with less need for my services (never much in the first place), I, too, was laid off.

SELLING, THE ART OF SEDUCTION

Through friends and family connections, I got jobs at other stores further down the food chain on 42nd Street, as stockboy and salesman (apprentice). It was relatively easy selling the miniature Japanese cameras featured in the show window as loss leaders for ninety-nine cents. In fact, they sold themselves. I thought I was doing great until I realized what I was selling like hotcakes . . . *were* hotcakes!—pilfered off some freighter at the docks. They could afford to be given away—

no loss there. I soon realized that, without pushing harder, I was not much of a salesman, nor did I aspire to be.

Once a Brazilian sailor came in and asked the reason for the big difference in price between two porno movies featured in the window, to which one of the salesmen replied, "Two strokes."

What I did learn working there was: walk into a store and you're fair game for the hunters leaning on the counters, or playing cards in the back, waiting to "T.O." (take over). Top salesmen, "clip men," roving freelancers to the highest bidder, were made overtures (behind the scenes, at a bar mitzvah or a wedding or in shul) and hijacked by rival store owners, bribed to break their verbal contract (nothing was written down or legally binding), moving from store to store, like itinerant, high-priced gypsies (depending on their current reputation) on that expensive and "fashionable" (the word hugs you to its cushy bosom) strip of high-rent real estate. From the swankiest, perfume-misted department store to the tiniest hole-in-the-wall coffee shop wedged between a building's front entrance and its neighbor's freight exit, location in the right areas (no matter the rent) brought high visibility and foot traffic, which meant sales. Arts, antiques, clothes, carpets, handbags, jewelry, linens, were magnets for the charge accounts of wives of bank managers and executives, who strolled and shopped while waiting for their husbands to finish work and take them to dinner and a show. Attractive, expensively outfitted, and well-coiffed, these young and middle-aged women, with the flair of showgirls, would saunter into the stores.

For women, especially those with leisure and charge accounts, shopping was more than a functional business transaction; it was adventure. The closer blew the whiff of the romantic, the better and more to be desired. During those years I worked on both 5th Avenue and 42nd Street, and, especially during the summer, you'd hear stories about mothers and their daughters being bedded and "shtooped" by the resident "C-man" (cocksman) on the piled Persian rugs in the back or in the basement, either in exchange for some item they fancied and couldn't or wouldn't pay for (perhaps the very rug they were bedded on), or for the daring escapade.

What went on when their husbands came home? ("Hi, hon, guess what *we* did today!") Or was it all a lie? After all, I never saw pictures, but I do recall seeing some young and middle-aged women reappear from the basement with grins on their flushed faces, carrying a small rug rolled up under their arm, or clutching their handbag as they wove, a tad wobbly, out the door.

The T.O. was often used on women customers. On completing the sale of a small item, like a handkerchief or a piece of costume jewelry, the salesman, backing off and giving his cue, would smoothly pass the customer on to a veteran clip-man who, all smiles, with shooting cuffs, took over, drawing the woman's interest to a more expensive item, and in gradual stages cajoled her, catering to her inborn desire "for the best." For the major maxim in the unwritten manual of salesmanship is that in every person—no matter how plebeian—there lurks an aristocrat waiting for a chance to acquire (at a big discount, of course) what they have always secretly craved.

If neither this nor other usual techniques succeeded in clinching the sale, there was the self-effacing fallback (such as when a potentially high-end customer was about to "B.O.," or "back out") to at first a subtle, then if need be, gradually unashamed appeal for help in saving the business that, contrary to appearances, was on the verge of bankruptcy. If that ploy failed, the salesman would finally abandon all pretense of self-respect and descend to shameless pleading, falling to his knees and working himself up to a show of tears, throwing himself on the mercy of the horrified woman who'd suddenly find herself being beseeched, and at whose expensively shod feet this miserable wretch was laying his heart-wrenching case: his family was facing eviction (in fact he lived alone), his wife (he was a bachelor) was threatening to leave him, his children (he had none) were in need of food and clothing. Somehow the shock of tears and the aching, breaking, bereaved voice would so unnerve and frazzle the woman who, in an instant elevated from matronly housewife to beneficent monarch, had no chance to think before her maternal instinct somehow impelled her into signing a generous check for the rescue of the beggar with the expensive Alencon lace or Madeira tablecloth thrown over his head, prostrate before her, trembling as if in a grand operatic tragedy from which she, only she, and her open purse of a heart, could save him.

After being signaled to lock the front door, I had witnessed such scenes on several occasions. Often the woman would be offered, and accept, a quality blue label scotch, whiskey, or brandy kept especially for such occasions; after some time had passed, she'd be approached by (and accept) slippery hands, lips, tongue—to lubricate the touchy art of checkbook seduction.

Once, after such a sale closed, and the check was safely in the register, and the staggering woman, after straightening her clothes, was ushered out the door to a waiting cab back to her hotel, the boss warned the salesman (more ecstatic about the large commission he'd just earned than his near-consummated sexual exploit) against following the woman to her hotel, which address he knew since he had called the cab. She had mentioned that her husband was out-of-town overnight.

The following morning, before the check could be taken to the bank, the woman's husband showed up early and threatened a law suit if his wife's check was not returned. The fool salesman, inflated with the success of his sales seduction, had in fact later gone to the hotel, gained entrance to her room with more affectionate cajoling, and tried going further with the drunken woman, only, by his crude actions, to have her come to her sober senses, and order him to leave.

Whatever she told her husband of what had happened resulted in his showing up early the next morning, threatening to notify the police. Needless to say, our boss was furious with the salesman; that was one clip man whose cupid wings were abruptly clipped. We never saw him again or heard anything more about him through the coast-to-coast grapevine of gossip.

WORKING AT BARCLAY HANDKERCHIEF CO.

The next job I had was as a shipping clerk in the garment center at Barclay's Handkerchief Company on 32nd Street, off 5th Avenue. After my shortened school day was over at 1:30 p.m., I'd take the train and arrive around 2:15 at the 34th and 7th Avenue station, walk through the crowds past Macy's, to reach my job by 2:30 and work till 7:00 p.m. Owned by two brothers, Barclay's shipped out cartons and cases of handkerchiefs so rapidly, in such bulk, at such wholesale prices to chain stores throughout the Midwest and South, you'd have thought the country was in the midst of staving off a national nasal emergency.

All of us employed there were S.Y.s. As relatives of the bosses, or friends of relatives, or relatives of friends, we were from families that could be vouched for in our small, closely knit community. The young women secretaries in the front office were also related to the Barclay brothers, but I noticed that that didn't dissuade the older brother Moe from patting the office babe's tight skirt with his free hand as he passed her in the narrow aisle, while his other hand busily unzipped his fly, on his way to the toilet.

The back-room shipping manager at Barclay's, Jakie Schwecky, was a boss's dream: dependable, thorough, and utterly honest. I see him in a characteristic still shot: pencil behind his ear as he holds a 6"x 9" white cardboard box he is busy filling with various styles of handkerchiefs to complete the back orders from retail chains preparing for an upcoming Mother's Day or Valentine's or (most chaotic) Christmas. We shippers would then pick up the stacks of filled boxes, carry them to a work table, pack them in cartons or wooden cases, and ship them by freight.

No matter how busy he was—with the phone ringing and some store manager in the Midwest wanting to know the status of an order he'd put in the day before, or one of the bosses calling him out to greet an important customer in the front showroom, or the freight men needing his signature, or noticing one of us screwing up, mixing orders—Jakie managed to run the shipping room with a clear head and a steady, unruffled demeanor. And, as I would soon learn, he was a most patient and forgiving supervisor.

BOBBY ADIS

Bobby lived on my block, down the street from me, with his parents and older brother. I had often seen him on the street or in the synagogue, but never playing ball, though his brother was one of the most powerful long-ball hitters in the neighborhood. Being swarthy—almost as dark-skinned as the movie character Sabu—gave Bobby's usual look of seriousness an even more somber aspect. He was a couple of years older, a serious reader of literature, and kept mostly to himself. It was only when we both worked at Barclay's as shipping clerks that I got to know him, though not much. Earnest and not given to easy laughter, he seemed to brood about something he preferred not to share, veiled, perhaps out of fear or embarrassment. I sensed he was even more secretive than I was.

Like others who share similar interests, we began to slowly, cautiously feel each other out. When we did talk about books, Bobby seemed tentative in his remarks, even hesitant about offering any opinion about a book he was reading. I got the impression from his passing remarks that he may have entertained the notion of becoming a writer himself, but he never showed me anything he'd written, nor I him.

On the long train ride home from work, we'd talk about books. Once, Bobby mentioned that he had begun reading Faulkner's *Absalom! Absalom!*, a novel whose endless, convoluted sentences I had earlier tried to follow but—masterpiece though it was considered by critics—I soon gave up on. The next time we talked, Bobby looked and sounded even more somber than usual. He said trying to follow the novel's dense, delirious complexity had frightened him and stirred disquieting thoughts and emotions that I could see troubled him.

He sounded as if he'd experienced a threat to the already delicate equilibrium of his mind, and added that, if this dread was what writing brought on, he would give up any further thought of becoming a writer. He was, he said, also strongly urged in this decision by his older brother who was suspicious of literature to begin with, and was now adamantly opposed to Bobby's further reading in it. After that, we did not broach the subject again, and I had the definite impression that he stayed away from me to ensure that the subject would not arise.

Soon after this, I would learn the extent of Bobby's sensitive nature while we were at work. One day in the course of our packing and shipping duties, a bill of lading for a carton of merchandise was needed to confirm that it had been shipped out. When asked about it, Bobby, who had done the packing, said that he had put the receipt in the drawer we used for that purpose, but when the drawer was searched, it could not be found. All of us—Jakie, Sonny (Jakie's assistant), Bobby, and I—went through all the bills of lading, but could not find it. Through it all, Bobby's face grew dark with apprehension.

At first, he claimed that he had, in fact, put the bill in the drawer, but as Jakie and Sonny exchanged looks of barely disguised skepticism that grew to open disbelief, Bobby began to sweat, betraying his own doubt. He'd been mistaken and absentminded on the job before, as I had been. In fact, not too long before, I had thought I'd locked the freight elevator door before we left work one evening, only to discover the next day that Jakie had been called at home late that night by the watchman and told that the elevator door was unlocked, so that he, Jakie—the only one besides the bosses who had a key—had to drive all the way back to the city from his home in Brooklyn and lock the door. Jakie told me this the next day with what felt like—given the circumstances—only mild annoyance, though I sensed no trace of rancor.

But now, facing Bobby, Jakie was showing more than irritation: he was exasperated, disdainful . . . so much so that Bobby, looking sheepish and crestfallen, dropped his assertion and began to mumble and stutter, disclaiming his original contention. The next day he called in and quit.

CHAPTER TWENTY-NINE

NOCTURNE

While education was not encouraged at home, we were still required by law to finish high school as we continued working at the jobs we had in order to contribute to the household. The expectation was, hopefully, that we would move up from our stock clerk and salesman jobs in stores owned by relatives and family friends, and start our own retail or wholesale businesses, a future I did not envision. My idea of education was to concentrate my attention (in as well as out of school) on subjects I was interested in (literature, history, science), and to more or less get by with the least amount of work to pass the required subjects.

After graduating in 1953, and despite my aversion to continuing any formal education in "required subjects," I was curious about what further academic studies had to offer, applied to Brooklyn College, took the entrance exam, and was accepted. Since I was working at Barclay's in Manhattan during the day, I registered for night classes. After I got off work at seven, I could take the train back to Brooklyn and arrive in time for my class at eight. During my first few weeks attending classes, I noticed a yellow flyer posted in the hallway of the English building asking for submissions to the night school's literary magazine, *Nocturne,* as well as an invitation to join the editorial board, which met on Friday evenings to consider submissions.

About that time, enamored of Dylan Thomas's poems and having heard him read them on the Caedmon record, I noticed an announcement in a newspaper that he would give a reading at the uptown YMHA in the coming week. It was a chance to hear him in person, as well as attend my first poetry reading.

While at work that day, along with the excitement at the prospect of hearing and seeing a poet I so admired in the flesh, I began to feel a growing unease, even apprehension at the possibility that the famous poet, more noted for his drunken behavior than his readings, might, in fact, live up to his reputation. As the time approached, I could not shake off a sense of imminent disaster, and envisioned Thomas disheveled and drunk, falling down the stairs. The image of a poet I admired, humiliated, was enough to dissuade me from the chance of witnessing such a scene, and I decided not to go. Rather than witness a debacle, I preferred not seeing him at all.

That same week, after a performance of *Under Milk Wood,* his play for voices, Thomas, having boasted that he'd downed more than eighteen whiskies and beer chasers in the White Horse Tavern, later reportedly died of an "alcoholic insult to the brain."

Curious about others around my own age interested in writing, I decided to attend the *Nocturne* meeting, although, by doing so, I would break my own dictum against showing my writing to anyone.

From my house, the college was a slow bus ride along Avenue J, a teeming shopping area of restaurants, clothing stores, single-family homes, and a noisy extension of the elevated train system overhead. Popularly known as the college you didn't need to leave home for, Brooklyn College was made up of several blocky, redbrick buildings set on a few acres at the far end of Bedford Avenue. Its appearance was squat and functional. From the look of the large areas of grass between buildings, it looked as if the campus had not too long ago been open farmland. For Brooklyn dwellers like myself—used to busy streets and crowded traffic—this was close to "country": any patch of grass larger than a few yards had the feel of open pasture.

ARTHUR ALTENBURG

We met at the first *Nocturne* meeting I attended.

I was eighteen, just out of high school; and he, in his early thirties, living with his parents in their brownstone in Brooklyn, was (not too purposefully it seemed) working toward a degree in English literature long after most people his age had been in academic life for a decade or more. Diffidence, indecision, and ambivalence were his modes of being. On shaky ground regarding his own aims, and so critical of his abilities, so hesitant to begin, or, if begun, to complete a project, he was nevertheless decisive and adamant about encouraging others to pursue the talent he sensed in them.

Arthur was a natural spotter of seriousness, which to him was as much a sign of promise—if not actually proven yet—and as much to be encouraged as fulfilled talent. From the first time we met, he granted me, generously, what he seemed unable to give to himself: permission to come out from under the cloak of a past that bound him in its shadow.

He usually wore the same outfit: slacks and a brown tweed jacket with elbow pads, and a shirt without a tie—academic-looking but short of formal—and had a habit of running his hand over his soft, thinning hair in a gesture to cover over the thin spot in front that billowed in the slightest breeze. When ill at ease, he'd absentmindedly start scratching—hard, till it reddened—the back of one hand with the nails of the other as he spoke or listened to you, as if in response to an inner nagging agitation that could not be assuaged.

Ambivalence was his strong suit, mostly about himself. His acute—painfully so, I'm sure—critical sense registered shadings of subtlety in the smallest choices, so many, and so at odds, and so paradoxical, as to leave him immobilized. He talked vaguely about wanting to get a degree, but didn't seem to work enough to finish the required courses; that would have been too definite. He talked about writing an essay on J. D. Salinger, but he hadn't gotten far with it. At the same time, he was interested in an attractive female student in one of his classes, and became both intrigued and distressed when he learned that she posed as a cover model for sexy detective thrillers.

He was interested in your writing because what he saw in your present work promised future achievement. His praise fired in me a drive (even when it resulted in derivative imitations) to continue writing in order to bring new work to the Friday night meeting.

Though I think he may have written or attempted to write a story or two, his talent seemed to be in appraising the work of others. Art, as I soon called him, in college longer than most doctoral candidates, seemed to have made a career of prolonging his stay, perhaps as a buffer against having to make a career choice. Although he never showed me anything he had written, or submitted any work to the magazine, when he'd ask to see poems of mine, as a senior editor of

Nocturne, he published them in the next issue. After I attended several meetings, he invited me to join the editorial staff, which I did. Without using hyperbole or critical jargon, in his unassuming, measured way, his encouragement meant a great deal.

After meetings, Art would give me a ride in his car back to my house, and as he drove, we would talk, discovering our common interests, though I cannot recall the details of our conversations, except for his curiosity about my writing and our shared preoccupation with literature. Up until then, I had not confided my thoughts or feelings about my writing, nor did I suspect they'd be of interest to anyone. Art, almost twice my age, allowed me to feel at ease and be forthcoming, more so perhaps than if he were closer to my age. In his support and reassurance, I never sensed him trying to impress or flatter.

When we'd arrive at my house, we'd continue our discussion in near-darkness. In the driver's seat, Art would face me at an angle underneath the yellow streetlight that made me squint under its glare, but also created a kind of lulling dream-space cast in an atmosphere of hesitant, hovering possibilities. When he'd ask which poets I liked, I'm sure he knew my poems were derivative of Hart Crane and Dylan Thomas, but that in my heart I meant poetry no harm. He suggested that *serious* imitation was the first step toward an originality of one's own.

Under the streetlight, talking about books and writers was a connection with a secret, privileged hierarchy. After a number of such talks, having handed in several batches of poems, one night I confessed to Art that writing was becoming too difficult and I was beginning to seriously question whether I could continue. I had come to feel so overwhelmed by the difficulty of writing about feelings I did not want to face or explore further, sensing that if I did enter that obscure, shadowy realm, once entered, it could not be ignored; I felt a dread for my sanity. In these moments, Bobby Adis's fear came to mind and I shared a sense of what must have overwhelmed him.

What I most wanted was relief, a numbness against the peril that writing seemed to threaten: the poignant loneliness in Sherwood Anderson's *Winesburg, Ohio* stories; the aching, impossible longing for home that echoed in Thomas Wolfe's "A stone, a leaf, a door," and the haunting refrain, "O lost, and by the wind grieved, ghost come back again."

After hearing me out, Art turned, "Do you have a choice?"

He paused longer than usual, as if he'd been holding his question in reserve, expecting mine, with a backwards-bending weariness in his voice. I wasn't sure what he meant. After a moment in which he waited, he asked again, "Do you?" He waited. "If you do, then make one." His usual note of good-natured humor was absent as he then said, "Can you *not* write? Because if you *can't* then there's no choice. It's made."

If I had a choice . . . but did I? It was possible, but at what price? Without the effort of articulating one's true feelings, where was sanity? Certainly not at home, nor in school, nor in the jobs I had and would have in the future. That, I saw, and could foresee, clearly. Going with what you had no choice over would be cleaner.

Then, as though a door had opened, he began telling me about his own difficulties: trying to begin a piece he had given thought to, that he couldn't start, or finishing a piece he had started. Having asked me whether I had a choice, he was as much as saying that, unlike me, he did not feel that nagging pull, which, given no choice, would be liberating, and he was paying the price of that indecision in self-doubt, the ground pulled out from beneath him. Elaborating his difficulties and misgivings seemed as difficult as writing itself, and gave no sense of total engagement with his abilities. All his ingenuity and intelligence seemed aimed at prolonging hesitation and postponement. Was he saying that he, unlike I, *did* have choices, and being pulled between them, had nothing to show for it?

Much of what he said about himself was rife with disappointed aspirations and self-deprecation. He said his conditions for writing had to be so precisely calibrated, the words so weighted, measured, and shaded with premeditated meanings, the burden was paralyzing. He told me of a method he'd devised to get himself writing: as a smoker, only after he finished writing a page would he allow himself a cigarette, thereby making writing a by-product of the craving for nicotine. At that rate, I thought, smoking as a reward, if he were to write an extended piece, would be disastrous. To be tied to such a bargain seemed a no-win situation, and though I refrained from saying so, I'm sure he knew.

Instead, I believed that jumping in—somewhere, anywhere— would be better than inertia. And as for my having no choice, he said finally that he considered that enviable.

To break the pall of such passivity made me instinctively try to counter with something active, however glib I may have sounded. When I suggested to perhaps allow accident to be an ally, he gave me that enigmatic smile of commiserating rebuke for my naïve, impulsive remedy. For him, indecisiveness had become a currency that transmitted meager psychic coin through the nerves into insubstantial emotional states and vague physical gestures.

At other times, in editorial meetings or when people were discussing literary matters, I'd notice that slightly indulgent grin playing behind his raised hand as he'd turn slightly to cover his grimace at what had just been said, revealing the speaker's naïveté. I felt the grin was of an irony polite, pitying, and permanently fixed beneath his face. If a self-imposed restraint kept that expression within bounds, there was a despairing sense of its fragililty on the edge.

After several weeks of riding the train from my job in the city to night classes, one of my bosses at Barclay's, urging me to stay late and work extra hours for the approaching busy Christmas season, reached into his pocket and offered me a deal I found hard to refuse: besides the overtime pay, an extra bonus of twenty dollars a week! This meant I couldn't attend night classes. I decided to accept. No more college . . . which I considered no real loss. Having not been an eager student, I wondered what I could gain from pursuing a college degree when what I really wanted was to write and travel. Writing on my own time, I'd work and save enough to travel. I wanted a break from my surroundings, from my family, from more years of formal education, and from my job. I wanted a future that would be open-ended, and I was willing to wing it.

At the next *Nocturne* meeting, when I told Art I intended to drop out and save enough to travel, no doubt feeling our bond about to loosen, he told me that he, too, had been thinking about travel.

"Where to?" I asked.

"Oh, anywhere. The South Seas, Tahiti . . ."

Was he serious, or just playing along?

"How would you get there?"

"I'd build a boat out of lumber and put a sail on it . . ."

"O.K., O.K.," I said. I got it.

"Or I could take a job on a ship," he added. "But I'd need seaman's papers."

"And how would you get them?" I asked for my own benefit.

From his pause, I could tell he was not about to volunteer the answer before drawing out the difficulty a bit longer.

"By having been to sea," he replied, wide-eyed, as if the catch was apparent there. Then he capped it, pleased with the lilting sound of the irony:

"And you can't go to sea without seaman's papers."

When I asked what could be done, he said most shipping companies would not hire you without seaman's papers, but he'd heard that a place to try was the Scandinavian line. There, you might not need papers. They might hire without your having been to sea. I told him this sounded promising and that I'd look into it.

"You'll need a passport," he said.

"How long would that take?" I asked.

"Not sure; a week, two weeks. If you're serious, apply now and you might get it before you land a job, and even if you don't, you'll need it when you leave the country," then added, "for Paris, like Hemingway," with a grin.

I decided to take Art's advice and save time by applying for a passport before I began my search for a ship. I received my passport about two weeks later; meanwhile I put in a lot of overtime at my job to earn extra money.

With passport in hand, I tracked down the Scandinavian Seaman's Office in a downtown Brooklyn building and entered a large bare hall on the ground floor where young men in work clothes were scanning small cards pinned to a cork board on the wall for job listings on outbound ships. The language typed on the cards was unfamiliar. When I asked to speak to someone, I was pointed to an office in the back.

I knocked and heard a gruff voice: "Yah!"

Opening the door, I saw an older, thick-set man on the phone, seated behind a counter; he wore a green eyeshade. He didn't look up, so I waited.

"Yah, yah," he said into the phone, and jotted something down. With one hand, he cupped the phone and glanced up at me.

"Yah!" he said. "Vaht is it?"

I told him I was looking for a job on a ship. From the moment I had started searching, I'd been entertaining the notion of signing on a cruise ship or a luxury liner—something in the way of a paid vacation—for not too long a time: a few weeks, perhaps, and not too far away. Sunny, festive scenes of exotic tourist sites from travel posters flashed before me: the Bahamas, Port-au-Prince, Trinidad . . .

"I was hoping . . ." I began, but he cut me off.

Nodding toward the phone he cradled, he said, "Dere's a freighter to Vest Africa needs a mess-boy. Tomorrow morning."

Africa had never occurred to me. I hadn't given it a thought. Was it real?—and not created by the fevered imaginations of writers like Conrad and Rimbaud? Instantly I envisioned forests, turbulent rivers, blinding heat and deserts, the paraphernalia of literature become life.

"Vell? . . . Yes, no?"

In a flash of dread that froze me, I saw myself standing on an edge and having to make a sudden decision I hadn't foreseen. Was this a danger to avoid or an opportunity to grasp? I quickly calculated: if I declined, I might never get this chance again; if I accepted, I might not return. . . .

He held up the phone to me. "The first mate is vaiting."

Against my fear, a counterforce, more reckless than resolute, took me over. It was not adventure I wanted so much as escape.

Tipping over the edge in a rush of free-fall, I heard myself say, "Yes."

After relaying my acceptance on the phone, he had me sign some papers, then showed me a list of the ports at which the ship would stop: Cape Verde, Dakar, Lagos, Monrovia, Abidjan, Luanda, Matadi. . . .

I returned home, packed some clothes, a pen, and a notebook in a small bag, and checked a map. Matadi was on the Congo River; we would be traveling up the same route as did Conrad. I was excited, and slipped a paperback volume of *Heart of Darkness* into the bag to take along and compare the details of the story with what I would encounter.

When I told my mother I'd be leaving on a ship to Africa, her eyes widened and she threw up her hands in a gesture of final surrender.

"*Laesh* (Why)?" she asked. "Things aren't good enough here? You have to go to the *teshmaeh fil din'yaeh* (the world's toilet) to see for yourself? *"Ruuhh, Allah ma'aak* (Go, God be with you)." When I told my father that night, he gave me a long, resigned look. "My dear boy, you'll do what you want. Be careful. We'll be anxious to know what you're up to."

Next morning, at 8:00 a.m., I arrived at the pier of the New York harbor and as I walked up to the SS *Ferngrove* at its dock, my heart sank when I saw its small size against the wide harbor water and the sky, and the peeling paint along its rusted hull. It looked like a twisted tin can that could hardly withstand the weather, much less the steady beating of an ocean voyage.

Several crew members were taking on stores; winches revolved overhead, men were shouting and pointing. I showed my papers to a man at the foot of the gangplank and he motioned me aboard. I walked up and, at the top, jumped onto the deck, a steel plate reverberated beneath me like a metallic drum. I was taken to the first mate, a tall, bulky blond fellow in the clean white shirt and dark blue trousers of a ship's officer. He told me my job was to help in the mess, clean up, give a hand storing supplies, and to be on call when needed by the bosun's crew and help them scrape paint and rust off the deck, washing it down, hauling ropes. I was to be a multipurpose hand.

After storing my bag in the cabin I'd share with a fellow crew member, and being assigned the top bunk, I went out on deck as we took on a pilot who was to steer the ship out of the harbor toward the open sea.

For a last look at what I was leaving, I went up to the top deck and stood with the ship under me sliding away from the Brooklyn shore. Already, as the buildings and landmarks slipping past began to appear unfamiliar, I had a sense of lifting closer to the sky, a feeling—which would grow over time in the open sea—that sailing would be not so much floating as flying.

COLOPHON

From Baghdad to Brooklyn was designed at Coffee House Press in the historic warehouse district of downtown Minneapolis. The text is set in Spectrum with Officina Sans titles.

FUNDER ACKNOWLEDGMENT

Coffee House Press is an independent nonprofit literary publisher. Our books are made possible through the generous support of grants and gifts from many foundations, corporate giving programs, individuals, and through state and federal support. This book received special project support from The Rosen/Litman Family. Coffee House Press receives general operating support from the Minnesota State Arts Board, through an appropriation by the Minnesota State Legislature and from the National Endowment for the Arts, a federal agency. Coffee House receives major funding from the McKnight Foundation, and from Target. Coffee House also receives significant support from an anonymous donor; the Buuck Family Foundation; the Bush Foundation; the Patrick and Aimee Butler Family Foundation; Consortium Book Sales and Distribution; the Foundation for Contemporary Performance Arts; Stephen and Isabel Keating; the Lerner Family Foundation; the Outagamie Foundation; the Pacific Foundation; the law firm of Schwegman, Lundberg, Woessner & Kluth, P.A.; the James R. Thorpe Foundation; the Archie D. and Bertha H. Walker Foundation; West Group; the Woessner Freeman Family Foundation; and many other generous individual donors.

This activity is made possible in part by a grant from the Minnesota State Arts Board, through an appropriation by the Minnesota State Legislature and a grant from the National Endowment for the Arts.

 MINNESOTA STATE ARTS BOARD

 NATIONAL ENDOWMENT FOR THE ARTS

 TARGET.

To you and our many readers across the country, we send our thanks for your continuing support.

Good books are brewing at coffeehousepress.org